AF568168

Preparation and Training of Library Staff

Preparation and Training of Library Staff

K. P. Singh

RANDOM PUBLICATIONS
NEW DELHI (INDIA)

Preparation and Training of Library Staff

ISBN 978-93-5111-247-1

Published in 2014 in India by

RANDOM PUBLICATIONS

4376-A/4B, Gali Murari Lal, Ansari Road
New Delhi-110 002
Phone : +91-11-43580356, +91-11-23289044
e-mail: randomexports@gmail.com, sales@randompublications.com, info@randompublications.com

Reprinted 2019

Type Setting by : Keystoneprintads, Delhi-110051
Digitally Printed at : Replika Press Pvt. Ltd.

Preface

Training is the acquisition of knowledge, skills, and competencies as a result of the teaching of vocational or practical skills and knowledge that relate to specific useful competencies. Training has specific goals of improving one's capability, capacity, productivity, and performance. It forms the core of apprenticeships and provides the backbone of content at institutes of technology. In addition to the basic training required for a trade, occupation, or profession, observers of the labor-market recognize as of 2008 the need to continue training beyond initial qualifications: to maintain, upgrade and update skills throughout working life. People within many professions and occupations may refer to this sort of training as professional development.

Some commentators use a similar term for workplace learning to improve performance: "training and development". There are also additional services available online for those who wish to receive training above and beyond that which is offered by their employers. Some examples of these services include career counseling, skill assessment, and supportive services. One can generally categorize such training as on-the-job or off-the-job.

The on-the-job training method takes place in a normal working situation, using the actual tools, equipment, documents or materials that trainees will use when fully trained. On-the-job training has a general reputation as most effective for vocational work.It involves Employee training at the place of work while he or she is doing the actual job. Usually a professional trainer serves as the course instructor using hands-on training often supported by formal classroom training.

Off-the-job training method takes place away from normal work situations - implying that the employee does not count as a directly productive worker while such training takes place. Off-the-job training method also involves employee training at a site away from the actual work environment. It often utilizes lectures, case studies, role playing and simulation, having the advantage of allowing people to get away from work and concentrate more thoroughly on the training itself. This type of training has proven more effective in inculcating concepts and ideas.

With the ever-changing nature of our work, library staff needs fresh and innovative training opportunities to say current and to continue to meet the needs of our patrons. Managing staff training involves assessment of training needs, planning and evaluating staff development, and keeping on top of all the learning methods and formats available. Whether conducting training face-to-face or online, a blend of both or augmented with social media tools, managing staff learning can be the basis for a transformative and accessible learning organization for all.

I thank all members of my team who have helped in the preparation of the book. My special thanks go to "Random Publications" who have published the book.

– K. P. Singh

Contents

1

Introduction

WHAT IS LEARNING AND DEVELOPMENT? WHY IS IT SO IMPORTANT?

UNDERSTANDING LEARNING AND DEVELOPMENT

It's amazing how so many of us go through so many years of schooling, but have such little understanding of learning and development. Before reading about the many aspects of learning and development in this topic in the Library, including learning and development programmes and practitioners, it's best to start with a basic understanding of what learning and development is and how to best benefit from it. Also, it's useful to understand the common terms and the sometimes subtle differences between them. If you will be doing training and development with yourself (and almost every adult will be at some time in their lives) or with others, you should know the differences between training children and teens versus training adults. Adults have very different nature and needs in training. Also, there are some common beliefs about training that just aren't true. Understand those misconceptions so you don't build your training around those illusions.

BENEFITS OF LEARNING AND DEVELOPMENT

We often think that the biggest benefit of learning is that we get a diploma or credential. As we get wiser, we realize there are so many more benefits than that. Knowing the benefits will help motivate you to design your own training plans and programmes, and to motivate others to participate as well. Perhaps one of the biggest benefits is the appreciation that you can be learning all the time, even if you are not in a formal training programme.

RELATIONSHIP OF LEARNING AND DEVELOPMENT TO PERFORMANCE

We tend to assume that training leads to learning, which leads to doing better in our lives and work — it leads to increased performance. However, you will very likely get more out of your trainings and be more successful in promoting trainings to others if you understand more about the relationship between training and performance. That understanding is especially useful when designing training to increase performance or to redesign training programmes that don't seem to be as successful as you wish.

DIFFERENT TYPES OF TRAINING AND ACTIVITIES

INFORMAL VERSUS FORMAL TRAINING, SELF-DIRECTED VERSUS OTHER-DIRECTED TRAINING

There are different major forms of learning and development. We're most familiar with formal and other-directed forms of learning and development, that include the strong attention to the systematic structure and evaluation of the learning and development, especially as used in schooling. That is somewhat ironic, because the most common forms of learning and development are informal and self-directed — they occur without strong attention to a systematic design and evaluation and without many experts guiding us through those experiences.

TYPES OF ACTIVITIES FOR LEARNING AND EVELOPMENT

There are many approaches to learning and development and many types of activities that can be undertaken to learn. We're most used to thinking of the formal, other-directed activities, such as attending courses or lectures. However, most of the types of learning are informal and unstructured. An awareness of these other types will broaden your possibilities for intentional learning and for designing training for yourself and others.

MOVEMENTS IN ORGANIZATIONAL TRAINING AND DEVELOPMENT

The field (or many would argue, the profession) of training and development has undergone dramatic improvements, especially with the inclusion of computer- and Web-based technologies. We're also expanding the concept of learning beyond the learning of individuals — we're thinking that groups and organizations can learn, too. (Although the topics of the learning organization and knowledge management are fairly recent and still popular, many people would disagree that they're actually learning and development programmes — those people might assert that they're actually forms of organizational performance management. However, the two topics still seem to be so broad and changing, that they're referred to here as movements.)

PREPARATION FOR DEVELOPING TRAINING AND DEVELOPMENT PROGRAMMES

EXAMPLES OF PROGRAMMES IN THE WORKPLACE

Before this Library topic goes on to explaining how to design and develop training programmes, it's useful to get a quick impression of various types of training programmes. A training programme is an intentionally designed, (hopefully) highly integrated set of activities that are aligned to accomplish a certain set of results among learners. Many of us might not be used to thinking of the following as programmes in the workplace.

HOW TO ENSURE TRANSFER OF TRAINING — TRAINING THAT STICKS

One of the biggest concerns of trainers — and those paying for training — is whether the learners will indeed understand and apply the new information and materials from the learning and development activities, that is, whether the new information and materials will transfer to the learners.

DEVELOPING SYSTEMATIC TRAINING AND DEVELOPMENT PROGRAMMES

INSTRUCTIONAL SYSTEM DESIGN (ISD) AND THE ADDIE MODEL

Formal approaches to learning and development often have the highest likelihood of transfer of training. A formal approach to learning and development usually follows a systematic and consistent framework. Systematic means that the framework is designed to guide learners to achieve an overall set of goals — goals to address a need or situation, then associates objectives and activities to achieve those overall goals, and evaluates the activities and results to be sure the goals were achieved. Instructional system design (ISD) is the activities to ensure that the design of training is very successful in achieving the goals of the training. One of the most common ISD models is ADDIE, which is an acronym for assessment, design, development, implementation and evaluation — you can discern from the acronym that ADDIES is a systematic design of training.

- *ADDIE Phase 1 — Assessing Your Training Needs:* Needs Assessment to Training Goals: What overall results or outcomes should be accomplished by learners? Those outcomes usually are identified from the results of assessments, or measurements, of what a person or workplace needs to accomplish in order to achieve some desired level of performance. An outcome might be the ability to perform a complex job.
- *ADDIE Phase 2 — Designing Training Plans and Learning Objectives:* What learning objectives must be accomplished by learners in order to achieve the overall outcomes, and what activities must be undertaken by trainers and learners to accomplish those objectives? The integration of the overall outcomes, objectives and activities and also how they will be evaluated comprise the design of the learning and development programme. Learning objectives often

are described in terms of new learning — new knowledge, skills and competencies.

- *ADDIE Phase 3 — Developing Training Activities and Materials:* Now it's important to get even more clear on what resources must be obtained and developed in order to undertake the activities to achieve the objectives. Resource might include certain expertise, facilities and technologies. Development might include several trainers and learners reviewing the design of the training to ensure it meets their nature and needs.
- *ADDIE Phase 4 — Implementing Your Training Programme:* Now you're ready to have trainers and learners participate in the programme, to undertake the activities and evaluations of learning. Implementation often results in refining the original design of the training programme.
- *ADDIE Phase 5 — Evaluating Your Training Programme:* As trainers and learners participate in the programme, evaluation should occur of the quality of the activities and the extent of achievement of the objectives. After the programme, evaluation should occur to assess the extent of achievement of the overall goals of the programme. Evaluation might focus on short-term, intermediate and long-term outcomes.

HOW DO MANAGERS MANAGE?

The studies by researchers showed that from street gang leaders to the President of the United States, managers do not spend their time planning, organizing, coordinating, and controlling as the French industrialist, Henri Fayol said they did in 1916 and as most writers on management have continued to repeat ever since. They are not like the orchestra leader who directs the component parts of his organization with ease and precision. Instead, they spend their time reacting to crises, seizing special opportunities, attending meetings, negotiating, talking on the telephone, cultivating interpersonal and political relationships, gathering and disseminating information, and fulfilling a variety of ceremonial functions. Researcher says:

- I was struck during my study by the fact that the executives I was observing—all very competent by any standard—are fundamentally indistinguishable from their counterparts of a hundred years ago (or a thousand years ago. for that matter). The information they need differs, but they seek it in the same way—by word of mouth. Their decisions concern modem technology, but the procedures they use to make them are the same as the procedures of the 19th Century manager. Even the computer, so important for the specialized work of the organization, has apparently had no influence on the work procedures of general managers. In fact, the manager is in a kind of loop, with increasingly heavy work pressures but no aid forthcoming from management science.

The Mintzberg view is by no means unique. There is a growing number of management scholars who are questioning the conventional view of management and what managers do. In a critical review of *On Management*, a book of articles selected from 25 years of the *Harvard Business Review*, Albert Shapero, a management professor at the University of Texas, strikes a similar note:

- The term "management" conjures up images of control, rationality, systematics; but studies of what managers actually do depict behaviours and situations that are chaotic, unplanned, and charged with improvisation. The Managerial life at every level is reflexive—responding to calls, memos, personnel problems, fire drills, budget meetings, and personnel reviews. Occasionally, however, we find at managerial levels individuals who go 24 hours without being interrupted by meetings or phone calls. They are the longrange planners, the people in O.R., E.D.P., financial or market planning, or market research. Management is really for them. The bulk of the articles in *On Management* are concerned with ideas from the world of the staff functionary.

ARE MANAGEMENT SYSTEMS REALLY USED?

What about the claims of widespread use of new scientific management systems and techniques? Is it really true that managers in business, government, and other institutions are using them extensively while we library administrators are lagging far behind? Let's first look at what a few of the management experts say about the use of these systems in general, and then we will look at their use in libraries. William R, Dill, dean of the Graduate School of Business Administration at New York University, makes this sober assessment:

- For all the progress we have made in developing good approaches to planning, forecasting, budgeting, and control, and for all the enthusiasm we in schools of management have helped to build for these approaches, their use has been fitful and sporadic, even in the most analytically sophisticated and goal-oriented institutions. In corporations that are pointed out as models for what can be accomplished. the outputs of planning, budgeting, and modeling staffs are often quietly ignored by operating people when times are good: these outputs often seem irrelevant in times of sudden challenge or change. Analysis and planning are still far from foolproof ways to anticipate change and potential crises.

Aaron Wildavsky, dean of the Graduate School of Public Policy at the University of California, Berkeley, has written a number of articles in which he argues convincingly, citing evidence and authorities, that the major modern information systems like PERT, MBO, PPBS, Social Indicators, and Zero Based Budgeting have not worked and cannot work. About PERT (Programme Evaluation Review Technique), he says that: "the few studies that exist suggest that outside of construction, where one activity tends to follow another, PERT is rarely successful." On MBO (Management by Objectives), he says: "The trouble with MBO is that the attempt to formalize procedures for choosing objectives without considering organizational dynamics leads to the opposite of what was intended—had management, irrational choice, and ineffective decision-making."

"The main product of MBO, as experience in the United States federal government suggests, is, literally, a series of objectives. Aside from the unnecessary paper work, such exercises are self defeating because they become mechanisms for avoiding rather than making choices. Long lists of objectives are useless because rarely do resources remain beyond the first few." On PPBS, Wildavsky is equally harsh. He says that "Programme budgeting does not work anywhere in the world it has been tried," and that "no one knows how to do programme budgeting." His assessments of Social Indicators and Zero Based Budgeting are in a similar vein. hese realistic assessments that we are getting from authorities like Mintzberg, Shapero, Dill. Wildavsky, and others should serve to remind us to maintain a healthy skepticism whenever we read about the effectiveness and widespread use of new management systems and techniques.

We librarians should guard against the tendency we have to look for panaceas and to accept uncritically the claims and promises made on behalf of each new management theory or system that appears. onsider the minimal impact on libraries as compared with the initial promise, for example, of PPBS, Operations Research, MBO, and even Participative Management. To the best of my knowledge, PPBS has not been successfully implemented in a single library and I doubt that it ever will be. Interest in it is rapidly waning. he practical application of Operations Research in libraries has been extremely limited to date. One of the earliest and best known economic analyses of library decision making was done in the MIT Libraries in 1969. The report of that study came to this sobering conclusion: "Although helpful, an economic analysis of a university (or public) library is insufficient because libraries operate as political systems and thus improving libraries requires political analysis."

In an excellent article on library decision making, Jeffrey Raffel, an economist and co-author of the MIT study begins by saying that "in general, the more important the decision, the less beneficial a cost-benefit analysis is to library decision makers," and concludes by saying that "it is time that we all recognized the politics of libraries and acted accordingly." In a classic paper on Management by Objectives in academic libraries, James Michalko, after a thorough, critical review of the literature, recommends against the use of MBO in libraries on the grounds that it is a limited approach which is costly and difficult to implement and which yields uncertain results. Participative management is another "new" management technique that has been particularly oversold in the last decade. In fact, it is considered by many librarians to be the perfect management system. Good management has always included consultation and participation, it is just the name, the faddishness, and some of the formal structures that are new.

When used properly and honestly, participative management is a useful process at all levels, and not just by top managers on major decisions as is sometimes assumed. It is essential that there be appropriate consultation and participation of interested and competent staff members on important decisions affecting them. But participative management will not bring on the management millennium in libraries. Participative management is not decision making by committee or by staff plebiscite. Good management requires that when all the facts have been gathered and analyzed and all the advice is in, the appropriate administrator has to make the decision and take responsibility for it. Knowing when and how to seek and take advantage of consultative advice and prior approval of decisions where appropriate is one of the most important managerial skills. Decisions should be made at the lowest competent level.

The library's critical strategy decisions involve a world outside the library and must usually be made by the director and his chief associates. Staff committees can give good advice on such matters, but they simply do not have the information, the knowledge, or the perspective required to make those decisions—and they cannot take responsibility for the results. ne extreme form of participative management, the collegial or faculty system of governance, was developed for academic departments: it works badly there and worse or not at all in libraries. Where it appears to work, it is because those involved have tacitly made concessions to traditional hierarchical systems and the demands of the environment while preserving the collegial form. A library is not an academic department, it is a service organization and should be so administered.

A librarian by any other name is still a librarian and it is time for mature acceptance of that fact. Perhaps the reason that participative management has been embraced so enthusiastically and uncritically by librarians in recent years is not because of its management benefits, but because it appears to be the model that best justifies faculty status. t is assumed that because faculty members participate in a collegial academic decision-making process, that model is the appropriate one to use in libraries—if librarians are to achieve faculty status.

Much of the library-based management literature since 1970 is self-serving and reflects a direct or indirect preoccupation with matters of staff status and benefits frequently hidden behind arguments for participative management.

It is time that we recognized this natural bias and took steps to overcome it by giving more attention and weight to the more objective management literature from outside the library field.

Two recent articles on participative management in libraries, one by James Govan and the other by Dennis Dickenson, give encouraging evidence that the library profession is beginning to take a more realistic and balanced view of the advantages and limitations of participative management and collegial governance. Govan reminds us that:

- Librarians cannot afford to degrade services nor alienate their users in an effort, however enlightened or well-in-mentioned to make their jobs more challenging and satisfying. Participation and consultation cost time and money and often, like faculty deliberations, produce rather conservative results. In this connection, it is useful to remember Maslow's belief that Theory Y is possible only in periods of affluence. It is also healthy to recall Drucker's statement that service institutions do not operate for the people who work in them.

In his perceptive article, Dickenson tries to provide "an antidote for some of the more extreme and sometimes naive interpretations of participative management that appear from time to time in library literature." Peter Drucker summed up an important truth about management when he said in response to an interviewer's question about the efficacy of new management techniques: "The young people today expect to see business run by theory, knowledge, concepts, and planning. But then they find it is run like the rest of the world—by experience and expediency, by who you know, and by the hydrostatic pressure in your bladder." his is not just the way business is run, it is the way libraries are run as well.

And it is the way they will continue to be run despite the current rhetoric about the managerial revolution that is being ushered in by the use of new quantitative and psychological management systems and theories. Why? Because a library operates in a political environment and nearly all the really important decisions that are made at the highest levels have an overriding political component. They are rarely the product of cost benefit analysis or Operations Research where the various factors are weighed and compared and the "best" or most cost-effective course is chosen. These management techniques can be useful sometimes to implement a programme or a project in the most effective manner after the political decision to proceed has been made.

They can also be useful in providing a rationale to support some essentially political decision that is being proposed or advocated, or to impress higher authorities or constituents with the competence of the managers and the rationality of their decision making process. Management systems, particularly PPBS, ZBB, and PERT are used in government and military bureaucracies largely because they are mandated by law or regulation. n the library world, as in education, business, and government, few major programme decisions are made solely or even largely on the basis of careful studies of needs and costs. Consider, for example, decisions to build a new library building, to open a new departmental or branch library, to achieve excellence in some special subject discipline, or to embark on a major automation programme.

These programme decisions are usually the result of an initiative or vision by an imaginative and powerful person, perhaps a library director a dean, a president, a mayor, or other official. They are political, emotional, or even personal decisions—justified, rationalized, and perhaps implemented with the assistance of various kinds of analyses and studies, but seldom derived from them. It is important that librarians understand how and why these really critical decisions are made so that they will not be disillusioned or discouraged when they discover that the "best." the most efficient, or the least expensive solution frequently loses out to the one that is the most politically expedient or attractive.

THE QUANTITATIVE APPROACH

Scholars think it is important to make a distinction between the claims made on behalf of complex quantitative management systems such as Operations Research and Cost-Benefit Analysis, and the collection and analysis of quantitative data in libraries to assist in rational decision making. Scholar is questioning the validity and usefulness of these complex systems, but scholar is not questioning the need for and use of quantitative studies for measuring and evaluating library services. Quite the contrary, we need to know more about libraries, their resources, and how they are actually used. We have relied historically upon input data, e.g., the number of books acquired, the number of serials subscribed to, the number of books circulated, the dollars spent, etc.

The qualitative characteristics of these data are dubious; we desperately need reliable measures of library effectiveness. Following the pioneering work by Fremont Rider in 1940 on the growth of research libraries, there has been an increasing number of extremely valuable quantitative studies such as those by Fussier, Lancaster, Buckland. and other works of solid quality. The findings of such studies provide the theoretical foundations and practical knowledge that working library managers need to draw on to help them think clearly and creatively about library management and to make sound decisions based on valid data.

This is especially true in this time of transition when the conventional wisdom of our profession will not suffice to see us through. s one of the library managers for whose benefit and use such studies are presumably made, researcher thanks the authors and urge them on to greater productivity and precision. Researcher also urge them to try to keep their studies as simple as possible and to summarize their findings in readable English. nfortunately, a good deal of the quantitative research that is done in the library field is unintelligible, irrelevant, or too complicated and theoretical for any practical use in libraries.

Much of it is written in the language of higher mathematics which is incomprehensible to most managers. This is particularly true of studies that are made by academics outside the library field such as statisticians, economists, psychologists. Operations Research people, etc. Their goal is not necessarily to do studies that are useful, but to demonstrate their mathematical prowess, to test theories and methodologies, to get published, and to award doctoral degrees to deserving graduate students. They select the library as their laboratory because it is convenient and because they think it is virgin territory ready for easy exploitation. They are more interested in the process than in the results.

The most useful library research is done by librarians or others with a serious long-term interest and involvement in libraries who work with librarians in a spirit of genuine collaboration. They are trying to make an impact. It is the difference between a class assignment and the real thing, between war games and war. notable exception to this criticism of academics is the landmark work by William J. Baumol and Matityahu Marcus, Economics of Academic Libraries. These two economists went to unusual lengths to explain their statistical methods and to summarize their conclusions with refreshing brevity and clarity. s a consequence, their work is widely read and frequently cited. anagement scientists and other quantitatively oriented researchers frequently wonder why the results of quantitative research studies are not used more by practicing library managers in the decision making process.

One reason is that the mathematics and the methodologies required are far too complex and difficult for operating managers to learn and apply in their busy work environments. Few senior library administrators have the kind of staff support needed to successfully carry out complex analyses. Another and equally important reason is that the quantitative approach does not and cannot take into sufficient account the complex of political, organizational, and psychological factors that characterize the real work where people are more potent than numbers or logic. The quality of many decisions could be significantly improved if we had more and better data, but many of the more important decisions have a relatively small quantitative component. As a library director, I seldom have a critical need for more quantitative data than are available from regularly kept statistics or by having someone make a special and usually simple survey and analysis of the problem.

When the data are simply not available or too difficult to assemble, researcher can usually find a satisfactory way to manage without them. My real problem has nearly always been to correctly assess the political rather than the economic or quantitative factors. It is fairly easy to determine the most cost-effective course of action with or without detailed data. It is much harder to map out and implement a successful strategy for achieving it, to assess how the various persons and groups affected will perceive the manager's intentions, and how they will react to the decision. Someone said that quantification is not synonymous with management. Finding the best or most cost-effective course of action is not the same as getting it accepted. Sometimes the quality of a decision is critical, other times, it is acceptance.Effective decision-making processes in large academic and public libraries involve complex sets of policies, procedures, and problems which require a variety of different kinds of information and approaches. Some decisions will be authoritarian, some will be collegial, some will be made by committees, and some will be made by combinations of the above.

Library directors are not all-knowing, nor are the collective judgments of library faculties and committees infallible. Different situations call for different approaches. There are no simple formulas and no easy answers. The new management systems that we have been discussing in this article divide into two general categories. There are quantitative systems such as Operations Research, PPBS, and ZBB, and psychological or behavioral systems such as Theory Y (and its variants) and MBO. In each system, there are a number of concepts, ideas, tools, and techniques that have validity and can be used to advantage by library managers, but as comprehensive systems they are all far too theoretical, complex, and simplistic to be applied successfully by ordinary managers in the day-to-day work environment. Few managers have the time or the specialized knowledge and skills required to make these systems work, and those that do are probably astute enough to manage as well or better without them.

In the hands of amateurs—and this is most of us— the quantitative systems frequently produce misleading and wrong solutions, while the psychological or behavioural systems can lead to the manipulation and misuse of people. The real danger with both kinds of management systems is that they offer mechanistic formulas for dealing with complex realities and keep us from thinking about and solving our management problems in practical, realistic, and common sense ways. Despite the many claims to the contrary, management is not yet a science. It is still an art, but is very much an art that can and should be mastered and practiced by librarians.

TRAINING AND SUPPORT TO USERS

The importance of the library as a resource centre and the endeavor of the management to exploit the resources gathered over the years with a lot of investment, need not be over emphasized. However, it has been the experience of many a library, especially those attached to organisations, the use of their resources appear to be little compared to the efforts put in building up the resources. As such there appears to be a constant need to initiate outreach programmes in order to enhance the usage of the library to the maximum extent. Library is looked upon as a centre for learning. The Library has to strive to repackage the material that is received in the library in the form of Alerts, reviews, digests, abstracts and databases to enhance library utilization and improve readership.

Also, in view of the rapid developments in Information and Communication Technologies, the role of a librarian is not like what it used to be a few decades ago. Added to IT, satellite communication systems, networking, Internet and intellectual property rights, have all made the library environment more complex. Further, the budgetary constraints, inadequate infrastructure, falling standards in human resources are all compelling the librarian to change his attitude from a mere custodian of information to that of a facilitator. As the library is a service institution there should be close interaction between the information providers, processors and users to enhance the effectivity of any resource centre Keeping in view the above factors, National Institute of Rural Development (NIRD) conducted a learning programme on. This programme provided a forum for the users of information and the library personnel to come together, to understand each others way of dealing with information and how the information barriers can be overcome and what best practices are to be adopted to increase the utilization of the resources of the Library through various training programmes.

LIBRARY UTILIZATION AND READERSHIP ENHANCEMENT (LURE)

When CORD conducted the one-day programme LURE I in 1991, had a modest goal to find out the ways and means to increase the library utilization by adopting innovative methods tolure the readers. This was based on a feeling that we have been investing in the library huge amounts of money year after year, trying to equip the library with more relevant reading material and also recruit trained personnel to make the resources more useful. While we are trying to build up a tempo, we had a feeling somewhere along the line that the readers or users are still not coming along with us. This feeling lead us to an introspection which gave rise to the impetus for conducting a programme for the first time on LURE in 1991. As stated earlier, the learning programme provided an opportunity for interaction between the library professionals and our own users in understanding the lacunae in promoting exploitation of library resources. In the first workshop on LURE in 1991 several issues were thrown up such as the following:

ISSUES FOR CONSIDERATION

As the reader is reluctant to come to library, it may be necessary that the library has to go to the reader. Naturally, that situation will determine the kind of services that are planned or envisaged to enhance the usage of the library. The issues that influence the usage hinge upon how the information needs are gauged and the methods that are adopted to identify those needs. Some of the other major issues identified are:

- Focus of the parent organisation
- Information collection
- Information processing
- Information search in the Internet era
- Information dissemination
- Information barriers

The workshop offered a set of simple but effective steps to increase the library use with suggestions like involvement of users in procurement of literature, client based services etc., The other major recommendations include:

- The book selection and acquisition are both important and modalities like participatory practices have to be followed;
- User education and user services have to be frequently conducted by the library to improve the interaction between users and the library personnel;
- A brochure on the library highlighting the library collection, cataloging and classification system followed and the services offered would be more useful;
- immediate computerization of all activities of library;
- creation of new services like abstracting, alerting service, reference and making digests on specific topics etc.,
- augmentation of facilities for document supply and other physical facilities like proper sign boards, stools to reach higher shelves, etc., and
- strengthening of the resource sharing at the local level.

These recommendations were taken seriously as they were particularly important in the over all development of the library utilization. Fortunately, most of the suggestions would be implemented with a telling effect on the positive response of the readers.

LURE – II

After a gap of nearly two years, CORD thought of again reviewing the library utilization with the completion of library automation. Accordingly, in 1993 a second programme on LURE was conducted. This time with a difference. The impetus came from the management of parent organization. There was a constant refrain from the management that with automation is there any improvement in the utilization of library resources? How many faculty are visiting the library? What is the ratio between faculty and participants of various training programmes that visit the library? What special arrangements were made to familiarize the participants with the new automation etc., These were a few of the questions that were bothering the management. Also, with computerization of library procedures, a new barrier is likely to be perceived by the users. Such 'Automation anxiety' may have to be taken into consideration in designing training programmes on library initiation.

Accordingly, the participants were chosen from not only the users of the library but also the participants of the then running courses, besides other librarians of neighbouring institutions. The programme was conducted in 3 sessions. In these sessions several papers based on cases illustrating the circulation facility, visitors register, pattern of usage of library on different dates and use of various information products of CORD were presented. Several suggestions emerged based on the discussions and some of which are as follows:—

- *Information Products:*
  - The coverage of indexing and abstracting services done through CORD Index and CORD Abstracts is found to be satisfactory. However, emphasis may have to be given to the immediate interest of the faculty members depending on their research and training programmes.
  - The journals that are covered in CORD Alerts may have to be displayed at a designed place for their immediate location and identification of articles given in the service.
- *Maintenance:*
  - Upkeep and maintenance of various sections will provide the necessary incentive for the users to browse.
  - Library staff should be trained and motivated to assist the readers.
- *User Studies:*
  - Though the faculty members are patronising the library, there is a scope for improvement.
  - Visitors to the Library are not always recording their visits in the prescribed register and so it did not reflect the total visits made by the academic staff in comparison with non-academic staff. A strict vigil on the visitors register may have to be maintained to satisfy the management.

The other major recommendations include:

- Promotion of library with a professional image is essential;
- Library staff should be trained in inter-personnel communication skills;
- There is a need to display current journals in more attractive and useful manner like displaying latest issues at a prominent place, rearranging of primary journals in alphabetical sequence, etc.,
- NIRD publications should be displayed prominently for outside visitors.

- A marketing approach to its library and information products is essential. For this purpose Library counters and surrounding areas should be used for display of not only for acquired publications but also NIRD publications.
- There are about 3000 participants in a year coming to NIRD to participate in the training programmes, who should be given orientation tour to the library for better appreciation of the resources. Also, a session on information resources, and information management relevant to the theme of any course wherever possible should be arranged apart from display of the publications pertaining to the training programme.
- A faculty directory, user manual, training of staff on information technology etc., are other suggestions that emerged from the programme.

After LURE-II in 1993 there was marked improvement in the appreciation of library services, the physical facilities and the environment in the library. Non-book material like CD-ROMS, videos, electronic journal have slowly started to show their presence. In the mid 90s internet opened gates to the Information sources world wide, and made possible access to information from a remote location. As a result it has become more important to look into the problems of transforming a traditional library into an information clearing house.

LURE – III

Against this backdrop a 3rd LURE programme was conducted in the year 1998 after a gap of 5 years. This learning programme was made into a National Workshop inviting papers from all over India on various themes such as library utilisation; techniques of readership enhancement; evaluation of library services; internet and changing role of the librarian etc. Participants from several parts of the country made their presentations based on their own back-home experience in user education and identification of user needs. This workshop revealed various kinds of experiments that are on-going in several parts of the country by innovative librarians and demystifying the Internet for the librarian and the user. Information search in the Internet era has totally changed the way the readers look for information. Searching Internet should become a matter of routine in any special library, to make the expression "Internet is Librarianship" truly applicable. Some of the other major recommendations of the workshop were:

- Continuous study of user needs.
- Development of communication skills of the library personnel.
- Role of parent organization in recognising the contribution of their libraries and supporting their activity.
- Design and update of user manual in the fast changing information technology environment.

- Change of attitude of librarians to the market driven economy and interact with the users more closely and make users appreciate the library services.
- A thematic approach to all the library services have to be i.e., the information products of the library like CORD INDEX, CORD ABSTRACTS should follow the themes identified for the research and training of the institute.
- The Selective Dissemination of Information (SDI) service can perhaps be concentrated on a faculty or a discipline at a time. Once a faculty is studied for a period of 6 months or so as a focussed group the impact on the group and its activities perhaps be quantitatively measured.

CORD is giving continuous training to the Library staff in the above areas in order to serve the clientele for effective use of Library Resources. They are also deputing the staff to other training programmes to get trained in these as well as new emerging areas. Simultaneously providing training and support to the users for better utiliztion of the resources without any barriers. Thus a new era emergd where information driven activities gained importance which will hopefully energize the users as well as information specialists to come together and work for the better uilization of information following the best practices in information dissemination through regular training programmes.

INTERNET TRAINING FOR ACADEMIC LIBRARY STAFF

Educational institutions are being encouraged by the Government and other organizations to upgrade their resources for research and education. Consequently the academic libraries of the higher education institutions are also being upgraded. Internet has proved to be boon in this endeavor. Internet has helped these libraries to be interconnected and share their resources and also to access resources in remote locations. Internet connections have been growing in the recent years with good connectivity and access. But are these libraries fully geared up especially in terms of their employees' skills to be able to fully utilize the Internet for the benefit of the academic community? It has already been widely discussed that training is essential for the staffs to work in a network and automated environment. The Library Association Working Party on Training cites in its Policy Statement that training "is of fundamental importance to all levels of staffs working in all types of library", contributing to "greater efficiency and continuity, with real cost benefits". Since technology keeps on changing it becomes even more necessary for the staff to be trained in Internet.

OBJECTIVES

The present study aims to understand the status of Internet training for the academic library staff within greater Guwahati. Since the importance of

Internet is growing in today's academic environment therefore the issue of training the academic library staff in handling Internet is becoming important. So this study will investigate the various training methods used in the academic libraries, the content of such training, problems encountered and whether any evaluation is undertaken for such training. The investigation will also try to reveal the attitudes of the library managers with regard to training their staff on Internet. In order to understand the status of Internet training for the staffs of the academic libraries a sample of six academic libraries was taken. A questionnaire-based survey of the sample was conducted. The questionnaire contained both close-ended questions and open-ended questions. The questionnaire was prepared based on some existing studies already done on understanding the Internet training of academic library staff. Comprehending the importance of the study the author personally went to the respective libraries to collect the data.

INTERNET AND ITS USE IN ACADEMIC LIBRARIES

Many of us by now are familiar with Internet especially those working in the academic libraries. This is because the academic libraries have been the pioneer in the field of automation and Internet. Internet has become essential for today's education and research in the academic institutions. Library being a hub of research and academic activities are therefore being provided with Internet connections. The Internet is a unique information resource, bringing a wide range of material from around the world to a local machine. One of the earliest usages of the Internet was to access the OPAC i.e. the Online Public Access Catalogues of different libraries or within a campus. The union catalogues which lists the holdings of several libraries was another important tool accessible through net.

Another area of growing importance for academic libraries is that of electronic journals. Big publishing houses like Elsevier, Springer, ACM etc. are providing packages of their journals to libraries in electronic form via Internet. So at nominal subscription the libraries can access to these costly journals, which are becoming increasingly popular with the users. hus grew consortia based subscription in India. INDEST, INFONET and CSIR Consortium are the examples of library consortia for sharing journals and bibliographic information. These consortia based journal subscription are available through the Internet.

The Indian National Digital Library in Engineering Science & Technology i.e. INDEST was set up by the Ministry of Human resource Development (MHRD) for subscription to electronic resources for 38 institutions including IISc, IITs, NITs, IIMs, etc. Over 6000 e-journals are accessible through this consortium, which has its headquarters in IIT Delhi. Infonet Contortia is set up by UGC and operated through its INFLIBNET Centre, Ahmedabad. Over 100 Universities are its members. It covers disciplines like Arts, Sciences,

Mathematics and statistics etc. About 4000 full text electronic journals from 25 publishers are currently accessible. CSIR e-journal Consortia provides access to 3300+ e-journals from 11 publishers to all CSIR S&T staff of different CSIR institutions located around India.

These consortia not only provide full text access but they also give access to bibliographic databases like COMPENDEX, INSPEC SciFinder Scholar, and Web of Science etc. Many open access materials important for education and research are available on the Internet. They are very useful in the context that they are not fee based and also don't have restricted access and are thus becoming very popular with students and researchers. Communicating with users is very important in academic libraries. Widespread access to the Internet has also created new means of communicating with users. In some cases, Internet technologies (e.g. email and publishing on Web pages) are used to reproduce an existing service in another medium, such as online "suggestion boxes".

However, there is "added value" to such a service as users can mail in their suggestions from terminals on or off campus at a time convenient to them. Email enquiry or reference services also represent an extension of mainstream library activity - although some academic librarians initially had concerns about being able to meet the demand of such a service. Reference and enquiry services in academic libraries in the main seek to teach their users how to search for information themselves, rather than answering the enquiries themselves, as is more likely to be the case in a special library. A significant number of British academic libraries have adopted electronic mail enquiry or information services - at the University of Hull the "email help line" is treated as an extension of the Enquiry Desk service. Anecdotal evidence suggests that electronic enquiry services are not overwhelmed, and most users do stay within the parameters of the service. The most successful email enquiry services have developed their procedures and boundaries prior to the service going live.

As many enquiries fall into the category of Frequently Asked Questions, these can thus be answered by existing position statements. Electronic mail also has great potential to cut down on the mountain of paperwork involved in sending out recall notices, notifying readers that items can be collected etc. Some library systems allow students to renew loans (provided no other reader is waiting for the book) directly via the OPAC or to request a renewal via email.

Similarly, weblogs or simply blogs are now becoming very popular on the Internet as a communication medium. A library weblog can be used to:

- Providing news information for users
- Providing links to recommend internet sources
- Book reviews, information about new books
- Providing entertainment or amusement for users

- Providing news or information for librarians
- Book discussions
- Provide news or information for the trustees
- Provide research tips
- Communication among the librarians (in a library system).

The library can make good use of the electronic mail system of Internet i.e. Email to communicate reservation alert, current awareness services like SDI, new arrivals of books and journals, receiving interlibrary loan request and sending overdue notices to the users. In addition to these specialist services academic librarians also make use of the Internet information that is available to all users. Much bibliographical and price information can be found from online bookstores and Web sites for professional organizations and publishers. A wide range of factual information from government and NGO sources is available too. Although librarians have more skepticism about the well-publicized Web search tools than most users, such services can be valuable, particularly for easily defined topics (such as names or abbreviations) and the sheer range of material indexed, subjects covered and the speed with which they search can make them useful when a clear starting point is not obvious. They may not always retrieve a full answer, but may give helpful clues. Internet resources are just another information medium academic librarians are extending their skills to encompass it. So they may offer a current awareness service to teaching and research staff to inform them of new Web sites and discussion lists; they will apply established criteria to assessing the content of information sources or the effectiveness of secondary services like search tools. The hypertext nature of the Web makes it easy to make additional explanation or instruction for a resource as an optional choice. This concept of instruction at the point and time of use is harder to achieve in the physical library.

WHY INTERNET TRAINING IS NECESSARY

In the Internet age there is acute need of Internet specialists. These specialists will be armed with the necessary skills and training to help the users to locate their information pin pointedly and efficiently on the net. Libraries specially the academic libraries would have a great demand for these specialists. Internet connectivity in the academic libraries is growing day by day. So, the present administration of the academic institutions should take necessary steps to equip the library staff with the required skills and training on Internet. Training can help to understand many essential aspects of the Internet such as follows:

- Are we using the right type of Internet connection for our needs? Are we getting a good deal?
- How quickly can we find what we looking for on the Internet? We should be able to find useful information about virtually any topic in less than a minute. If you're taking longer, you're doing something wrong.

- How do we know if we are safe? Most people who contract viruses or other nastiest thought they were protected.
- Are we using email correctly? Or are we really annoying we our colleagues and they are too polite to tell us? We might be unpleasantly surprised to learn the truth.
- How do we avoid those terrible pop-up windows?
- How do we know if information is real or a hoax?
- How can we make surfing faster?
- How can we get the maximum satisfaction without spending more time on net?

As noted by Paula L. Matthews while employing Internet in academic libraries one of the important issues for the administrator is the implementation library staff training. "A lack of training can result in:

- Poor staff performance;
- Lack of motivation;
- High staff turnover;
- Resistance to change;
- Costly errors or accidents;
- Unfulfilled objectives;
- Undesirable low standards of service.

Academic librarians may well draw on training materials available on the Internet for the higher education community. Recently the issue of whether librarians should learn HTML (Hyper-Text Markup Language) was debated on a North American discussion list. The conclusion was that knowledge of basic HTML was necessary in order to prepare presentations and information guides, which are an integral part of the librarian's professional role. As an increasing number of academic libraries experience some measure of "convergence" with other academic support services, library staff has many opportunities to augment their IT skills and collaborate with colleagues in other services. The combination of technical knowledge and the ability to evaluate information sources is a powerful argument for the continued need for LIS professionals in higher education.

The users of the Academic libraries including some faculty member do not have net skills. In such cases the academic library staff has to come forward to help them. For readiness the staff should have some kind of net skills. The transition of traditional library resources to technology based library resources has put a lot of pressure on the academic library staff. Unless the staff is kept up to date on Internet skills he will face more pressure to work in such conditions. So training of staff has become a necessity in today's context

RESEARCHING AND BENCHMARKING BEST PRACTICE IN LIBRARY STAFF DEVELOPMENT

Most university libraries throughout the world are engaged in some level of staff development. Benchmarking of staff development activities however is not widespread and little useful data exists to enable meaningful comparisons between university libraries within national borders, let alone provide meaningful international perspectives. Three studies in the first half of this decade examined staff development policy and practice in the university library sector in Australia and the United Kingdom. Significantly, the studies enabled limited international comparisons where none had been previously possible.

In January 2008, two university library organisations – CAVAL in Australia and EMALINK in the United Kingdom - commenced a joint project to further develop this process of comparison by benchmarking staff development practices within their member libraries. Although located in different hemispheres and literally half a world away from each other, CAVAL and EMALINK were assessed as good candidates for a benchmarking study. Both organisations are roughly similar in terms of their size, composition and orientation. Prior to 2008, they had also already shared expertise relating to staff development and key personnel had worked together as members of IFLA's Continuing Professional Development and Workplace Learning Section. A collaborative project thus appeared to offer CAVAL and EMALINK a unique opportunity to provide value to their member libraries in two key ways:

- By identifying, comparing and generally sharing knowledge about current staff development practices and processes; and,
- By establishing common measurement points, indicators and best practice benchmarks to assist with planning improvements in future staff development practices and processes.

On the ground, the project aimed to obtain data and test various assumptions that would enable the development of a practical tool to facilitate ongoing benchmarking between CAVAL and EMALINK member libraries. Longer term, the project hoped to inform the development of a marketable "dashboard" of indicators for benchmarking staff development activities in other libraries at national and international levels. CAVAL also planned to establish a database of indicators in order to build up a longitudinal data set to facilitate trend analysis.

In tandem with these aims, the project also sought to demonstrate how recent developments in information and communications technology (ICT), particularly social networking technology, have helped to facilitate international collaborative library research projects. Originally projected for completion in late 2008, the project encountered logistical challenges on the Australian side within several months of commencement. Rather than delay or compromise the entire project, CAVAL withdrew temporarily, thereby allowing EMALINK to push ahead with a pilot survey of its members in the United Kingdom. In this way, EMALINK was able to complete base level data collection already undertaken by CAVAL in 2006. This chapter constitutes a progress report and case study of the CAVAL – EMALINK library staff development benchmarking project to July 2008. The chapter outlines the drivers for benchmarking in library staff development and discusses why applied research of this kind is of potentially such great value to university and other libraries in the context of current issues impacting staff development: for example, recruitment and retention of staff. Details are provided of the research methodology agreed by CAVAL and EMALINK, and the benchmarking dimensions investigated by the project. With preliminary data from EMALINK available in early July 2008, the paper reports on initial findings and considers important practical lessons in international collaboration learned to date.

UNDERSTANDING THE VALUE OF BENCHMARKING

In the context of libraries, benchmarking may be defined as an ongoing structured process by which we evaluate the functions, work processes and services of other organisations (not always libraries) recognised for their leadership and innovation.

This process of evaluation is undertaken for the purpose of organisational comparison and improvement. The concept of *competitive benchmarking*, later 'benchmarking', was first popularised by the Xerox Corporation in the late 1970s as an innovative response – at that time – to strong competition in a market segment that it had hitherto dominated. Xerox refined the concept of benchmarking through the 1980s and eventually promulgated a ten-step benchmarking process.

Despite there now being many competing process models for benchmarking, most can trace their origins back twenty years to the original Xerox process, and early variations. Other influences cited as significant in the development of the concept of benchmarking include the quality assurance movement and just-in-time manufacturing methods. Indeed, Deming's classic four step quality improvement process still forms the basis of many benchmarking exercises.

Benchmarking is essentially concerned with understanding how processes work – through observing and studying work methods and practices – and then identifying good or best practice. Benchmarking seeks to learn from the observation of such good and best practice, and to make improvements necessary to reach identified standards of good and best practice. Assessment of improvement is based on review and comparison with other like organisations; hence the significance of a good match between CAVAL and EMALINK.

Drawing on Deming's four step process, Ford and Longbottom each propose useful models for benchmarking; Ford specifically in the context of benchmarking human resource development (HRD). It is Longbottom's 'PAIR' approach however that resonates through the methodology applied in the CAVAL-EMALINK project:

- *Planning:* Investigation, measurement and examination of the strengths and weaknesses of current processes;
- *Analysis:* Identifying potential benchmarking partners and then exchanging information, and observing and comparing processes;
- *Implementation:* Adaptation and modification of processes based on learning from the analysis stage;
- *Review:* Ongoing review and refinement with the intention of achieving continuous improvements.

Within the higher education sector, libraries have frequently been early and enthusiastic adopters of benchmarking techniques. University libraries in Australia, New Zealand and the United Kingdom, for example, have all been at the forefront in adopting and applying benchmarking processes to various aspects of their operations. In the case of Australia, the work of scholars has been important in outlining suitable frameworks and encouraging the adoption of benchmarking methods in university libraries.

Noting the need to identify benchmarks which would assess efficient use of resources and the quality of the contributions which university libraries make to the realisation of university objectives, McKinnon *et al* proposed a range of criterion reference benchmarks with the intention firstly of identifying attributes of good practice and then using those attributes as benchmarks for further evaluation. The *Council of Australian University Librarians* has encouraged benchmarking between its members and has facilitated a range of studies in various operational areas including client satisfaction with library services, performance and effectiveness of document delivery services, availability of sought materials, cataloguing, and the re-shelving of library materials. Several trans-national benchmarking projects have also been undertaken with Australian libraries as a key partner, for example between libraries in Australia and New Zealand and Australia and the United Kingdom.

STAFF DEVELOPMENT RESEARCH IN AUSTRALIA AND THE UNITED KINGDOM

Attempts to examine and benchmark staff development practice in Australian university libraries can be traced back more than twenty years; with more recent work in Australia and the United Kingdom attempting to update and expand that work. Both early Australian surveys by Trask and Gray revealed a paucity of human resource development in the university library sector, albeit balanced by an emerging recognition at that time of the importance of developing people. In 2001 and then again in 2005, Smith explored the extent of commitment to staff development, linkages to strategic organisational priorities, and the focus of staff development activity. The overall picture presented by these 2001 and 2005 surveys was of a strong commitment to investment in human resource development – a picture very different to that found in the earlier 1983 and 1986 analyses. Smith concluded that the major influences on the focus of staff development programmes in Australian university libraries included:

- Increasing scope and volume of electronic publishing, with consequent changes in required staff skills and knowledge;
- Increasing involvement of university library staff in teaching information literacy (with needs for skill development on the part of those staff doing such teaching);
- Changing organisational demographics (in particular ageing workforces), and actual or impending retirements of staff (particularly senior staff) – this resulting in the need for succession planning and development of new leadership and management capability; and,
- The imperative for regionally isolated libraries to grow and develop skills and capability within their existing workforce.

For the first time, the 2005 survey explored budget allocations for staff development. This was interesting as a measure in its own right of the level of commitment to staff development activity. It also enabled benchmarking against a comparable survey undertaken in the United Kingdom, and several other available benchmarks including those of the *American Society for Training and Development* and *UNESCO*. In 2004, motivated partly by the 2001 Australian study, Yeoh investigated staff development in a cross section of university libraries in England, Scotland and Ireland. That survey found, inter alia:

- A strong commitment to staff development as part of institutional strategic organisational management;
- Formal written statements of commitment to staff development in just over half of the organisations surveyed;
- A planned and structured approach to staff development in most organisations; and,
- A structured appraisal and review of these activities in two thirds of organisations.

It was also keen to develop common staff development indicators and a database to enable longitudinal studies. In retrospect, the survey instrument developed by the project team was arguably too broad, encompassing 97 questions over 46 pages, and too complex; partly a outcome of trying to align the survey with international studies. As a result of the CAVAL survey's complexity, details of staff development practice within member libraries were largely obscured by other issues relating to recruitment and retention and succession planning.

Although providing a highly detailed and ultimately fascinating snapshot of human resources in CAVAL member libraries in late 2006, the project stalled after presentation of the preliminary findings in March 2007. "The research project generated an immense amount of data that is of varying degrees of completeness and indeed of value." The research instrument itself was complex, which potentially added further complications to the ability to undertake an effective comparative analysis and interpretation of the responses." Interestingly, researcher comments echo those of Ford, writing on benchmarking HRD: "choosing the wrong set of metrics is one of the surest ways to doom a benchmarking study."

For CAVAL, the over-riding challenge of the 2006 *Benchmarking of Staff Development Practice in CAVAL Member Libraries* project was how to go about "extracting the desired key measurement points needed if benchmark levels of practice and processes are to be established within the membership of the consortium." With resources allocated to the CAVAL project exhausted by early 2007 and other projects moving to the fore, further progress on benchmarking staff development seemed unlikely in the short term. As one door closes, however, sometimes another opens. Enter at this point EMALINK, the East Midlands Library Information Network, representing the 10 university and higher education libraries comprising the United Kingdom's East Midland University Association (EMUA).

WHY BENCHMARK BEST PRACTICE IN LIBRARY STAFF DEVELOPMENT?

Before reporting on the methodology and early findings of the 2008 CAVAL-EMALINK study, it is important to understand the significance of benchmarking best practice in staff development to libraries in general. Libraries, it was long argued, were simply the sum of their collections – print and later electronic. A big library was ipso facto a good library. The majority of contemporary library measures still reflect this preoccupation with the physical item, even where electronic resources have taken precedence.

The rise of the internet and increasing demands from customers have however progressively turned the focus of library managers to their people – arguably always their best information 'assets'. People and the environments in which they live and work are not static though, and the parallel processes of personal and professional development must be ongoing. Thus libraries, particularly university libraries, have come to realise the significance of better understanding staff development through benchmarking. Many are returning to the origins of benchmarking as an organisational improvement tool, and Spendolini's simple elevator definition of benchmarking as "learning from others".

Researcher that "changes in the academic library workplace mirror those of other workplaces in the new millennium." Expanding on this theme, researcher observes:

- Following the nature of the work, the organisation of the institution is constantly shifting, requiring staff in all areas to perform a greater variety of tasks. The operations daily become more automated and more technical. The workforce becomes more diverse. The pace quickens. The budget tightens. And the tensions mount.

For libraries, particularly university libraries, there are also specific challenges to address. The last two decades have seen greatly increased emphases on access to information and knowledge management. Changes and developments in the ways and means of organising and accessing recorded knowledge have been both rapid and profound; with increasingly sophisticated information systems evolving as a result. As IFLA acknowledges, libraries and those who work in them have an increasingly important role to play in such an environment:

- The quality of service provided to the public by library and information science institutions depends on the expertise of their staff. Constant flux in the needs of societies, changing technologies, and growth in professional knowledge demand that information workers must expand their understanding and update their skills on an ongoing basis.

As a consequence of this transformation, human resource professionals in libraries are observing a range of issues impacting on and influencing staff development.

Focusing on university libraries, the issues are as follows:

- The need for library staff to keep current with continuous changes in information technology and with information itself;
- A related need to coordinate technical training for library staff, and find the expertise and resources to provide it;
- A strengthening of libraries' traditional customer service orientation in order to compete with Internet search engines and online booksellers;
- Further development of libraries' orientation towards teamwork, made necessary by shrinking budgets, decreases in staff numbers, and the rise of multifunctional teams;
- Additional support required for both new and experienced managers;
- Growth of the teaching and training role of university library staff, particularly but not exclusively those in professional positions; and finally,
- The need to provide meaningful staff development as a means of recruiting and retaining staff.

The imperative to maintain and upgrade the skills, knowledge, and abilities of library and information staff has been recognised, and is reflected, in the significant priority allocated to human resource development (HRD) activity in many libraries. As a strategic organisational priority it is important that HRD is assessed and, where necessary, improved and that this be a continuing cyclical activity. Benchmarking has clear potential to achieve that end. Indeed, benchmarking has particular applicability for HRD because the activity naturally lends itself to cooperative and collaborative working between institutions. Ford proposes a series of metrics which may be usefully applied to benchmarking staff development. Some are relatively straightforward to measure and calculate, while others are more challenging. In broadly escalating degrees of difficulty in measurement these metrics include:

- Expenditure on staff development activities expressed as a percentage of payroll;
- Average hours spent on staff development per employee per annum;
- Average staff development cost per participant per hour;
- Percentage of employees undertaking staff development activity per annum;
- Average percentage of positive ratings of staff development activities by participants;
- Average percentage of gains in learning reported by participants in staff development activities;
- Average percentage of improvement in on-the-job performance as a result of participation in staff development activities;
- Cost savings and efficiency gains as a result of participation in staff development activities.

The eventual goal is to take raw data and convert it to ratios or percentages that can be monitored easily over time – in effect, a staff development 'dashboard'. Although nowhere near this level of sophistication, IFLA's *Continuing Professional Development and Workplace Learning Quality Guidelines Project* has published useful best practice indicators for staff development. IFLA requires that there be:

- Regular learning needs assessment.
- Broad range of learning opportunities, both formal and informal; formal offerings in a choice of formats, designed to meet identified needs, in modules structured to cover topics from introductory through advanced.
- Organizational commitment and leadership from staff development and continuing education administrators with expertise in adult continuing education.
- Widely disseminated information about continuing education and resources, accurately described.
- C[ontinuing] E[education] activities design that includes learning objectives aligned with identified needs; follows principles of instructional design and learning theory; selects course instructors on the basis of both subject knowledge and teaching ability; attends to transfer of training and feedback.
- Consistent documentation of individuals' participation in learning and recognition of continuing learning in hiring and promotion decisions.

- A minimum of 0.5 to 1.0 % of institutional budget earmarked for staff development, as stated in *The public library service: IFLA/ UNESCO guidelines for developmen.*
- About 10% of work hours provided for attendance at workshops, conferences, in-service training, and other educational activities, and for informal learning projects.
- Evaluation of continuing education and staff development offerings and programmes.
- Research that assesses the state of CPD and examines the efficacy and outcomes of continuing education and staff development programmes.

CAVAL-EMALINK STUDY METHODOLOGY

In October 2007, Ian Smith and Graham Walton proposed that CAVAL in Australia and EMALINK in the United Kingdom undertake a joint study to identify best practice in staff development in member libraries. They highlighted a number of benefits to individual member libraries, including:

- Acquisition of staff development data to inform and guide ongoing change processes;
- Opportunity to undertake national and international level comparisons; and,
- Opportunity for international partnering and skills exchange.

Within the context of developing and delivering the project, the proposal acknowledged that university libraries are busy organisations and that no funds had been budgeted for the project by CAVAL or EMALINK in 2008. It was considered crucial therefore that the work should not be time or resource intensive, particularly in relation to project management and data collection. A relatively brief web based questionnaire was suggested to minimise the time and effort required for survey development, administration and analysis. Smith and Walton proposed that the project should be jointly overseen by a small team of nominated representatives from the CAVAL Human Resources Group and EMALINK. This working group would take responsibility for jointly developing and administering the survey questionnaire, analysing the data obtained, and producing a summary report for dissemination to individual member libraries. The proposed study methodology called for data collection to take place through a web based questionnaire, with questions taking no more than 20 minutes in total to complete. In scoping the 2006 staff development benchmarking study involving CAVAL member libraries, Smith originally proposed eight benchmarking dimensions:

- Budget allocation for staff development expressed as a percentage of total payroll costs. Further, what elements are covered by that budget and what budget model is applied for staff development (e.g., centralised or distributed)?

- Approval criteria and processes – how are staff development applications assessed and approved?
- Links between staff development priorities and strategic planning;
- Organisational approaches to the development, documentation and evaluation of staff development plans;
- Common themes and priorities in staff development plans;
- Application of *Rodski* results in setting staff development objectives - have staff development investments in turn improved *Rodski* ratings?
- Coordination of staff development in CAVAL member libraries – how and by whom?
- Evaluation of staff development programmes by the organisation and measurement of the return on investment (ROI).

By mid-July 2008, EMALINK had received an encouraging seven responses from a total membership of ten university libraries. In 2006, CAVAL received responses from all eleven members.

2

Library Staffing

CONCEPT AND IMPORTANCE OF STAFFING

CONCEPT

Staffing is one of the important management functions which is mainly concerned with proper arrangement and management of the required manpower for the organisation. After having prepared plans, as well as the structure of organisation for seeking the objectives, various positions are created. Effectiveness is not uni dimensional or one sided. To be effective in work setting people must do many things well and they as people must derive same value from their efforts. to have an effective staffing process, it requires as a first step the explicit specification of exactly what is that people must do well and what they will be offered in reward for doing it. - Benjamin Schneider
Staff function of the management consists of the following features:

- To prepare manpower planning.
- To determine manpower requirements of organisation in terms of quantity and quality.
- To make all necessary arrangement for acquiring needed human force through proper and effective recruitment and selection.
- To maintain human force in organisation for a period of time.
- To formulating effective Labour policies for long period.
- To implementing the Labour policies in various projects.
- To develop manpower to its maximum by providing scientific training and conducting various development programmes.

IMPORTANCE OF STAFFING

- Staffing function is very closely related to other managerial areas of the business. It greatly influences the direction and control in the organisation. The effectiveness of other managerial functions depends on the effectiveness of the staffing function.
- Staffing function helps to build proper human relationships in the organisation. Smooth human relations is the key to better

communication and co-ordination of managerial efforts in an organisation.

- Skilled and experienced staff is the best asset of a business concern. The staffing function helps developing this asset for the business. It inculcates the corporate culture into the staff which in turn ensures smooth functioning of all the managerial aspects of the business.
- Staffing decisions have long term effect on the efficiency of an organisation. Qualified, efficient and well motivated staff is an asset of the organisation. Staffing function assumes special significance in the context of globalisation which demands high degree of efficiency in maintaining competitiveness.
- Staff selection should be based on the ability of the prospective employees to meet the future challenges that the organisation need to address. Therefore the potential contribution of the staff in their anticipated future roles should also be taken into account in staff selection.

STAFFING AS PART OF HUMAN RESOURCE MANAGEMENT

It is a function which all managers need to perform. It is a separate and specialised function and there are many aspects of human relations to be considered. It is the job of managers to fill positions in their organisation and to make sure that they remain occupied with qualified people. Staffing is closely linked to organising Since, after the structure and positions have been decided, people are required to work in these positions. Subsequently, they need to be trained and motivated to work in harmony with the goals of the organisation.

Thus, staffing is seen as a generic function of management. The staffing function deals with the human element of management. Managing the human component of an organisation is the most important task because the performance of an organisation depends upon how well this function is performed. The success of an organisation in achieving its goals is determined to a great extent on the competence, motivation and performance of its human resources. It is the responsibility of all managers to directly deal with and select people to work for the organisation. When the manager performs the staffing function his role is slightly limited.

Some of these responsibilities will include placing the right person on the right job, introducing new employees to the organisation, training employees improving their performance, developing their abilities, maintaining their morale and protecting their health and physical conditions. In small organisations, managers may perform all duties related to employees salaries, welfare and working conditions. But as organisations grow and number of persons employed increases, a separate department called the human resource department is formed which has specialists in managing people. The management of human resources is a specialised area which requires the expertise of many people. The number of human resource specialists and sise of this department gives an indication of the sise of the business as well. For a very large company, the Human Resources Department itself will contain specialists for each function of this department. Human Resource Management includes many specialised activities and duties which the human resource personnel must perform. These duties are:

- Analysing jobs, collecting information about jobs to prepare job descriptions.
- Defending the company in law suits and avoiding legal complications.
- Developing compensation and incentive plans.
- Handling grievances and complaints.
- Maintaining labour relations and union management relations.
- Providing for social security and welfare of employees.
- Recruitment, *i.e.,* search for qualified people
- Training and development of employees for efficient performance and career growth.

STAFFING PROCESS

- The very first step in staffing is to plan the manpower inventory required by a concern in order to match them with the job requirements and demands. Therefore, it involves forecasting and determining the future manpower needs of the concern.
- Once the requirements are notified, the concern invites and solicits applications according to the invitations made to the desirable candidates.
- This is the screening step of staffing in which the solicited applications are screened out and suitable candidates are appointed as per the requirements.
- Once screening takes place, the appointed candidates are made familiar to the work units and work environment through the orientation programmes. placement takes place by putting right man on the right job.
- Training is a part of incentives given to the workers in order to develop and grow them within the concern. Training is generally given according to the nature of activities and scope of expansion in it. Along with it, the workers are developed by providing them extra benefits of indepth knowledge of their functional areas. Development also includes giving them key and important jobs as a test or examination in order to analyse their performances.
- It is a kind of compensation provided monetarily to the employees for their work performances. This is given according to the nature

of job-skilled or unskilled, physical or mental, etc. Remuneration forms an important monetary incentive for the employees.

- In order to keep a track or record of the behaviour, attitudes as well as opinions of the workers towards their jobs. For this regular assessment is done to evaluate and supervise different work units in a concern. It is basically concerning to know the development cycle and growth patterns of the employeesin a concern.
- Promotion is said to be a non-monetary incentive in which the worker is shifted from a higher job demanding bigger responsibilities as well as shifting the workers and transferring them to different work units and branches of the same organisation.

RECRUITMENT: MEANING AND SOURCES

Acquiring and retaining high-quality talent is critical to an organisation's success. As the job market becomes increasingly competitive and the available skills grow more diverse, recruiters need to be more selective in their choices, Since, poor recruiting decisions can produce long-term negative effects, among them high training and development costs to minimise the incidence of poor performance and high turnover which, in turn, impact staff morale, the production of high quality goods and services and the retention of organisational memory.

At worst, the organisation can fail to achieve its objectives thereby losing its competitive edge and its share of the market. Traditionally, Public Service organisations have had little need to worry about market share and increasing competition Since, they operate in a monopolistic environment. But in recent time, the emphasis on New Public Management/ Public Sector Management approaches has forced public organisations to pay closer attention to their service delivery as consumers have begun to expect and demand more for their tax dollars. No longer are citisens content to grumble about poorly-produced goods and services and the under-qualified, untrained employees who provide them.

As societies become more critical and litigious, public service organisations must seek all possible avenues for improving their output and providing the satisfaction their clients require and deserve. The provision of high-quality goods and services begins with the recruitment process. Recruitment is described as "the set of activities and processes used to legally obtain a sufficient number of qualified people at the right place and time so that the people and the organisation can select each other in their own best short and long term interests".

In other words, the recruitment process provides the organisation with a pool of potentially qualified job candidates from which judicious selection can be made to fill vacancies. Successful recruitment begins with proper employment planning and forecasting. In this phase of the staffing process, an organisation formulates plans to fill or eliminate future job openings based on an analysis of future needs, the talent available within and outside of the organisation, and the current and anticipated resources that can be expended to attract and retain such talent. Also related to the success of a recruitment process are the strategies an organisation is prepared to employ in order to identify and select the best candidates for its developing pool of human resources.

Organisations seeking recruits for base-level entry positions often require minimum qualifications and experience. These applicants are usually recent high school or university/ technical college graduates many of whom have not yet made clear decisions about future careers or are contemplating engaging in advanced academic activity. At the middle levels, senior administrative, technical and junior executive positions are often filled internally. The push for scarce, high-quality talent, often recruited from external sources, has usually been at the senior executive levels. Most organisations utilise both mechanisms to effect recruitment to all levels.

THE RECRUITMENT PROCESS

Successful recruitment involves the several processes of:

- Development of a policy on recruitment and retention and the systems that give life to the policy;
- Needs assessment to determine the current and future human resource requirements of the organisation. If the activity is to be effective, the human resource requirements for each job category and functional division/unit of the organisation must be assessed and a priority assigned;
- Identification, within and outside the organisation, of the potential human resource pool and the likely competition for the knowledge and skills resident within it;
- Job analysis and job evaluation to identify the individual aspects of each job and calculate its relative worth;
- Assessment of qualifications profiles, drawn from job descriptions that identify responsibilities and required skills, abilities, knowledge and experience;
- Determination of the organisation's ability to pay salaries and benefits within a defined period;
- Identification and documentation of the actual process of recruitment and selection to ensure equity and adherence to equal opportunity and other laws.

Documenting the organisation's policy on recruitment, the criteria to be utilised, and all the steps in the recruiting process is as necessary in the seemingly informal setting of in house selection as it is when selection is made from external sources. Documentation satisfies the requirement of procedural transparency and leaves a trail that can easily be followed for audit and other purposes. Of special importance is documentation that is in conformity with Freedom of Information legislation, such as:

- Criteria and procedures for the initial screening of applicants;
- Criteria for generating long and short lists;
- Criteria and procedures for the selection of interview panels;
- Interview questions;
- Interview scores and panellists' comments;
- Results of tests;
- Results of reference checks.

Recruitment Strategies and Processes

Recruitment may be conducted internally through the promotion and transfer of existing personnel or through referrals, by current staff members, of friends and family members. Where internal recruitment is the chosen method of filling vacancies, job openings can be advertised by job posting, that is, a strategy of placing notices on manual and electronic bulletin boards, in company newsletters and through office memoranda. Referrals are usually word-of-mouth advertisements that are a low-cost-per-hire way of recruiting. Internal recruitment does not always produce the number or quality of personnel needed; in such an instance, the organisation needs to recruit from external sources, either by encouraging walk-in applicants; advertising vacancies in newspapers, magazines and journals, and the visual and/or audio media; using employment agencies to "head hunt"; advertising on-line via the Internet; or through job fairs and the use of college recruitment.

Public service agencies enjoy greater exposure to scrutiny than most private sector organisations; therefore, openness and transparency in recruitment and selection practices are crucial. The discussion that follows will identify some of the options available for attracting applicants to the public service job market and discuss strategies for managing the process.

POSTING VACANCIES

As indicated earlier, job posting refers to the practice of publicising an open job to employees and listing its attributes, such as criteria of knowledge, qualification, skill and experience. The purpose of posting vacancies is to bring to the attention of all interested persons the jobs that are to be filled. Before posting a vacancy, management needs to decide whether:

- It intends to retain the job in its present form and with its present title, remuneration and status;
- Selected attributes of the job, for example, skill or experience, will change;
- There are sufficient qualified, potential applicants serving in other positions within the organisation who may be potential candidates for that job;

- The existing organisational policy on recruitment is still applicable;
- The organisations stands to benefit more, in the long-term, from recruiting applicants from external sources.

Also necessary is the availability of a functional human resource information system that supports recruitment.

An effective, computerised system would:

- Flag imminent vacancies throughout the organisation to ensure that the recruitment process is timely;
- Ensure that no candidates are lost but, instead, move through the process and are kept informed of their status;
- Ensure that good candidates whose applications are pending are kept in touch to maintain their interest in the organisation;
- Assist in analysing hiring, transfer and exit trends and provide other data that are helpful in planning, evaluating and auditing the recruitment process;
- Identify any adverse impacts of the recruitment process on vulnerable groups;
- For internal recruiting, control the internal job posting process, generate the notices, and then match internal applicant qualifications with job specifications;
- Where jobs are not being posted, generate a list of qualified internal candidates.

An organisation needs to analyse the benefits and disadvantages of recruiting its personnel through internal or external sources and, where the latter is selected, whether formal or informal systems should be used.

Recruiting from Internal Sources

There are sound reasons for recruiting from sources within the organisation:

- The ability of the recruit is known so it is easy to assess potential for the next level. By contrast, assessments of external recruits are based on less reliable sources, such as references, and relatively brief encounters, such as interviews.
- "Insiders" know the organisation, its strengths and weaknesses, its culture and, most of all, its people.
- Promotions from within build motivation and a sense of commitment to the organisation. Skilled and ambitious employees are more likely to become involved in developmental activities if they believe that these activities will lead to promotion.
- Internal recruitment is cheaper and quicker than advertising in various media and interviewing "outsiders". Time spent in training and socialisation is also reduced.

At the same time, several disadvantages exist:

- Sometimes it is difficult to find the "right" candidate within and the organisation may settle for an employee who possesses a less than ideal mix of competencies.
- If the vacancies are being caused by rapid expansion of the organisation there may be an insufficient supply of qualified individuals above the entry level. This may result in people being promoted before they are ready, or not being allowed to stay in a position long enough to learn how to do the job well.
- Infighting, inbreeding, and a shortage of varied perspectives and interests may reduce organisational flexibility and growth, and resistance to change by those who have an interest in maintaining the *status quo* may present long term problems.
- In times of rapid growth and during transitions, the organisation may promote from within into managerial positions, regardless of the qualifications of incumbents. Transition activities and rapid organisational growth often mask managerial deficiencies; it is not until the growth rate slows that the deficiencies become apparent and, then, the organisation finds it difficult, if not impossible, to undo the damage. The resulting cost of remedial training can prove prohibitive.

Recruiting from External Sources

External recruiting methods can be grouped into two classes: informal and formal. Informal recruiting methods tap a smaller market than formal methods. These methods may include rehiring former employees and choosing from among those "walk-in" applicants whose unsolicited résumés had been retained on file. The use of referrals also constitutes an informal hiring method. Because they are relatively inexpensive to use and can be implemented quickly, informal recruiting methods are commonly used for hiring clerical and other base-level recruits who are more likely than other groups to have submitted unsolicited applications.

Former students who participated in internship programmes may also be easily and cheaply accessed. Formal methods of external recruiting entail searching the labour market more widely for candidates with no previous connection to the organisation. These methods have traditionally included newspaper/magazine/journal advertising, the use of employment agencies and executive search firms, and college recruitment.

More often, now, job/career fairs and e-Recruiting are reaching the job seeker market. Posting vacancies externally through the various arms of the media or via employment agencies reaches a wider audience and may turn up a greater number of potential candidates from which the organisation can choose. At the same time, this method is relatively expensive and time-consuming as the organisation works through initial advertisements, short-listing, interviewing and the other processes that precede selection. Even then, there is no guarantee that the results will be satisfactory to the organisation, Since, the cost of advertising often limits the frequency and duration of the job posting, as well as the amount of information made available, thus making it difficult for a job seeker to accurately judge the worth of the position being offered. In addition, the organisation may hire a candidate who fails to live up to the high potential displayed during the selection process.

Recruiting firms/employment agencies are gaining in popularity, especially in the search for management level/executive talent. Recruiting via this medium is expensive, whether the organisation uses a contingency firm or has one on retainer. Executive search firms tend to match candidates to jobs faster that most organisations can, on their own, primarily because the recruiting firms/employment agencies possess larger databases of, and wider access to, persons and have a greater awarene of the location of competencies needed by the client agencies.

Of course, it is possible to for an organisation to reduce the risks and high costs of recruitment by maintaining a small cadre of full-time, permanent employees and meeting an unexpected and temporary need for staff through the use of *ad hoc* and short-term contract workers who come to the position already trained. It is frequently said that the best jobs are not advertised; their availability is communicated by word of mouth. Networking, therefore, continues to be a viable mechanism for recruiting, especially at the senior management level in certain industries. In many instances, networking is a strategy used by the recruitment firms/ employment agencies.

ON-LINE APPLICATIONS/RECRUITING ON THE INTERNET

Using the Internet is faster and cheaper than many traditional methods of recruiting. Jobs can be posted on Internet sites for a modest amount, remain there for periods of thirty or sixty days or more - at no additional cost - and are available twenty-four hours a day. Candidates can view detailed information about the job and the organisation and then respond electronically.

Most homes and workplaces are now using computerised equipment for communication; the Internet is rapidly becoming the method of choice for accessing and sharing information. First-time job seekers are now more likely to search web sites for job postings than to peruse newspapers, magazines and journals. The prevalence of eadvertising has made it easier. The Internet speeds up the hiring process in three basis stages:

- Faster posting of jobs.
  - The submission of information to the media house and its appearance in print disappears. On the internet, the

advertisement appears immediately and can be kept alive for as long as the recruiter requires it.

- Faster applicant response.
  - Jobs posted on the Internet and requiring responses via the same medium receive responses on the same day.
- Faster processing of résumés.
  - An applicant sending a résumé electronically can immediately have the application processed, receive an acknowledgement, be screened electronically, and have details of the application and résumé despatched to several managers at the same time.

On-line recruiting also provides access to passive job seekers, that is, individuals who already have a job but would apply for what appears a better one that is advertised on the Internet. These job seekers may be of a better quality Since, they are not desperate for a job change as are the active job seekers who may be frustrated, disgruntled workers looking for a new position. Companies that are likely to advertise on-line usually have a Web site that allows potential candidates to learn about the company before deciding whether to apply, thus lowering the incidence time-wasting through the submission of unsuitable applications.

The Web site can be used as a tool to encourage potential job seekers to build an interest in joining the organisation. Job web sites offer unlimited space which can be used, by management, to sell the organisation. The site can then be used, not only to post vacancies, but also to publicise the organisation. That will allow candidates to become more familiar with the company, know what skills the company is looking for and get to know about its culture. Most importantly, the system will provide a proper path to securing quick responses to job openings. On-line recruiting facilitates the decentralisation of the hiring function by making it possible for other groups in the organisation to take responsibility for part of the function.

- Some applicants still place great value on face-to-face interactions in the hiring process. Such applicants are likely to ignore jobs posted, impersonally, on-line.
- Companies are overwhelmed by the volume of résumés posted on the Internet. This can, in fact, lengthen the short-listing process. If the screening process is not well done, the quantity of applications/ résumés logged-on may be more of a hindrance to the process that an aid to selection.

Job seekers who demand confidentiality in the recruitment process may be reluctant to use the Internet as a job search mechanism. For effectiveness in the use of the strategy of e-Recruiting, companies are advised to:

- Use specialised Job Sites that cater to specific industries; interested in joining the company;
- Take advantage of the fact that Internet job advertisements have

no space limitations so recruiters can use longer job descriptions to fully describe the company, job requirements and working conditions offered;

- Use valid Search Engines that will sort candidates effectively, but will not discriminate against any persons or groups;
- Create attention-grabbing newspaper advertisements that prompt people to visit the company's Web site. They will then see all vacancies that are advertised;
- Encourage employees to e-mail job advertisements to friends;
- Design and implement a successful e-Recruitment strategy.

COLLEGE RECRUITMENT

College recruiting – sending an employer's representatives to college campuses to prescreen applicants and create an applicant pool from that college's graduating class – is an important source of management trainees, promotable candidates, and professional and technical employees. To get the best out of this hiring strategy, the organisation and its career opportunities must be made to stand out. Human resource professionals are aware that few college students and potential graduates know where their careers will take them over the next fifteen to twenty years.

Therefore many of the an opportunity for recruiters to select the potential employees with the personal, technical and professional competencies they require in their organisation. The personal competencies identified may include, *inter alia,* a positive work ethic, strong interpersonal skills, leadership capacity and an ability to function well in a work team. The opportunity to discuss a student's current strengths and potential future value to an organisation cannot be replicated in any other setting. Two major advantages of this strategy are the cost (which is higher than word-of-mouth recruiting but lower than advertising in the media or using an employment agency), and the convenience (Since, many candidates can be interviewed in a short time in the same location with space and administrative support provided by the college itself). nfortunately, suitable candidates become available only at certain times of the year, which may not always suit the needs of the hiring organisation.

Another major disadvantage of college recruiting is the lack of experience and the inflated expectations of new graduates and the cost of hiring graduates for entry-level positions that may not require a college degree. To make college recruiting effective, the recruiting organisation must first determine how many and which schools should be targeted. It may prove cost-effective to do intensive recruiting in a few, carefully-selected institutions, establishing a presence and building the organisation's reputation among students and faculty. Timely and frequent dissemination of literature, the offer of internships and the award of prises for academic and/or social prowess help to advertise the organisation as a preferred place of employment. Subsequent invitations to the organisation's offices, made to students identified as potential employees, may serve to solidify the firm's image. Public Service organisations are usually unable to compete financially with their Private Sector counterparts and are therefore less likely to pay competitive salaries.

However, most public service agencies provide their employees with a wealth and range of experiences that are available nowhere else. It is for that reason that many college graduates use the Public Service as an employer of first resort to gain the experiences that will make them marketable in the short term. The strategies may not work as smoothly for public service recruiters, Since, the laws that govern their organisations' recruitment practices may be more stringent than those that apply in private sector companies. There may also be questions about the legality of the on-line application form. If this strategy were to be employed, public service recruiters must first decide on the criteria that should guide the process. The Public Service is seldom immediately seen as an attractive employer, mainly because salaries are uncompetitive.

Except for those students who have a commitment to public service, the top ten percent of college graduates will select the Private Sector as the employer of choice, partly because of the prestige value but primarily because of the remuneration package and because the recruiters may have been more successful in marketing their company. Therefore, it is understood that many of the graduates who enter the Public Service will stay for a short time and either return to school or proceed to another sector once they have acquired the requisite skills and experience that make them marketable. Recruitment and retention strategies in the Public Service must, therefore, reflect this reality and efforts made to get the most out of college graduates before they move on; conversely, the organisation may need to plan to recruit those students whose academic records suggest that they will remain in an organisation that pays less.

Retention strategies will focus on ensuring opportunities for intense training and development for skill enhancement and personal satisfaction. College recruitment also offers opportunities for internships. These programmes may provide the organisations with quality employees at low cost per hire. Some interns are hired at low cost (perhaps minimum wage) and are offered work experience.

Interns are able to have business skills, check out potential employers, and learn more about employers' likes and dislikes before making final career choices. Some of the better interns are recruited after graduation. College recruitment is relatively expensive and time consuming for the recruiting company. The process involves screening the candidate, that is, determining whether he/she is worthy of further consideration and marketing the company as a preferred place of employment. An alternate strategy for college recruitment is the career planning workshop. These activities are usually (but not exclusively) associated with adolescent school leavers. They do not immediately produce ready candidates for the job market but provide the opportunity for an organisation to present itself as an employer worthy of consideration. Co-ordinators of career planning workshops co-opt professionals and organisations to present career options to potential school leavers in a controlled setting so as to lay out the range of possibilities to young job seekers. Career planning workshops are used mainly as information-giving tools which the school leaver can use to make informed career choices. Some organisations use the workshops as a base for internships.

Job Fairs

The concept of a job fair is to bring those interested in finding a job into those companies who are searching for applicants. Job fairs are open fora at which employers can exhibit the best their companies have to offer so that job seekers can make informed choices. They are considered one of the most effective ways for job seekers to land jobs. At the job fair, employers have a large pool of candidates on which to draw, while job seekers have the opportunity to shop around for dozens – sometimes hundreds – of employers, all in one place. Notwithstanding the fact that the atmosphere at the fair is more relaxed than at an interview, employers are still on the look out for qualified, potential employees who have interest, dedication and initiative.

Maintaining Fairness/Equity in the Recruitment Process

It is often difficult to ensure and maintain fairness/equity in the recruitment process although, in every jurisdiction, there are laws that protect individuals and vulnerable groups from the negative impact of discriminatory practices. Where necessary, systems, detailed procedures and processes exist or must be established to minimise discrimination. Each country designates/identifies a group or groups for special notice; women, visible minorities and the disabled are usual targets. The Government of Canada, in articulating its "Employment Equity Act and Regulations", identified four designated groups as employment equity targets: women, Aboriginal people, members of visible minority groups, persons with disabilities. In the legislation, managers' responsibilities for employment equity are stated as:

- Ensuring effective overall performance and continuous progress of the employment equity goals within the operation;
- Achieving, fostering and maintaining a representative workforce;
- Showing leadership in employment equity and demonstrating commitment to it by ensuring that discrimination and stereotyping are not tolerated; and
- Informing and educating employees in the organisation about employment equity and diversity.

The Australian Public Service Commission, in ensuring that there were no infringements against individuals rights, issued general guidelines on workplace diversity, some of which related to recruitment:

- Integrate workplace diversity with the agency's goals and business.
- Reflect agency workplace diversity objectives in workplace agreements and certified agreements.
- Integrate workplace diversity principles into human resources policies and practices.
- Include implementation of workplace diversity objectives in the corporate plan, business plan and client service charters.
- Ensure information about employment opportunities is available in accessible formats.
- Review recruitment and selection processes to ensure that current and potential employees are not discriminated against.

Gather information on demographics. It is the goal of every jurisdiction to minimise or eliminate any instance of obvious discrimination against individuals or groups. In discussing policies on employment equity, scholor explains: "Employment equity policies and Programmes are about fairness in the workplace, not about reverse discrimination. Fairness is achieved when no one is denied employment opportunity and no one benefits for reasons unrelated to ability.

Employment equity Programmes attempt to change the composition of the Workforce so that employees better reflect the community. The facts (both historical and current) show that members of the four designated groups face discrimination, enjoy less access to educational Programmes and training, and are often denied employment and promotions even when they have the necessary skills and experience." The University's policies give special attention, *inter alia,* to the existence of systemic barriers and instances of intentional discrimination in the process of recruitment. Service Commissions were enshrined in the Independence Constitutions of the territories of the Commonwealth Caribbean and given *inter alia,* the power to recruit/appoint persons into the Public Service and, in so doing, reduce the influence of politicians on the staffing process.

In order to discharge their authority for making appointments, the Commissions have influenced the development of legislation and regulations that circumscribe the practice of recruitment, primarily to ensure that no discrimination attends the exercise.

To this end, entry into the Public Service follows the procedures of:

- Application on prescribed forms;
- Selection on the basis of seniority of application; application of age limits for entry into certain defined grades/classes; the use of written examinations and/or competitive interviews as the basis for permanent appointment to certain grades/classes.

The rules established by the Commissions enforce compliance in an attempt to minimise or eliminate the possibility of bias in staffing on the basis of race/ethnicity, creed, age, social status or physical disability.

SELECTION—PROCESS

In the context of evolution, certain traits or alleles of genes segregating within a population may be subject to selection. Under selection, individuals with advantageous or "adaptive" traits tend to be more successful than their peers reproductively—meaning they contribute more offspring to the succeeding generation than others do. When these traits have a genetic basis, selection can increase the prevalence of those traits, because offspring will inherit those traits from their parents. When selection is intense and persistent, adaptive traits become universal to the population or species, which may then be said to have evolved.

Scientists who do experimental genetics employ artificial selection experiments that permit the survival of organisms with user-defined phenotypes. Artificial selection is widely used in the field of microbial genetics, especially molecular cloning. Whether or not selection takes place depends on the conditions in which the individuals of a species find themselves. Adults, juveniles, embryos, and even eggs and sperm may undergo selection. Factors fostering selection include limits on resources (nourishment, habitat space, mates) and the existence of threats (predators, disease, adverse weather). Biologists often refer to such factors as selective pressures. Natural selection is the most familiar type of selection by name.

The breeding of dogs, cows and horses, however, represents "artificial selection". Sub-categories of natural selection are also sometimes distinguished. These include sexual selection, ecological selection, stabilising selection, disruptive selection and directional selection. Selection occurs only when the individuals of a population are diverse in their characteristics—or more specifically when the traits of individuals differ with respect to how well they equip them to survive or exploit a particular pressure. In the absence of individual variation, or when variations are selectively neutral, selection does not occur. Meanwhile, selection does not guarantee that advantageous traits or alleles will become prevalent within a population. Through genetic drift, such traits may become less common or disappear. In the face of selection even a so-called deleterious allele may become universal to the members of a species.

This is a risk primarily in the case of "weak" selection (*e.g.*, an infectious disease with only a low mortality rate) or small populations. Though deleterious alleles may sometimes become established, selection may act "negatively" as well as "positively." Negative selection decreases the prevalence of traits that diminish individuals' capacity to succeed reproductively (*i.e.*, their fitness), while positive selection increases the prevalence of adaptive traits. In biological discussions, traits subject to negative selection are sometimes said to be "selected against," while those under positive selection are said to be "selected for," as in the sentence Desert conditions select for drought tolerance in plants and select against shallow root architectures.

TYPES AND SUBTYPES OF SELECTION

Patterns of Selection

Aspects of selection may be divided into effects on a phenotype and their causes. The effects are called patterns of selection, and do not necessarily result from particular causes (mechanisms); in fact each pattern can arise from a number of different mechanisms.

Stabilising selection favours individuals with intermediate characteristics while its opposite, disruptive selection, favours those with extreme characteristics; directional selection occurs when characteristics lie along a phenotypic spectrum and the individuals at one end are more successful; and balancing selection is a pattern in which multiple characteristics may be favoured.

Mechanisms of Selection

Distinct from patterns of selection are mechanisms of selection; for example, disruptive selection often is the result of disassortative sexual selection, and balancing selection may result from frequency-dependent selection and overdominance.

EMPLOYEE SELECTION PROCESS

Employee Selection is the process of putting right men on right job. It is a procedure of matching organisational requirements with the skills and qualifications of people. Effective selection can be done only when there is effective matching. By selecting best candidate for the required job, the organisation will get quality performance of employees. Moreover, organisation will face less of absenteeism and employee turnover problems. By selecting right candidate for the required job, organisation will also save time and money. Proper screening of candidates takes place during selection procedure.

All the potential candidates who apply for the given job are tested. But selection must be differentiated from recruitment, though these are two phases of employment process. Recruitment is considered to be a positive process as it motivates more of candidates to apply for the job. It creates a pool of applicants.

It is just sourcing of data. While selection is a negative process as the inappropriate candidates are rejected here. Recruitment precedes selection in staffing process. Selection involves choosing the best candidate with best abilities, skills and knowledge for the required job. The Employee selection process takes place in following order:

- It is used to eliminate those candidates who do not meet the minimum eligiblity criteria laid down by the organisation. The skills, academic and family background, competencies and interests of the candidate are examined during preliminary interview. Preliminary interviews are less formalised and planned than the final interviews. The candidates are given a brief up about the company and the job profile; and it is also examined how much the candidate knows about the company. Preliminary interviews are also called screening interviews.
- The candidates who clear the preliminary interview are required to fill application blank. It contains data record of the candidates such as details about age, qualifications, reason for leaving previous job, experience, etc.,
- Various written tests conducted during selection procedure are aptitude test, intelligence test, reasoning test, personality test, etc. These tests are used to objectively assess the potential candidate. They should not be biased.
- It is a one to one interaction between the interviewer and the potential candidate. It is used to find whether the candidate is best suited for the required job or not. But such interviews consume time and money both. Moreover the competencies of the candidate cannot be judged. Such interviews may be biased at times. Such interviews should be conducted properly. No distractions should be there in room. There should be an honest communication between candidate and interviewer.
- Medical tests are conducted to ensure physical fitness of the potential employee. It will decrease chances of employee absenteeism.
- A reference check is made about the candidate selected and then finally he is appointed by giving a formal appointment letter.

TRAINING AND DEVELOPMENT: CONCEPT, IMPORTANCE AND METHODS OF TRAINING

Changes in technology, especially information technology, generate knowledge spreading up at tremendous speed, as well as its quick obsolence. In the period between 1900 and 1950, the amount of human knowledge doubled, and Since, then it has doubled every 5 to 8 years. Knowledge is becoming obsolete so quickly that all of us need do double our knowledge every 2 to 3 years in order to keep up with the changes. On the other hand, the increasing complexity, turbulency and uncertainty of the environment requires different and greater knowledge. Modern business requires more and more knowledge and skills that are still inadequatly present in the formal school education, *i.e.*, the gap between business reqiurements and the knowledge acquired at school is growing. The period of mass producing is over and the customers are very selective. Increased consumer demands require new solutions and knowledge.

Due to increasing competition, the organisation is required to constantly revise its product and service mix, managerial methods, and to increase productivity. Modern conditions of dynamic competition, sophisticated information technology, knowledge economy, market globalisation, has changed the relation to importance of human resources in organisation. These conditions actualise the human capital as the strategic resource of every organisation. Differences between the organisations exist exactly due to the differences between human capital, *i.e.*, the organisations human resources, ways of their management and development. In a more and more global, complex and turbulent environment, knowledge is the only reliable source of competitive advantage.

Traditional factors of manufacturing as the soil, Labour and capital did not disappear, but their significance is not primary anymore. Knowledge is viewed as the key of realisation of a competitive advantage. And therefore the question of where the corporative knowledge is located, how to release it and develop to achieve organisational goals has become very important.Since, the organisational knowledge is largely located inside the human mind, *i.e.*, the head of employees, as carriers of knowledge and activities, human resources are becoming the key factor of business success. Organisational development is always conditioned by human knowledge and skills. That is why, contemporary organisations pay more and more attention to the development of their emplozees.

Thus, employee education and training are becoming an optimal answer to complex business challenges, and the management of human resources is taking central role in modern management. Through the process of employee training and development, the management of human resources provides constant knowledge innovation, creates conditions for mutual knowledge and experience exchange and proactive behaviour, in this way contributing to competitive advantage and satisfaction of all participants in business procedures. As a consequence of these procedures a learning organisation has formed.

The aim of this chapter is to point to the fact that education and development of human potential are the basic factor for creation of basis for transformation from traditional to a learning company. Learning organisation is organisation that promotes learning of all of its members and it transforms permanently. Individuals and societies that do not have enough knowledge are in inferior position, compared to societies and organisations that have it and even permanently acquire new knowledge. That is the reason why we say that success is not among the educated but among those that are learning permanently, and everything changes except knowledge acquirement, which is constant.

EMPLOYEE TRAINING AND DEVELOPMENT

Understanding the phenomenon of employee training and development requires understanding of all the changes that take place as a result of learning. As the generator of new knowledge, employee training and development is placed within a broader strategic context of human resources management, *i.e.*, global organisational management, as a planned staff education and development, both individual and group, with the goal to benefit both the organisation and employees.

To preserve its obtained positions and increase competitive advantage, the organisation needs to be able to create new knowledge, and not only to rely solely on utilisation of the existing. Thus, the continous employee training and delopment has a singnificant role in the development of individual and organisational performance. The strategic procedure of employee training and development needs to encourage creativity, ensure inventiveness and shape the entire organisational knowledge that provides the organisation with uniqueness and differentiates it from the others. Education is no longer the duty and privilege of those in higher positions and skilled labour, but it is becoming the duty and need of everyone. The larger the organisations, the more funds they spend on education and provide their employees with greater and diverse possibilities of education and development.

Understanding the tremendous significance of education for the modern organisation and confident that it represents a good and remunirative investment, present day organisations set aside more and more resources for this activity. Most of the organisations invest 3 to 5 per cent of their revenue into adult education. It is estimated that the organisations that desire to keep the pace with changes need to provide their employees with 2 per cent of total annual fund of working hours for training and education. Thus, it is necessary to accept the model of permanent, continuous learning. That truth has been known for more than two centuries.

Denis Diderot, a French philosopher and literate of the Age of Enlightment, wrote the following: "Education shouldn't be finished when an individual leaves school, it should encompass all the ages of life . . . to provide people in every moment of their life with a possibility to maintain their knowledge or to obtain new knowledge". The only way for present day organisations to survive is the imperative to innovate or perish. Since, this depends on the knowledge the organisation possesses, this imperative could be read as: learn faster than competition. The logical sequence is: knowledge creation – innovation – competitive advantage. If knowledge is good, is it not true that the more knowlegde we have, the better we are? Many organisations which consider knowledge as a good thing are trapped into the pitfall of gathering as much knowledge as possible. Knowledge that is not necessary is exatly what it is: unnecessary. And the efforts to obtain it are wasted efforts. The only important knowldege is the knowledge with strategic importance to the company, knowledge that helps to increase the value of the company, knowledge with significance to the strategy of the company. It is not about knowledge for the sake of knowledge, but rather knowledge according to the needs, applicable knowledge, knowledge to create innovation and competitive advantage.

Obtaining knowledge, learning, education, all could have a real effect on the quality of labour only if they are harmonised with the needs of a particular organisation, its goals and the goals of its employees. The further choice of educational contents and educational methods, and the efficiency of educational effectiveness control depend on clearly defined educational goals and needs, answers to the questions of which knowldege is necessary to realise the strategy and the survival of the organisation in general, which employees need to possess this knowledge and will this knowledge solve certain problems. Employee training and development does not imply only obtaining new knowledge, abilities and skills, but also the possibility to promote entrepreneurship, introduce employees to changes, encourage the changes of their attitude, introduce the employees to important business decisions and involve them actively in the process of decision making. To precisely define expectations and attract skilled workforce, more and more employment advertisings offer a certain number of annual hours or days for education.

The most wanted resources are the people with particular knowledge, skills and abilities. Managers must learn to manage them, and the organisations to employ and retain them. Knowledge based organisations must preserve their competitive advantage by retaining skilled workforce, workers of knowledge, strengthening their motivation and improving the reward and compensation systems according to the workers' performances. Within the context of learning organisation, it is not sufficient for the worker only to add value to the organisation based on his knowledge, but he also has to receive knowledge. He gives as much knowledge as he receives. For the present day employees the wage by itself is not a sufficient incentive, but they also need investment into themselves in a sense of investing in their knowledge. Empolyees no longer work for money alone, nor can they be influenced by traditional attractive financial packages.

CONCEPT OF A LEARNING ORGANISATION

Every individual should appreciate lifelong learning, and every successful organisation has to become a permanently learning organisation. Many successful organisations describe themselves as learning organisation or one of their strategic goals is to become such an organisation. Companies such as Coca-Cola, Motorola, General Electrics and Cisco have assigned vice presidents for knowledge, learning or intellectual capital whose task is to create knowledge management systems that enable them to quickly adopt development tendencies, influencing in that way the customers, competitors, distributors and suppliers. The organisation is not only the user of knowledge, but also its creator.

Peter Senge described in the book named "The Fifth Discipline", the learning organisation implies free flow of knowledge, *i.e.*, lifting of all barriers on developing knowledge and new ideas at the very beginning. In the future it will not be possible to "unthread things from above" and for all the others to follow the "big brother's" instructions anymore. The top organisations of the future will be distinguished by their knowledge about how to encourage engagement and develop the learning potential on each organisational level. Peter Senge's model of a learning organisation is very interesting Since, it recognises the organisation as a whole, *i.e.*, in his organisation, through their functions and sectors within the organisation, all the employees influence the course of business procedures, and the knowledge creation, consequently the creation of new values both for the organisation and its customers. With this definition, Senge has made significant qualitative progress compared to the classical organisation, Since, he emphasised the necessity of ability development through the process of learning.

Besides Senge, Chris Argyris was a great populariser of a learning organisation as well. In his book "Teaching smart people how to learn", he says: "Any company that aspires to succeed in the tougher business environment must first resolve a basic dilemma: success in the marketplace increasingly depends on learning, yet most people don't know how to learn. What's more, those members of the organisation that many assume to be the best at learning are, in fact, not very good at it. I am talking about the well-educated, highpowered, highly committed professionals who take up key leadership positions in the modern corporation." Organisations learn only through the learning individuals.

Individual learning does not guarantee organisational learning. But without it there is no organisational learning as well. The ablity to learn faster than the competitors may be the only sustainable competitive advantage. Thus, the learning organisation is the organisation that learns and encourages people to learn in the organisation. It motivates information exchange between employees and creates staff with different knowledge. Chris Argiris explains this: "On the other hand, there is a problem of existence of individuals within the organisation who know how to learn, but that doesn't create automatically conditions for the organisation to learn as well. This is due to the indisputable view that knowledge is still the only private property the man owns. This means that individual learning, and even learning of all the employees, doesn't imply the existence of a learning organisation. To have a learning organisation, it is necessary to know how to transfer individual into organisational knowledge, *i.e.*, into organisational learning." The starting point of knowledge management concept is in the fact that power does not come from knowledge, but from the exchange of knowledge.

It starts from the synergic effect. By exchanging knowledge, combining individual knowledge, we get much more qualitative knowledge than the individual knowledge. Obtaining and sharing knowledge is the core of the learning organisation. The reasons to become a learning organisation are the following: people are developing (greater motivation, flexibility of employees, people are more creative, improved social interaction), better working teams and groups (knowledge sharing, mutual dependence), benefiting organisations (greater work productivity, more qualitative products/services/ procedures, competitive advantage, profit).

APPROACH TO TRAINING AND DEVELOPMENT WITHIN OUR ORGANISATIONS AND NEED FOR TRANSFORMATION

Unfortunately, the procedures of employee training and development within our organisations are undeveloped. They are mainly performed occasionally, and not connected with organisational strategy, nor do they have some strategic significance. They are mostly enforced when such business problems occur or are perceived that are considered relievable or solvable by organising a training, course or seminar for some of the employees. Employees view the training as an imposed obligation, rather than a way to maximise their potential and they do not realise that by improving their performances and innovation of their knowledge they may contribute to better business results of the organisation they belong to.

Unfortunately, top managers do not realise this as well. From their relationship with the employees it is plain to see that the employees are still treated as an expense, rather than an investment worthy of investing. In our organisations there is no culture of obtaining and sharing of knowledge. Many of our managers are under the influence of prejudices such as: training is expensive, training is an expense burdening the current business, it is not rewarding, training is for the young, etc., Knowledge is expensive, but ignorance is even more expensive.

Human possibilites to learn are unlimited, unless idviduals do not limit their abilities within their minds. Many studies have shown that investing in employee training and development has larger business effects than investing in equipment and other material resources. Our organisations must harmonise their approach to employee development with the changes. Employee training and development has to be connected with the organisational goals and strategy, they need to fulfil the new reqiurements of the environment. Employee training and development needs to become a managerial function.

It is a managerial challenge to consider the employees of the organisation from a strategic perspective (future orientedness) and constantly monitor and encourage the development of new skills and knowledge as the foundation of organisational development.

This is not about assigning the employees to appropriate jobs, but rather about the constant dynamic of encouraging and discovering new possibilities. This is a new type of leadership, significantly different from the classical model of organisational management. The leaders are no longer expected to be all-knowing bosses and supervisors, but rather moderators and inspirators. Since, people do not share the information which is the source of their power instictively, the leaders need to recognise, attract and release knowledge in the organisation. One of the main challegnes of modern organisations therefore is how to manage the process of knowledge transfer. "The answer is that wisdom, just because it is the most important, doesn't need to be located inside a tall building where the chief executive and his main assistants hang their hats (and soon their heads as well – unless they join the revolution of the mind).

This pictoresque answer of Tom Peters refers to decentralisation and substantivity of employees (turning every workplace into business), which implies a high degree of employee competence and orientation Towards the participative style of management. The process of democratisations, transitions, opening towards the EU, privatisations and arrival of foreign companies and praxis contributed considerably to transformation of approach to employee training and development within our organisations, from the *ad hoc* processes that originate from the goals and strategies, to a modern approach where human resources and their knowledge are gaining more and more significance.

IMPORTANCE OF TRAINING AND DEVELOPMENT

- Training and Development helps in optimising the utilisation of human resource that further helps the employee to achieve the organisational goals as well as their individual goals.
- Training and Development helps to provide an opportunity and broad structure for the development of human resources' technical and Behavioural skills in an organisation. It also helps the employees in attaining personal growth.
- Training and Development helps in increasing the job knowledge and skills of employees at each level. It helps to expand the horizons of human intellect and an overall personality of the employees.
- Training and Development helps in increasing the productivity of the employees that helps the organisation further to achieve its long-term goal.
- Training and Development helps in inculcating the sense of team

work, team spirit, and inter-team collaborations. It helps in inculcating the zeal to learn within the employees.

- Training and Development helps to develop and improve the organisational health culture and effectiveness. It helps in creating the learning culture within the organisation.
- Training and Development helps building the positive perception and feeling about the organisation. The employees get these feelings from leaders, subordinates, and peers.
- Training and Development helps in improving upon the quality of work and work-life.
- Training and Development helps in creating the healthy working environment. It helps to build good employee, relationship so that individual goals aligns with organisational goal.
- Training and Development helps in improving the health and safety of the organisation thus preventing obsolescence.
- Training and Development helps in improving the morale of the Workforce.
- Training and Development helps in creating a better corporate image.
- Training and Development leads to improved profitability and more positive attitudes towards profit orientation.
- Training and Development aids in organisational development, *i.e.,* Organisation gets more effective decision making and problem solving. It helps in understanding and carrying out organisational policies
- Training and Development helps in developing leadership skills, motivation, loyalty, better attitudes, and other aspects that successful workers and managers usually display.

IMPORTANCE OF TRAINING OBJECTIVES

Training objectives are one of the most important parts of training Programme. While some people think of training objective as a waste of valuable time. The counterargument here is that resources are always limited and the training objectives actually lead the design of training. It provides the clear guidelines and develops the training Programme in less time because objectives focus specifically on needs. It helps in adhering to a plan. Training objective tell the trainee that what is expected out of him at the end of the training Programme. Training objectives are of great significance from a number of stakeholder perspectives:

- Trainer.
- Trainee.
- Designer.
- Evaluator.

Trainer

The training objective is also beneficial to trainer because it helps the trainer to measure the progress of trainees and make the required adjustments. Also, trainer comes in a position to establish a relationship between objectives and particular segments of training.

Trainee

The training objective is beneficial to the trainee because it helps in reducing the anxiety of the trainee up to some extent. Not knowing anything or going to a place which is unknown creates anxiety that can negatively affect learning. Therefore, it is important to keep the participants aware of the happenings, rather than keeping it surprise. Secondly, it helps in increase in concentration, which is the crucial factor to make the training successful. The objectives create an image of the training Programme in trainee's mind that actually helps in gaining attention. Thirdly, if the goal is set to be challenging and motivating, then the likelihood of achieving those goals is much higher than the situation in which no goal is set. Therefore, training objectives helps in increasing the probability that the participants will be successful in training.

Designer

The training objective is beneficial to the training designer because if the designer is aware what is to be achieved in the end then he'll buy the training package according to that only. The training designer would then look for the training methods, training equipments, and training content accordingly to achieve those objectives. Furthermore, planning always helps in dealing effectively in an unexpected situation. Consider an example; the objective of one training Programme is to deal effectively with customers to increase the sales. Since, the objective is known, the designer will design a training Programme that will include ways to improve the interpersonal skills, such as verbal and non- verbal language, dealing in unexpected situation, *i.e.,* when there is a defect in a product or when a customer is angry. Therefore, without any guidance, the training may not be designed appropriately.

Evaluator

It becomes easy for the training evaluator to measure the progress of the trainees because the objectives define the expected performance of trainees. Training objective is an important to tool to judge the performance of participants.

TRAINING AS CONSULTANCY

Training consultancy provides industry professional to work with an organisation in achieving its training and development objectives.

Estimation of Training Outsourcing

It has been estimated that 58 per cent of the emerging market in training outsourcing is in customer education, while only 42 percent of the market is in employee education. The training consultancies offer various benefits such as:

Training Courses that Consultancies Offer

- Business Training Courses:
  - Management Development:
    a. Conflict Management;
    b. Managing Diversity;
    c. Project Management;
    d. Stress Management;
    e. Time Management; and
    f. Senior Management Workshops.
  - Sales:
    a. Negotiation Skills; and
    b. Sales Technique.
  - Customer Care:
    a. Customer Care Training; and
    b. Managing Customers.
  - Human Resource :
    a. HR Administration;
    b. Induction Training;
    c. Recruitment and Selection; and
    d. Successful Appraising.
  - Personal Development Courses.
  - Workshops on:
    a. Assertive Skills;
    b. Building Confidence;
    c. Coping with Change;
    d. Interview Techniques; and
    e. Maximise Potential.
  - One to One Coaching:
    a. Focused entirely on personal objectives;
    b. Move forward at individual pace;
    c. Material used in tailor made to specific development Need; and
    d. A strict code of confidentiality.

Importance of Training Consultancies:

- It helps in enhancing company's image.
- It helps in strengthening the team spirit.
- It helps in applying knowledge, developing core competencies, and reducing work load.

- It helps in improving the work relations.
- It helps in developing focused and inspired staff.
- It leads to greater chances of success.

Consultants can provide help on following areas:

- Management Development.
- Team Building Leadership.
- Health and Safety Training.
- Interpersonal Skills.
- Sales Training.

TRAINING AND HUMAN RESOURCE MANAGEMENT

The HR functioning is changing with time and with this change, the relationship between the training function and other management activity is also changing.

The training and development activities are now equally important with that of other HR functions. Gone are the days, when training was considered to be futile, waste of time, resources, and money. Now a days, training is an investment because the departments such as, marketing and sales, HR, production, finance, etc. depends on training for its survival. If training is not considered as a priority or not seen as a vital part in the organisation, then it is difficult to accept that such a company has effectively carried out HRM. Training actually provides the opportunity to raise the profile development activities in the organisation.

To increase the commitment level of employees and growth in quality movement (concepts of HRM), senior management team is now increasing the role of training. Such concepts of HRM require careful planning as well as greater emphasis on employee development and long term education. Training is now the important tool of Human Resource Management to control the attrition rate because it helps in motivating employees, achieving their professional and personal goals, increasing the level of job satisfaction, etc., As a result training is given on a variety of skill development and covers a multitude of courses.

Role of HRD Professionals in Training

This is the era of cut-throat competition and with this changing scenario of business; the role of HR professionals in training has been widened. HR role now is:

- Active involvement in employee education
- Rewards for improvement in performance
- Rewards to be associated with self esteem and self worth.
- Providing pre-employment market oriented skill development education and post employment support for advanced education and training.
- Flexible access, *i.e.,* anytime, anywhere training.

MODELS OF TRAINING

Training is a sub-system of the organisation because the departments such as, marketing and sales, HR, production, finance, etc depends on training for its survival. Training is a transforming process that requires some input and in turn it produces output in the form of knowledge, skills, and attitudes (KSAs).

THE TRAINING SYSTEM

A System is a combination of things or parts that must work together to perform a particular function. An organisation is a system and training is a sub system of the organisation. The System Approach views training as a sub system of an organisation. System Approach can be used to examine broad issues like objectives, functions, and aim. It establishes a logical relationship between the sequential stages in the process of training need analysis (TNA), formulating, delivering, and evaluating. There are four necessary inputs, *i.e.*, technology, man, material, time required in every system to produce products or services. And every system must have some output from these inputs in order to survive.

The output can be tangible or intangible depending upon the organisation's requirement. A system approach to training is planned creation of training Programme. his approach uses step-by-step procedures to solve the problems. Under systematic approach, training is undertaken on planned basis. ut of this planned effort, one such basic model of five steps is system model that is explained below. Organisation are working in open environment, *i.e.*, there are some internal and external forces, that poses threats and opportunities, therefore, trainers need to be aware of these forces which may impact on the content, form, and conduct of the training efforts. The internal forces are the various demands of the organisation for a better learning environment; need to be up to date with the latest technologies.

The three model of training are:

- System Model.
- Instructional System Development Model.
- Transitional model.

SYSTEMATIC MODEL TRAINING

The system model consists of five phases and should be repeated on a regular basis to make further improvements. The training should achieve the purpose of helping employee to perform their work to required standards.

- *Analyse and identify the training needs, i.e.,* to analyse the department, job, employees requirement, who needs training, what do they need to learn, estimating training cost, etc The next step is to develop a performance measure on the basis of which actual performance would be evaluated.

- *Design and provide training to meet identified needs*. This step requires developing objectives of training, identifying the learning steps, sequencing and structuring the contents.
- *Develop* - This phase requires listing the activities in the training Programme that will assist the participants to learn, selecting delivery method, examining the training material, validating information to be imparted to make sure it accomplishes all the goals and objectives
- *Implementing* is the hardest part of the system because one wrong step can lead to the failure of whole training Programme.
- *Evaluating* each phase so as to make sure it has achieved its aim in terms of subsequent work performance. Making necessary amendments to any of the previous stage in order to remedy or improve failure practices.

TRANSITIONAL MODEL

Transitional model focuses on the organisation as a whole. The outer loop describes the vision, mission and values of the organisation on the basis of which training model, *i.e.*, inner loop is executed.

- *Vision*—focuses on the milestones that the organisation would like to achieve after the defined point of time. A vision statement tells that where the organisation sees itself few years down the line. A vision may include setting a role mode, or bringing some internal transformation, or may be promising to meet some other deadlines.
- *Mission*—explain the reason of organisational existence. It identifies the position in the community. The reason of developing a mission statement is to motivate, inspire, and inform the employees regarding the organisation. The mission statement tells about the identity that how the organisation would like to be viewed by the customers, employees, and all other stakeholders.
- *Values*—is the translation of vision and mission into communicable ideals. It reflects the deeply held values of the organisation and is independent of current industry environment. For example, values may include social responsibility, excellent customer service, etc.

INSTRUCTIONAL SYSTEM DEVELOPMENT MODEL (ISD) MODEL

Instructional System Development model or ISD training model was made to answer the training problems. This model is widely used now-a-days in the organisation because it is concerned with the training need on the job performance.

Training objectives are defined on the basis of job responsibilities and job description and on the basis of the defined objectives individual progress is measured. This model also helps in determining and developing the favourable strategies, sequencing the content, and delivering media for the types of training objectives to be achieved.

The Instructional System Development model comprises of five stages:

- This phase consist of training need assessment, job analysis, and target audience analysis.
- This phase consist of setting goal of the learning outcome, instructional objectives that measures Behaviour of a participant after the training, types of training material, media selection, methods of evaluating the trainee, trainer and the training Programme, strategies to impart knowledge, *i.e.*, selection of content, sequencing of content, etc.
- This phase translates design decisions into training material. It consists of developing course material for the trainer including handouts, workbooks, visual aids, demonstration props, etc, course material for the trainee including handouts of summary.
- This phase focuses on logistical arrangements, such as arranging speakers, equipments, benches, podium, food facilities, cooling, lighting, parking, and other training accessories.
- The purpose of this phase is to make sure that the training Programme has achieved its aim in terms of subsequent work performance. This phase consists of identifying strengths and weaknesses and making necessary amendments to any of the previous stage in order to remedy or improve failure practices.

The ISD model is a continuous process that lasts throughout the training Programme. It also highlights that feedback is an important phase throughout the entire training Programme. In this model, the output of one phase is an input to the next phase.

METHODS OF TRAINING

There are various methods of training, which can be divided in to cognitive and Behavioural methods. Trainers need to understand the pros and cons of each method, also its impact on trainees keeping their background and skills in mind before giving training. Cognitive methods are more of giving theoretical training to the trainees. The various methods under Cognitive approach provide the rules for how to do something, written or verbal information, demonstrate relationships among concepts, etc., These methods are associated with changes in knowledge and attitude by stimulating learning.

The various methods that come under Cognitive approach are:

- Lectures.
- Demonstrations.
- Discussions.
- Computer based training (cbt).

- Intellegent tutorial system(its).
- Programmed instruction (pi).
- Virtual reality.

Behavioural methods are more of giving practical training to the trainees. The various methods under Behavioural approach allow the trainee to Behaviour in a real fashion. These methods are best used for skill development.

The various methods that come under Behavioural approach are:

- Games and simulations.
  - Behaviour-modeling.
  - Business games.
  - Case studies.
  - Equipment stimulators.
  - In-basket technique.
  - Role plays.

Both the methods can be used effectively to change attitudes, but through different means.

Another Method is Management Development Method

- The more future oriented method and more concerned with education of the employees. To become a better performer by education implies that management development activities attempt to instill sound reasoning processes. Management development method is further divided into two parts:
- The development of a manager's abilities can take place on the job.

The four techniques for on the job development are:

1. Coaching.
2. Mentoring.
3. Job rotation.
4. Job instruction technique (jit).

OFF THE JOB TRAINING

There are many management development techniques that an employee can take in off the job.

The few popular methods are:

- Sensitivity training.
- Transactional analysis.
- Straight lectures/ lectures.
- Simulation exercises.

3

Sustainable Library Design

INTRODUCTION

Prior to the germ theory of medicine, it was considered essential to health to be exposed to fresh air and daylight, for there was little else known to prevent infection or disease. In years following, medicine began to focus on increasingly sophisticated technology, abandoning experiential evidence of the benefits of contact with nature. As medicine and hospitals changed to meet this attitude shift, patients became further and further removed from the outdoors or any sign of it. As the strengths and shortcomings of technology have been revealed in practice, we have become aware that there lies a necessary balance between technology and nature. Studies conducted in the past two decades have shown a link between patient recovery rates and contact with nature.

As a result, the medical community is experiencing a shift towards balance between technology and nature, western and eastern medicine, aggressive medical treatments and holistic treatment. This is a change that parallels that of the design and construction of buildings. Architects are coming back to an ideological middle ground between advanced technology and traditional systems. For many years, architects have relied on mechanical systems to solve the indoor environmental and energy use problems that their aesthetically centered designs created. As a culture, we are coming face to face with the limitations of the technology that we have placed so much faith in. We are finding a need for using that technology appropriately, and in a way that supports design that is wisely collaborative with the laws of nature. Rather than suggest that we return to a primitive state, this shift suggests that we take inspiration from nature's design to use technology wisely to support design informed by thousands of years of experience.

It is essential to keep in mind that sustainable architecture is no different, in theory, from intelligent architecture. The challenge of building with minimal impact on resources provides architects with an opportunity to redirect their focus on elegantly simple design solutions, responsive to site, climate, and culture.

WHY ARE WE CONCERNED ABOUT BUILDINGS AND ENVIRONMENTAL IMPACT

Commercial, institutional and residential buildings and operations account for 30-40 per cent of total energy use, 50-60 per cent of total electricity use, 35-40 per cent of municipal solid waste, 25-30 per cent of wood and raw materials use, and 25 per cent of water consumption. Since, buildings represent such a large part of the consumption of earth's resources, an enormous opportunity for significantly reducing our environmental impact lies in our ability to optimise the energy and resource efficiency of the buildings we live and work in.

In the United States we spend, on average, 90 per cent of our time indoors. It follows naturally that we would want to make those spaces comfortable and healthy places to live, providing us with a connection to the outdoors when we are unable to be out in it.

In the energy crisis of the 1970's, many architects and engineers responded to the need to reduce flows of energy in and out of buildings by dramatically reducing window area, and effectively closing off any connection to daylight, views, or other source of natural diurnal rhythm. We have learned that shutting out daylight increases the lighting load of a building and balances out any benefit derived from increased heating load in winter or cooling load in summer that might have resulted from a window's thermal passage. For some it is helpful to imagine the sum of resources available on the Earth, in the form of materials, solar energy, wind and water.

These are all resources that we harness for our use. By imagining the sum of those resources that exist on a single building site, a designer can imagine what amount of materials, energy, and waste are appropriate for use. When considering energy, this is called a 'solar budget' or 'energy budget.' You can determine the total amount of sunlight available on a site that can be translated by current photovoltaic technology into usable energy using that light.

Once you know how much energy is available to that site, you then have a guideline for the maximum amount of energy you should design your system to use. For a library's level of energy consumption, this is typically not that great a challenge. The next step would be to consider the feasibility of actually harnessing solar power for the building's use, whether an onsite renewable source or through a green energy programme offered by utilities. A design team could also create an energy budget based upon the amount of wind that travels across a site.

Wind strong enough for effective power generation isn't as universal as the practicality of solar – but for a particularly windy site, it would be worth a study to determine the amount of energy that could be gathered using that renewable source. In addition to energy budgets, design teams interested in creating a building that doesn't use more than its share of water could calculate the amount of water that falls or flows through a site.

This is more challenging in some areas of California than in others – but at the very least, it creates an awareness of the disparity between available resources and those that are planned for use. This resource budgeting gives design teams a good tool for gauging the relative impact of their design compared against a tree, for example, which is not capable of using resources beyond what falls directly upon it or under it.

WHY SHOULD LIBRARIES BE SUSTAINABLE BUILDINGS

As Winston Churchill once said, "we shape our buildings and thereafter they shape us." Libraries serve as symbols of the attitudes and values of their creators and can serve to extend those attitudes and values to future generations of occupants and visitors. Communities with the opportunity to build a new library or update an existing library should prioritise sustainable design measures. Sustainably designed libraries would be built to last, to flexibly respond to changing functional demands, to provide an environment that is inspiring and safe, as well as to perform efficiently, providing great financial value to the community that supported its creation.

As we come to learn more about the psycho-physiological effects that buildings can have upon us, the importance of the health of libraries becomes ever clearer. Numerous studies have shown that strategies we use to reduce a building's environmental impact have ancillary benefits for improved occupant health and energy efficiency. The architectural firm Heschong Mahone conducted a study of the effect of daylighting on student performance and found that students who took their lessons in classrooms with more natural light scored as much as 25 per cent higher on standardised tests than other students in the same school district.

In her research into the connection between green building strategies and occupant wellbeing, Judith Heerwagen, PhD has found that, "much of the green building literature focuses on air quality and physical health, thereby ignoring the other dimensions that are equally as important. Ironically, many of the prominent features of green buildings are likely to have their greatest impact on cognitive and psychosocial well-being. For instance, contact with nature and sunlight penetration has been found to enhance emotional functioning. Positive emotions, in turn, are associated with creativity and cognitive "flow," a state of high task engagement."

Given that there is evidence to demonstrate a connection between green building strategies and occupant cognitive performance, library designers should be conscious of the opportunities inherent in those strategies for creating a quality space for occupants at the same time as delivering a building optimised for resource and energy efficiency. Whether an historic renovation, an adaptive reuse, or new construction, a library that is built with the intent to limit its impact upon the environment and community can serve to mark this time when our ways of thinking about resources are changing, much in the way libraries have always served as landmarks in their communities.

UNDERSTANDING SUSTAINABLE DESIGN IN THE LARGER CONTEXT

Historically, sustainability has referred to that which is economically sustainable. In the past several decades, further focus has been placed on environmental and social aspects of sustainability. Several theories have been developed to explain how caring for all three aspects will be essential for our survival.

THE TRIPLE BOTTOM LINE

The triple bottom line encourages organisations to broaden the focus of their goal setting and selfevaluation to include not only economic value but also social and environmental value – and impact. The three parts represent society, the economy and the environment. *SustainAbility's* John Elkington writes that, "Society depends on the economy - and the economy depends on the global ecosystem, whose health represents the ultimate bottom line. The three lines are not stable; they are in constant flux, due to social, political, economic, and environmental pressures, cycles, and conflicts." The idea of the three intersecting spheres of Economy, Environment and Social Equity is not unique to a single theorist. Many individuals have created variations on this same theme - perhaps a sign of its usefulness as a visual. By pursuing strategies that achieve positive results for all three of the spheres, an organisation can optimise its overall benefit. One organisation that has used this model as part of their purchasing policy is College Housing Northwest. They call the three intersecting spheres the sustainability nexus, and prioritise purchasing products and services that provide for the greatest intersection of the three spheres of concern.

THE NATURAL STEP

The Natural Step began with a Swedish Oncologist, who had noticed rising cancer rates in children, who do not display lifestyle factors that typically cause cancer. He took this to mean that more than likely the causes of these cancers were not linked to lifestyle but rather to environmental factors that he discovered such as atmospheric and indoor environmental toxicity, and bio-accumulation of toxic materials such as DDT and PCB's in mother's milk. He developed, along with about 50 other European scientists, the four system conditions, a set of conditions outside of which we will not be able to sustain ourselves as a species.

The four system conditions:

1. Substances from the Earth's crust must not systematically increase in the biosphere.
2. Substances produced by society must not systematically increase in nature.

3. The physical basis for the productivity and diversity of nature must not be systematically deteriorated.
4. There needs to be fair and efficient use of resources with respect to meeting human needs.

The Natural Step is a big picture theory of principle rather than detail. Rather than providing a prescriptive approach, it provides a compass for decision-making.

MCDONOUGH BRAUNGART DESIGN CHEMISTRY

The McDonough Braungart Design Chemistry, or MBDC, developed by Architect William McDonough and German Chemist, Michael Braungart, describes sustainability, similarly to the Triple Bottom line, as being made up of a balance of three considerations; ecology, equity, and economy. When too much attention is focused on one part of the triangle, the others become imbalanced. In an ideal situation, all three areas would be considered with equal weight. McDonough and Braungart have spent much of their time trying to help the design industry transform its thinking to setting its sights on "eco-effectiveness" as opposed to efficiency. When we describe a system as efficient, we are focusing on avoided damage. Eco-effectiveness is not merely the avoidance of negative change, but creating positive change and effect through design. McDonough asks: "How's your relationship with your spouse? Sustainable? Oh, I'm sorry! I would hope the answer was at least sustaining, better yet would be restorative!" The McDonough-Braungart Design Chemistry describes five steps to Eco-Effectiveness to help the market transition from its current unsustainable practices to ones that are sustainable and regenerative – taking into account that the change cannot happen overnight. In order to be economically viable, a significant change in design or practice must be understanding of the limitations imposed upon the organisation seeking to make the change. If a group were to set out to design a completely sustainable building right away, it would be impossible, due to the rest of the supporting markets/ industries not being prepared yet to offer products produced entirely sustainably.

So much of the success of a building's effort to be sustainable is dependent upon the transformation of the marketplace to one where sustainable products are available. The MBDC is one of a number of initiatives seeking to close the gap between design and product sustainability – between the consumers and the producers of goods and services. Economy, Community, Environment: without considering the success of all three, we will not succeed in sustaining ourselves. At a building level, what does this mean?

THE USGBC

The US Green Building Council is a national non-profit organisation, founded in 1993, to promote "the design, construction, and operation of buildings that are environmentally responsible, profitable, and healthy places to live and work." The USGBC is concerned with educating the public about green building, and with creating a standard for measuring a building's greenness. Before the USGBC, and without a consistent means of measurement, the potential for *greenwashing* was great. [Green washing is the practice of covering up aspects of a product or service that is unsustainable, by distracting consumers with a claim that it has some attribute that is environmentally preferable.] Many could claim that they had a green building, and there was no system in place for one to measure that claim.

In 1995, the USGBC began to develop the LEED™ rating system as a response to the need for defining what a green building is, and as a means for design teams to determine sustainable design goals, determine strategies for meeting those goals, and to track progress and success against those goals. So it offers a definition of successful resource and energy efficient design, as well as pushing designers to raise the bar on their own work. Prior to LEED™'s release, there were other systems in place for measuring a building's environmental performance, including BREEAM in the UK, and BEPAC in Canada; but none were based on building standards already in use in the United States. So, as the many creators of LEED™ began, they kept in mind the importance of creating a system that applies equally to all states, and using standards already in use by the construction industry, in order to reduce the burden of documentation. LEED™ is currently in its second version, Version 1.0 being the Pilot version under which only 12 projects were certified.

The pilot projects helped the programme administrators identify the weaknesses of the system in order to make improvements for Version 2.0. LEED™ version 2.0 is intended for use by new commercial, institutional, or high-rise residential projects only. Future versions will have more broad applicability to Tenant Improvement and Existing Building projects, with Version 3.0 anticipated for release in 2005. Site, Water, Energy, Materials, and Indoor Environmental Quality. These are the five impact categories the LEED™ credits are organised under. This is not to suggest that these areas are unrelated, or that some credits do not impact more than one category, but rather that they can be principally connected to one or another most simply, because of it's place in the design process, regulatory context, or the standards that are referenced to document the credit.

There are a total of 69 points available, 64 of which fall under the five impact areas. Four of the other five points are available to projects that can demonstrate that they have innovated outside the rating system's criteria. And the last point is available by having an individual on the design team who is certified to be a LEED™ accredited professional, having passed the exam proving proficiency with all aspects of applying the rating system.

Points	Section
14	Sustainable sites
5	Water efficiency

17	Energy and atmosphere
13	Materials and resources
15	Indoor environmental quality
64	Total
4	Design Process and Innovation
1	LEED Accredited Professional
69	Total points available

In addition to the 69 points, there are seven prerequisites without which a project cannot be certified. Measures were identified as prerequisites that were so fundamental to green building that the creators of LEED™ felt them to be inalienable qualities of a building designed to be energy and resource efficient. The points that a project earns determine what level rating it receives. The four levels are certified, silver, gold and platinum. The lowest possible score that a project can receive and be certified is 26, which is less than half the total number of points available.

- LEED™ Certified 26 – 32 points
- Silver Level 33 – 38 points
- Gold Level 39 – 51 points
- Platinum Level52 + points

AREAS OF IMPACT

SUSTAINABLE SITES

In many cases, a site has already been selected for a building before the design team is assembled. The library staff may not have the input of architects in the selection process. In fact, in many cases, the library staff may have no input in the site selection process either. It is as essential to select an appropriate site for construction, as it is to treat that site with care once design and construction begin. LEED™ considers not only environmental, but community and economic concerns in crediting a building with a wisely selected site. The USGBC has ascribed value to eliminating sites from consideration that are of environmental value greater than the building that would fill it. They have also prioritised the selection of sites which would encourage alternative transportation modes, or that would fill in unused urban space (taking pressure off of undeveloped land without existing infrastructure), or that would utilise and restore land that is labeled a brownfield for contamination.

Strategies

Alternative Transportation

A library can encourage the use of alternative transportation modes by providing facilities for bicyclists to store bicycles safely and to shower/change once they arrive to work. The facility can encourage the use of alternative fuel vehicles by providing electric car recharging stations. The City of Santa Monica, by providing free public access to recharging stations around the city, has created the opportunity for people to make that choice as a consumer. Libraries can also limit automobile use by reducing available parking, and providing preferred parking for carpools and vanpools.

Reducing Direct Site Impact

Maximize open space on the site, restoring as much of that open space to native vegetation and potential habitat as possible. During construction, the contractors can limit their staging areas to areas close to the actual building footprint to limit compaction.

Microclimate

Limit libraries' impact on the microclimate by reducing the amount of heatabsorbing and radiating materials on the site and on the roof. Try to pave as little as possible, and to shade as much of the paved area as possible. Parking can be put underground or made a pervious surface that can absorb storm water and retain little heat. A strategy that can reduce roof temperatures and reduce the necessity of handling and treating storm water run-off is the use of a vegetated roof, or green roof. This type of roofing can also provide benefits to building users when it is treated as a public green space.

Storm Water

When a building is placed on a site, more water runs off that area of land than would have previously. In a state where water is a precious resource, consider storing that water for use in landscaping, mechanical systems, or in the flushing of toilets, where potable water isn't required. This can reduce water consumption as well, relating to the following area of impact, water efficiency.

Night Sky

Night sky —polluting the night sky with excessive exterior lighting and poor control over interior lights can result in the disturbance of nocturnal animal habitat surrounding the building, and can disturb neighbours, and can contribute to a larger area problem of a night sky that is orange instead of starry.

WATER EFFICIENCY

Californians are reminded regularly of the precious nature of water as a resource. Water has a more political history in California than in just about any other state. Cities such as Los Angeles and San Diego owe their existence to the political and business dealings of a few in the early days with a very specific agenda for development of cities and agriculture in this state, which could not sustain itself without the infrastructure set in motion nearly a century ago. The droughts that Californians economise through, remind us that infrastructure can only go so far to serve a growing population in a desert. Like energy crises, water shortages also remind us of the importance of conservation and wise use. Strategies for reducing consumption of potable water are not unfamiliar to most Californians; but perhaps many do not realise, within the regulatory context of a drought, that conservation doesn't necessarily require sacrifice of quality of life.

Strategies

Landscape

One of the facets of a building that can consume enormous quantities of water is the landscape. Many public entities are set on having the conventional institutional appearance of a lawn with non-native shrubs. The benefits of using drought-tolerant native species have begun to reveal themselves through the popularity of xeriscaping – landscaping with plants that are adapted to their environment without the need of much irrigation, pest control, or maintenance. By selecting drought-tolerant plants, a designer opens up the possibility of using recaptured site water for irrigation, even in an arid climate with little annual rainfall. By recapturing site water with an efficient irrigation system; the use of potable water can be entirely eliminated for landscape purposes.

Efficient Fixtures

While not acceptable in some cities, alternative plumbing fixtures like waterless urinals can dramatically reduce con-sumption rates for public buildings. Waterless urinals also require less plumbing, and less maintenance, which can reduce first cost and life cycle cost for owners. Sensor faucets and gray water plumbing systems can reduce consumption as well.

Alternative Wastewater Treatment

Look into living machine technology as well as constructed wetlands, for treating the building's wastewater on site. Municipalities can consider treating the facility's gray water through reuse at one level, or have a demonstration system for sewage waste like the city of Arcata, CA. All of these strategies can be utilised while not requiring building users to alter their behaviour. In some cases, as with the native landscape, the strategies can serve to educate the community and connect the occupants with their immediate bioregion.

ENERGY AND ATMOSPHERE

Energy efficiency is often placed as the top priority for those considering greening their building or product, because of the broad range of impacts that energy production has on the environment, economy and global social equity. Because of the Carbon Dioxide (CO_2) produced in the production of energy in coal power plants, and the toxic waste generated by nuclear power, power production is named as one of the greatest polluters of our atmosphere and biosphere, contributing greatly to global warming, water pollution, and human toxicity. This is incredibly important once you realise that this is an impact that goes far beyond the user and could have implications for cultures completely unassociated with its cause. In addition to CO_2 emissions, there are the issues of diminishing fossil fuel resources, and the impacts associated with the extraction, delivery, and processing of those resources.

The USGBC promotes not only reducing a building's dependence upon energy, but in improving the sources of what energy it does consume. LEED™ promotes the use of onsite alternative energy sources as well as the brokering for green power to use for the building – options available to a deregulated market such as California's. In addition to energy use, this section of LEED™ is concerned with reducing the use of Ozone Depleting Materials in the HVAC&R systems of buildings, and with setting in place a commissioning plan to ensure that the building and its systems function as intended in design.

Strategies

There is an important relationship between the strategies that are effective in reducing the energy consumption of a building and ones that will be effective in improving the Indoor Environmental Quality. It will be important to not compromise daylight and views for lessened solar gain. In many cases there are strategies that can optimise both energy and environment.

Envelope Design

Rather than seeking to simply reduce glasing area, think about designing your glass to make maximum use of the type of light and solar gain you want to benefit from and eliminate that which you do not want. In the case of the Phoenix Central Library, this consisted of having glasing only on the North and South sides of the building, eliminating the deleterious effects of the extremely powerful rays of low sun at sunrise and sunset. There are exterior shading devices to ward off direct rays, to diffuse daylight, to bring light further into the interior, while maintaining any thermal gain from the mass of the shading devices on the exterior of the building, effectively keeping the re-radiation of that heat away from the interior.

Heating, Ventilation, and Air Conditioning

Strategies that reduce energy use of mechanical systems can be passive – using effective envelope design natural ventilation strategies in the design of spaces – as well as active – relying on developing technologies such as underfloor air or displacement ventilation. Due to the specific environmental parameters that a library environment must maintain in order to sustain the physical condition of the books, relying entirely on natural ventilation strategies might be viable in only a few select environments with steady temperatures that wouldn't threaten the library's treasures. If natural ventilation is ruled out, consider the feasibility of using the physics of the stack effect (where hot air rises, pulling cool air upward) in favour of drawing cool air through the space more easily. This strategy would be most viable in concert with a displacement ventilation system that relies on creating layers of temperature in a space with very low velocities of air being pushed by the mechanical system. This type of ventilation also generates very little stirring of particulate matter, lowering the amount of airborne dust. This strategy would be very much in line with a thermally comfortable environment as well as an effectively ventilated space, two concerns for Indoor Air Quality.

Water Heating

For a building type such as a library with relatively low demand for hot water, the use of solar water heaters could be of tremendous life cycle cost benefit. If the facility is to be constructed in an area with a reasonable amount of sunshine, this strategy should be studied for feasibility. Also consider the life cycle cost feasibility of an on-demand water heating system which doesn't require any energy use during times when hot water is not being used. A regular tank heater costs more to operate since, you are maintaining the temperature of an entire tank of water, whether or not there is demand for it. Heated water can also be considered for an HVAC strategy of using radiant heating through plumbed slab floors.

Lighting

Daylighting is a passive strategy which can improve the indoor environmental quality of a library – but it is a measure which will not reap energy savings unless there is a daylight sensor to control the lights in day lit spaces. Using photosensors in day lit spaces to control dimmable ballasts will allow a system to work without being actively operated by occupants. The importance of dimmable ballasts is in the way that the system operates on a cloudy day. Without dimming, lights might go off and then on and then off and on again in response to changes in light level. With dimming lights, the change would still be in response to ambient light levels, but it would be subtle and not distracting to occupants, as well as consuming less energy in the turning off and on.

MATERIALS

Did you know that for every 10 lb. laptop made, the amount of waste created in its construction totals 40,000 lbs? The materials we buy can be much more than they seem. Every material that is used in the construction of a building has a history. Armed with some knowledge about what materials are the most consumptive over their life cycles, consumers can make wise choices that can influence the markets to change to suit their preferences.

What Makes a Building Material Green

There are a number of different lists of criteria to define whether a building material is preferable environmentally. Ultimately, after consulting these lists to see what sorts of considerations need to be taken into account, it is up to the consumer to define what their values tell them is most important. Water efficiency is likely to be far more important to someone living in the desert than to someone living in a water rich environment.

It will be important too for you to hear why different groups place priority on different criteria before you choose what is the most significant for you.

Some of the most common aspects of a product's environmental performance that are considered by consumers include:

- Energy efficient and with low embodied energy.
- Made of renewable materials.
- Made of post-consumer recycled materials.
- Made of post-industrial recycled materials.
- Made of certified wood.
- Healthy for indoor air – low voc.
- Healthy for the atmosphere – no CFCs or HCFCs used in manufacturing.
- Non-toxic in use, production, or at end of useful life.
- Made of salvaged materials.
- Recyclable at end of useful life.
- Simple to install without dangerous adhesives, etc.
- Made near to the building site – low transportation impacts.
- Efficient/resourceful/reusable packaging.

One of the most significant barriers to successfully building green is to not have access to accurate environmental product data. It is a dangerous problem for consumers and specifiers. The consumer has to be incredibly savvy to differentiate a legitimately healthy product from that which is merely *greenwashed*. Many "green" products hang their hat on single attribute environmental claims, like, "contains 10 per cent recycled material," or "made with wood from sustainably managed forests." A word to the wise: If a product 'contains' 10 per cent recycled material, that means that one of the materials that make up the product could be 10 per cent recycled, and there could be as little as less than 1 per cent recycled content in the total product. Be aware that many manufacturers will attempt to skew the perceptions of consumers as long as there aren't simpler ways to identify the environmental impact of a product.

There are a few laws to protect consumers. The Federal Trade Commission has ruled that manufacturers can make only one environmental product claim. If they make more than one claim, they have to be able to back that up with third-party verified evidence that their claim is legitimate. There are a number of groups that are trying to promote the use of Life Cycle Assessment (LCA) to evaluate the environmental impact of products. LCA looks at the impact of a product through its entire life cycle, from cradle to grave, and generates a score (for lack of a better word) to show that product's performance against a series of criteria like ozone depletion or toxicity. The US government has invested a considerable amount of funding in the development of an LCA tool, called BEES, designed specifically for the US building materials market.

Simplification of Systems and Reduction of Use

What is the most sustainable material? Perhaps it is the material that is never used. When considering whether a building should be of new construction or a renovation project, keep in mind that for every material that can be simply reused, the impacts associated with its extraction, manufacture, delivery, installation, and eventual disposal are eliminated. In addition, simplifying systems that are either unnecessary or redundant can both lower first cost and environmental impact. For example, if a concrete slab floor is already being poured – consider the possibility of a stained and sealed concrete floor being an acceptable finish, rather than adding all of the various materials associated with a carpet or tile system.

LEED™ Materials Credits

LEED™ gives credit to projects that show that they have reduced the resource consumption of the building by specifying products that are renewable, recycled, salvaged, certified wood, or that are low-emitting materials. This impact category of LEED™ also is concerned with appropriate waste management during construction of the building and during operation of the building. By putting an advanced plan into place for the effective recycling and salvage of building materials during construction, projects can reduce significantly the burden placed on landfills, as well as reducing the demand for raw materials for use in new materials.

INDOOR ENVIRONMENTAL QUALITY

This aspect of green building is one that is influenced not only by the science of physiological response to environmental factors, but also our psychological response – recognising the link between the physical and emotional.

Studies have shown that people's psycho-physiological response to a natural environment is conducive to improved ability to focus, to be productive, to maintain health and to heal.

- "We need to create environments that sustain all life – including humans and their seemingly unique aesthetic, physiological, psychological, and spiritual needs. Aesthetics, beauty, health, well-being, and quality of life are as important to sustainable design as are redu-cing waste, energy consumption, and environmental impacts."

An indoor environment that is not only safe, but healthy and inspiring for occupants will take several environmental factors into consideration: fresh air, light, views or connection to the outdoors, thermal comfort, and the ability of the occupant to control their environment. As a building type, libraries have no intrinsic limitation to achieving any of the above goals. Not only that, but libraries are an apt opportunity for providing a rich indoor environment that is inviting, safe, and conducive to concentration. Several cases have shown that by providing occupants of a building with a healthy indoor environment, building owners can actually reduce their risk of liability, reduce absenteeism and improve worker productivity.

Sick Building Syndrome, multiple chemical sensitivity, and legionnaire's disease have been brought to public attention in the past several years. In some cases, individuals have had to abandon homes where mold spores in the building materials were threatening their health. The US Environmental Protection Agency lost a $1 million lawsuit over employees with sick building syndrome and multiple chemical sensitivity caused by the work environment in their new offices in Washington DC. These cases are causing people to take notice of the importance of indoor air quality.

So what are some Steps that can be Taken to Improve the Indoor Air Quality of a Library

Make sure that the effective delivery of fresh air is a priority to the design team. This is essential, but will not in and of itself create a healthy environment. If materials have been selected for the interiors that offgas dangerous chemicals, then the movement of air may not be enough. You must also be sure to isolate any sources of chemicals that could be hazardous to occupants. This includes separating copiers into spaces that can be properly ventilated so that the ozone from the copiers does not affect the entire library.

This will also include keeping the pollutants from the streets, sidewalks, and parking lots out of the library by having effective walk-off mats at all main entryways. In any public space, the mechanical system cannot respond to increasing occupancy rates without having some means for feedback. By providing CO_2 sensors in all occupied spaces, the mechanical system can "know" when there are more people needing more fresh air in a space and respond by increasing the rate of outside air into the ventilation. In addition to these health and safety concerns, there are psycho-physiological needs for daylight and views as a means for connecting to the outdoors and our internal clock that relies on cues from the environment.

These are needs that hadn't been taken seriously until the research of Roger Ulrich and others has shown their importance to our health and productivity. This is research that is still being deepened and authenticated, and is considered by some skeptics to be soft science. Whether validated by hard science or not, we all have an intuitive sense for the difference between a space that heals and inspires us and a space that distracts us or makes us feel uncomfortable. The qualities of those spaces that work for us will continue to reveal themselves as we investigate the spaces we live and work in.

INTEGRATED DESIGN TEAM APPROACH

Albert Einstein once said that one couldn't create a solution with the same thinking that created the problem. You have to imagine a new process, a new approach – only then can innovation find its voice. In the world of the design and construction of buildings, there is certainly a "way" of doing things that has stayed too long as a guest.

At this gathering of professionals that is a design team, each person is a wallflower, standing at the edge of the room, doing their own thing. When members of a team aren't communicating, there is no room for helping one another think through a concept, there is little of the free exchange of ideas that constitutes creativity.

Many in the design profession attempting to change their practices to be more sustainable are looking to deepen the partnerships of design team members, opening up the channels of communication early on, ensuring that all stakeholders in the end product have the opportunity to influence the project. There are a number of practices that help teams achieve this. One of the most effective means is the EcoCharrette.

The AIA has written a definitive guide to the EcoCharrette, but it may end up being an expression of the design team, the end user, the client, or even the community. The Charrette has a long history in architecture – an energetic exchange of design ideas/solutions, consisting of drawings, discussions, brainstorms, and setting of goals.

The EcoCharrette takes that concept and puts it to work as a means for setting a precedent for a project – so that all stakeholders are using the same compass to guide their work, and so that goals are set and clearly stated. EcoCharrettes are an opportunity to educate, to inspire, and to innovate solutions.

The reason for emphasising the EcoCharrette here is to advocate their use, certainly, but also as a metaphor for the integrated design team in which all team members are partnering together in the solution. Whether or not your project chooses to use the EcoCharrette as a tool, there can be a partnering of individual groups with an open collaborative approach. The sorts of people that should be involved in this process include: the owner, the occupant, the architect, the engineers, the landscape architect, the contractor, city or county representatives, and even groups like public utilities who often have incentives for green building strategies.

CASE STUDIES

PHOENIX CENTRAL LIBRARY; PHOENIX, ARIZONA

- Architect: Will Bruder, DWL Architecture
- Completed: 1995

The Phoenix Central Library is located in downtown Phoenix, and is constructed of tilt-up concrete walls to the East and West and Glass curtain walls to the North and South. The East and West walls are clad with copper mesh, which provides shade to the thermal mass of concrete. The North and South walls each have exterior shading device systems designed to respond to the challenges of those orientations. The ground floor of the library has a shallow pool of water over which air is drawn to assist the cooling of the interior. The interior is effectively daylit, with skylights designed to deflect any direct sunlight penetration that might harm the books.

LIBRARY AT MT. ANGEL ABBEY; MT. ANGEL, OREGON

- Architect: Alvar Aalto
- Completed: 1970

The feature for which this library is most known is its daylighting. Aalto made best use of the available light to this northern site – utilising the north light to its full advantage. The curves of the monitors in the ceiling assist in the reduction of glare from the light and broadcast the light throughout the interior space.

DELFT UNIVERSITY OF TECHNOLOGY LIBRARY; DELFT, NETHERLANDS

- Architect: Mecanoo Architects
- Completed: 1997

This enormous technical library houses approximately one million texts, under a tilted vegetated (green) roof. The daylighting is provided using enormous double-glazed curtain walls. Rising up through the massive library is a cone structure, which houses a number of study rooms. The cooling is provided using cold storage, a technique where cold is stored in a water table far below, and is then tapped for cold air in the summer.

LIBRARY AND CULTURAL CENTER; HERTEN, GERMANY

- Architect: Log I.D.
- Completed: 1994

This building is topped by a solar collector, which consists of a glazed roof that is raised above the building. Warm air is collected in this space, and in the winter when the warm air is needed for heating, it is pumped through a glazed rotunda in the interior, which is filled with plants. The oxygen generated by the plants in the rotunda enriches the air before it is passed through the rest of the interior. The glazed solar collector also contains solar water heaters between the glasing and the roof to provide hot water to the library.

4

Technology Infrastructure Design for Libraries

STECHNOLOGY SYSTEMS AND THE PROFESSIONALS

With the advent of the information age and the radical change in library materials, media and means of access to information, the nature of certain types of building systems have changed accordingly. The most dramatic of these changes was the evolution of building communications and its associated equipment into the broad category of *technology systems. Technology systems* in a building now encompass any digital device, digital media, routing devices, operating systems, digital networks and servers, audio-visual systems, cabling systems and digital wireless devices, that are used to provide access to sources of digital information, modify that information, or even create information. The *technology infrastructure* is the name usually given to the equipment, the control and operating subsystems, the network connections, and the cabling of the total *technology system* as it resides in the building.

The building's technology infrastructure is connected to utility services outside the building, such as telephone or cable service; this incoming service is referred to as the *technology utility*. The technology infrastructure in a building continues to evolve in complexity and in its features and characteristics, and a new type of design professional has emerged with the type of expertise required to analyse, plan and design the technology system and its infrastructure. The *technology consultant* must not only be an expert in state-of-the-art technology systems, but must also be capable of anticipating the directions of development of new technologies as well as understand the physical interaction of components of the system with users and with the building.

In the past, because of the simplicity of the communication system and its similarity with electric power systems, the consulting electrical engineer provided the basic design of this system for the building. Given the critical importance today of a well-designed technology infrastructure for the functioning of the library building for its primary use, the expertise of a technology consultant is now required as part of any library design team to bring both technical knowledge about advanced systems as well as planning and coordination to the total design process.

The technology consultant may be part of the electrical engineering team, or may be an independent consultant coordinating with the architect and the other engineering disciplines. The role of the technology consultant in library design is now as important as that of the electrical engineer or the HVAC engineer.

The technology consultant's specific scope of work may include:

- *Structured wiring system* design (cabling) supporting the technology infrastructure.
- The design of *distribution facilities* housing the technology equipment (*e.g.*, telephony PBX, voicemail system, voice-over-IP equipment, data network switches, routers, servers, etc.) and cable conveyance infrastructure elements supporting network and device interconnectivity throughout the building.
- *Audio/visual systems* design for multimedia presentations and information display.
- Voice, data, and video *network design* and configuration.
- Telecommunications *utility services* connections (*e.g.*, high-speed Internet service, DSL, T1 lines, etc.).
- *Universal control system design*, interconnecting voice, data, and video network equipment with other techno-logy system components such as audio/visual, security, information retrieval and systems, and even lighting controls.

The technology consultant can also provide valuable information to the architectural design team during both the development of the design programme and the initial space planning. Determining the appropriate characteristics and features of the technology system for library patrons and staff is an important element in the proper implementation of technology in a modern library building.

TECHNOLOGY SYSTEM PLANNING

A *Building Programme* is a document that outlines the expectations and design criteria for the building project. As such, the document provides a wealth of design information to be used and re-evaluated during the planning and design process. In addition to covering collections, services, and support requirements, the building programme will also typically address specific facility requirements, and should include a comprehensive plan for the technology systems and infrastructure, or a *Technology Plan*. Just as a collection development policy identifies goals for the number of reference volumes, current periodicals or audio books, a technology plan is also a key component to the process. The technology plan should address the library in the context of a larger technology plan, if one exists for the city or other jurisdiction. It should consider the library's relationship to any cooperative or consortium that may exist, as well as the general global context of how information will be managed and delivered in the digital world.

The Technology Plan can address issues and state intentions in a number of ways:

- By stating certain assumptions, such as "an increasingly higher percentage of the population will own laptop portable computers or other *Internet information appliances* in the near future".
- By setting general conditions for the library project, such as requiring all areas of the library to have library network access.
- By stating specific criteria or objectives, such as the requirement that the library network be wireless to the fullest extent possible.
- By setting a specific number of public workstations.
- By allocating a specific percentage of the acquisitions budget to electronic resources.
- By setting goals for instruction and training programmes.
- By making determinations about delivering print from digital sources.

At the very least, the Technology Plan will set forth the technology goals in the delivery of library services, and will develop a schedule and budget for acquisition and replacement of hardware and software required to meet these goals.

THE TECHNOLOGY UTILITY

The options and requirements for incoming communications service, or the *technology utility,* have changed as technology has developed. The technology utility now includes telephone, data, video, modem and fax lines, CATV, alarm systems, and Internet service. Voice service is available through a connection from a local phone service provider. This includes the copper trunk lines for analog circuits, which support incoming and outgoing telephone calls. Besides being used for voice applications, analog circuits are also used for modems and faxes. When considering voice service, provision must be made for both local and long distance calls. If the anticipated volume of long distance calls is high, then separate circuits for long distance can be more cost effective.

Voice lines can also support data and Internet services, although as bandwidth requirements increase this source of service is rapidly becoming obsolete. Fortunately, there are now many choices for high-speed data and Internet services that use dedicated lines. High-speed connections include DS3 (or T3), T1, DSL, and ISDN services. Recently, coaxial cable (typically used for CATV service) and small satellite antennae (dishes) have been used to deliver high-speed data services. Television and closed-circuit video services (*e.g.*, distance-learning, video conferencing) can be provided to modern buildings over a variety of transmission systems, including high-speed dedicated lines such as T1, CATV-type coaxial cable, fibre-optic cabling, and satellite antenna systems.

TECHNOLOGY INFRASTRUCTURE– DISTRIBUTION FACILITIES

TECHNOLOGY UTILITY SERVICE ENTRANCE (MPOE)

The main entrance facility, also know as the *Main Point of Entry* (MPOE) is the space where service providers for telephone, fibreoptic cable or CATV, locate their incoming connections for the building. Within the MPOE, the *outside plant* (exterior grade) cable is terminated and connected with the inside plant wiring for the building.

Fig. Typical MPOE.

The area should have good physical access from the outside of the building and be protected from flooding. The space should be located above the exterior high-water mark, be free from internal building plumbing, have water alarms around any air conditioning equipment that is located within the room, and be protected using fire sprinkler systems (pre-action, or "dry pipe" type fire sprinklers should be employed if electronic equipment is present within the MPOE). To economise on space use, the MPOE can be located within the *main equipment room* or the *main distribution facility* (MDF) for the building telecommunications. An additional advantage of co-locating the incoming services with the main technical center of the building is ease of maintenance.

The disadvantage, however, is that there is a potential security issue of allowing unsupervised telephone company service personnel access to a room that contains expensive equipment. The MPOE should be a minimum of 7′-0" x 5′-0" in dimension. A larger area may be required if any terminal equipment or racks are to be installed. This space should be thermally conditioned as though it was standard office space of equivalent size. The building electric power entrance facility can be located near the MPOE, and can be in many different configurations and capacities, but the MPOE should be separated from any building electrical rooms. The final configuration of the electrical entrance will take into account supply type, location, termination point and also site issues such as location of standby or emergency generators, supply transformers and cabling routes.

MAIN EQUIPMENT ROOM

The *main equipment room* is a central space used to house technological equipment of various types intended to service end users. This equipment may include the main telephone system (PBX), data network equipment and video distribution equipment. This space is a specialised area that must be designed for sensitive electronic equipment.

Fig. Main Equipment Room.

Should emergency power be required in the event of building power loss, it should be provided by installing a dedicated *uninterruptible power supply* (UPS) device so that controlled shut-down of servers and other technology equipment is possible. A separate *pre-action* or inert gas fire suppression system should be considered for this room. These systems minimize the possibility of water damage such as might result from a leaking sprinkler head or damaged pipe in a standard fire sprinkler system.

The pre-action fire suppression system, also known as a *dry pipe system,* keeps the water out of the sprinkler pipes within the room until smoke is detected. Only then will the pipes fill with water; when heat is detected to sufficient degree, the fire sprinkler system operates. The inert gas system avoids the use of water, but the gas supply is limited and the system is expensive compared to a pre-action system. Equipment installed within this area will operate and generate heat continuously. The airconditioning system servicing the main equipment room must be designed to operate whenever the technical equipment is operating, including during power outages. The space must maintain a controlled environment of 60°- 85°F and a relative humidity in the range of 30 per cent – 50 per cent.

Controls such as thermostats must be located within the space to be conditioned, and good airflow around the equipment must be maintained. The *main equipment room* should be located near, and possibly co-located with, the *main distribution facility* (MDF) for the Library. Typically, a space size of 13′-0" × 15′-0" provides adequate space for both the main equipment room and the MDF.

This area should also be located away from large electrical installations, such as electrical switchgear or line transformers, to avoid any electrical interference. (The main electrical room will contain the incoming service and the main disconnect point. Feeders from the main electrical room terminate at—*are connected to*—panels and motor control centers in the subelectrical rooms and from there, branch circuits are used to supply receptacles, light fixtures and equipment.)

TECHNOLOGY INFRASTRUCTURE DISTRIBUTION FACILITIES

The technology infrastructure distribution facilities contain the equipment and cable terminations necessary to connect the network backbone systems to user locations.

A modern distribution facility requires space to house the following:

- Data networking equipment (*e.g.*, switches, routers)
- Voice-over-IP (VoIP) equipment
- Voice cross-connect and cable termination points
- Data cable termination and patching points
- Broadband video distribution equipment (distribution amps, taps, splitters, transceivers)
- Wireless network resources

These spaces may also host local computing equipment such as departmental servers. Rooms selected for use as distribution facilities must not be shared with other functions such as janitorial, electrical, or storage. If other building control functions such as fire alarm and security systems must share space with this function, then the room size must be increased. The *main distribution facility*, or MDF, serves the entire building, and the *intermediate distribution facilities*, or IDFs, each serve a certain portion of the building as satellite distribution locations. Only about ten years ago, when most communications wiring within a building was used only for telephony services, these spaces were previously known as the *main telecom room* and the *telephone closets*.

Fig. Typical MDF.

Main Distribution Facility (MDF)

The *main distribution facility* (MDF) houses main termination patch panels and supports "core" technology equipment, such as the main data network router and switch. The main telephony and video distribution equipment is often co-located within the MDF. The MDF is the origination point for central network connectivity via backbone cable routed to the other distribution facilities within the building.

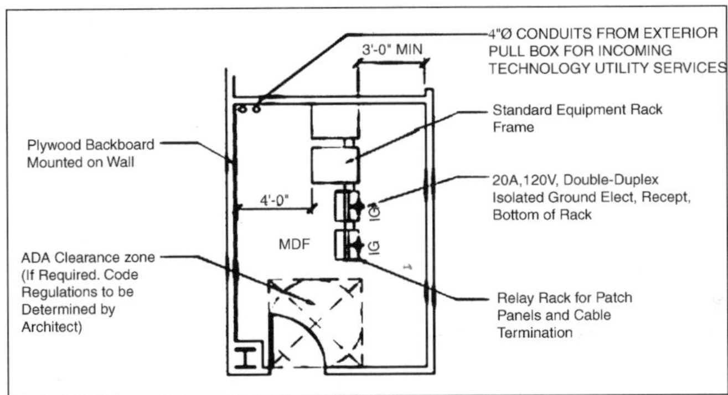

Fig. Plan Diagram of a Typical MDF.

Intermediate Distribution Facility (IDF)

IDFs should be located in the center of the area to be served, as this will allow the maximum floor area to be serviced. The increasing use of high-speed network cabling and the associated length limitations restrict the distance between an IDF and the technology outlet being serviced from that center. Industry standards governing performance of high-speed network cable require that the total distance (*channel length*) between distribution equipment (Ethernet switches) in the IDF and the end users' networked equipment (usually a personal computer) be no longer than 328 feet (100 meters). It is common practice to reserve approximately 40 feet of length for equipment cords, patch cords, and office connection cords.

Therefore, the distance between the patch panels in the IDF and the technology outlet being serviced from that center is limited to approximately 290 feet. Good engineering practice also suggests that each 15,000 square feet of floor space be allocated one IDF for medium to high-density space. In multi-story buildings, IDFs should be "stacked" to facilitate routing vertical backbone cabling or riser cabling. It is recommended to have a room on each floor (even though distance and area served may not strictly require it) to support the maintenance effort and to ease operational difficulties. IDFs (also known as the Tele/Data Rooms in some buildings) act as the transition points between horizontal station cabling serving technology outlets and vertical riser (or backbone) cabling that transports technology utility services between the MDF and each IDF.

Each IDF typically houses an equipment rack frame or cabinet containing the data network equipment that provide connectivity to those technology outlets served from the respective IDF. This connectivity is provided by interconnecting the data network equipment to the technology outlets via *patch panels* located in the IDF upon which the horizontal station cable is *terminated*. These patch panels are typically installed within "relay racks". The IDF also contains a backboard upon which copper riser cable and possibly coaxial cables are terminated. Typically, the copper cable, which conveys telephony signals, is terminated on *punch blocks*. Coaxial cable would be present if video services (CATV) are provided as part of the technology utility. This cable is typically terminated using *taps* or *splitters* mounted on the backboard providing connectivity to horizontal coaxial station cable.

ELECTRICAL SYSTEM CONSIDERATIONS

If an electrical ground is of poor quality, subject to circulating currents, or cannot withstand an electrical fault, high currents flowing through the equipment could damage technology equipment sharing the ground connection. A common approach to minimizing this effect is to use isolated grounding, also known as dedicated ground. This isolated ground provides a dedicated ground for the circuit, connecting the equipment ground of the device being powered to the main building ground. This not only protects the equipment, but also promotes "clean" power for computers and other technology devices. In addition, large motors, elevators, drives and even light fixtures cause harmonic disturbance (interference) to the power that can disturb the operation of technology equipment and cause data loss or permanent damage over time.

The solution to this problem is to isolate certain loads from the power supplying the technology equipment, either in the design of the electrical distribution or by using isolating transformers, or both. The primary method of protection is to design the electrical distribution so that loads that could cause interference are served from a separate part of the distribution system. The third cause of disruption by electrical power to technology equipment is due to power surges on the incoming supply to the building. By installing power electronic devices in parallel with the supply, the high surge current is diverted to earth (ground.) This method of protection is referred to as Transient Voltage Surge Suppression (TVSS).

The use of standby power and *Uninterruptible Power Supply* or *UPS* systems must be tailored to the requirements of the library, and should be verified at an early stage in the project. The UPS may be a simple stand-alone unit dedicated to each piece of technology equipment, sized to provide a limited capacity suitable for a controlled shut-down of the systems, or to provide power until a standby generator can start and pick up the load. A UPS can also be a large unit dedicated to providing a lengthy period of back up for a significant amount of load depending on the requirements of the project. The length of the backup period required will substantially increase both the size and the cost of the UPS. The typical length of backup period is 20 minutes to 45 minutes. The use of a standby emergency generator is generally governed by the other loads requiring standby power in the building. A generator, when used in conjunction with a UPS system, can provide a prolonged period of standby power in the event of a power supply failure.

TECHNOLOGY CABLE DISTRIBUTION METHODS

VERTICAL BACKBONE (RISER) DISTRIBUTION

Intra-building pathways are used to interconnect the service entrance, main equipment room, MDF and any IDFs that may exist as part of the infrastructure design. The interconnecting cable media required is typically referred to as *riser cable*. Generally, this riser cabling is categorised as part of the "vertical" distribution system within a building. However, this vertical distribution system in many cases may actually run in horizontal pathways, depending upon the building architecture and cable plant topology.

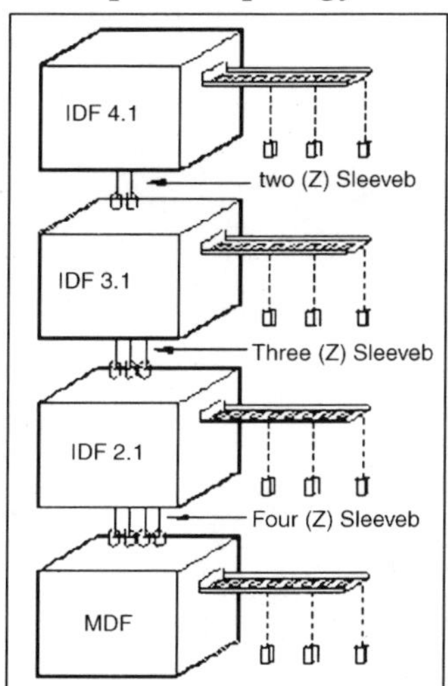

Fig. An Ideal Arrangement of Stacked Distribution Rooms.

In situations where distribution rooms are stacked, the vertical pathways may be conduit sleeves in the floor decks. The installation of these sleeves should be such that a minimum of one spare sleeve is provided within each distribution room. Where distribution rooms are horizontally separated, conduit runs, cable trays, or hanger systems may be used as the pathway for cable conveyance. If conduit is used in a horizontal run, large-radius (36" minimum) sweep bends are required and no more than two 90-degree bends are to be allowed between pull boxes in a run.

HORIZONTAL DISTRIBUTION

The horizontal pathways connect the distribution rooms to the actual outlets. These are the most heavily used pathways in the system. Horizontal pathways may have multiple sections that are not truly "horizontal." In a small building, all outlets on all floors may be served from one closet on one floor. There are a significant number of methods available for horizontal cable conveyance, which vary substantially in price and serviceability. This is typically an area that is overlooked, insufficiently budgeted, and/or under-designed for future cabling upgrades.

Cable Tray

Cable tray is widely used within modern communications cabling infrastructure, and is the preferred method of conveyance both exterior and interior to the distribution room. The type of cable tray selected depends upon the area of application.

In-Room Cable Tray

Tray within the various equipment and distribution rooms must convey the various OSP and ISP building cabling to the patch bays and must facilitate cable management of temporary patch cords and cross-connect wiring. A central-spine, upturned-tine cable rack as pictured in Figure is typically used.

Fig. Central Spine Cable Rack.

This product allows cables to be easily "hooked" over the tines, which facilitates the frequent changes associated with patching and cross-connects.

Cable Tray outside the Distribution Room

The preferred method for main arterial distribution (*e.g.*, corridors, main cable runs) within accessible ceiling spaces is cable tray. Cable tray should be sized per NEC requirements for 50 per cent cable fill. Product used in this application should provide semi-continuous supports for the cable and have built-in sidewalls. Ventilated-bottom trays are best for this application because they combine low weight with the ability to have cable pulled through after the initial installation has been completed. Ladder-type trays are not recommended for in-ceiling use as cable can "snag" on the rungs during installation. Also, subsequent cable installation attempted by pulling through the tray is not facilitated by ladder tray.

"Hanger" Cable Support Systems

A less expensive alternative to cable tray is the use of "J"-shaped hangers known as *J-hooks.* To ensure that cable is properly supported without kinks or danger of cuts or snags, the J-hook should have wide bearing surfaces (1 inch or more) and rolled edges.

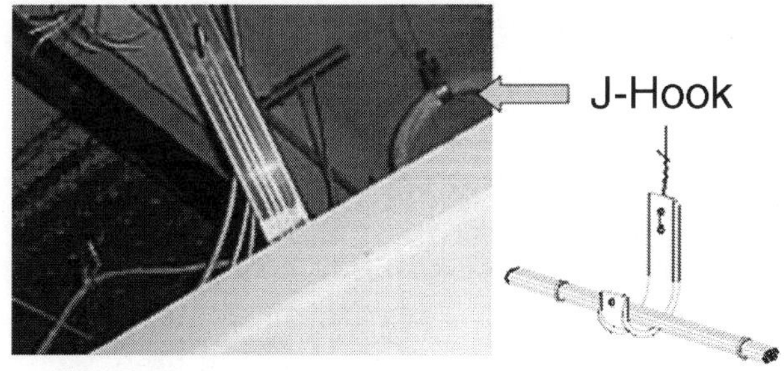

Fig. Typical J-Hook.

There are also several types of cable slings or "saddles" manufactured for communications cable conveyance. The saddles are made with a large metal plate that has rolled edges in the direction of cable flow. These devices can be attached to the building structure using various hanger-wire or rod support devices. The slings are similar in design to the saddles, but are treated with fire retardant, plenum-rated cloth. Slings may also be opened and closed many times.

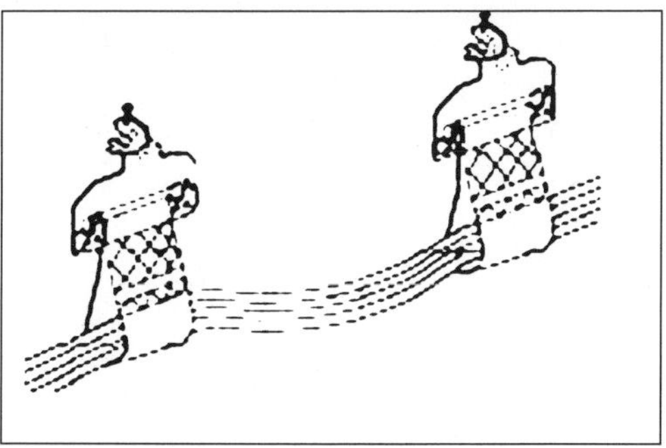

Fig. Cable Slings.

Floor Duct System

Floor duct systems are a network, or grid, of metal raceways with channels that can accommodate both electrical wiring and technology cable. The ducts are cast into and embedded in concrete floor, which allows horizontal distribution of the wiring and cables. The system allows a certain amount of flexibility for cable installation in open areas. Because of the construction technique, this distribution method can be considered only for new construction.

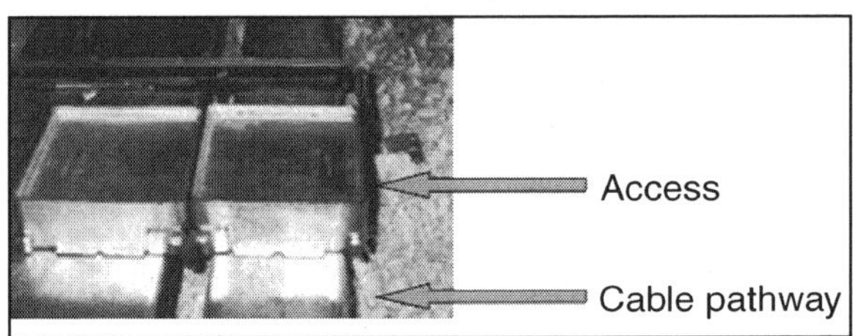

Fig. Two Compartement Underfloor Duct System.

The advantages of using floor ducts are the mechanical protection it provides for cables, a certain amount of power and data outlet layout flexibility and increased security. The major disadvantage of the floor duct system is its high initial cost of installation. The system is not supportive of furniture layouts that are subject to frequent changes, as an existing access point cannot be moved to a new location off of the original grid. Also, the limited volume of space within the ducts leads to packing of the raceways as cabling systems change and a large quantity of cable is left behind and abandoned in the floor system.

Raised Access Floor System

Distribution of cables can also be accomplished through various types of *Raised Access Floor System.* The low-profile type is usually 3" – 4" high and is used for cable and electrical wiring distribution. The relative cost of the low-profile system is high.

Fig. Low Profile Raised Floor System for Cabling and Electrical Wiring only.

In recent years, great success has been achieved at providing the high flexibility of raised access floor systems at low or no additional cost compared to other systems, by utilising a high framing system, minimum 14" to 18", and supplying air through this plenum.

Fig. Raised Floor System Used also as Air Plenum.

The elimination of conventional overhead air ductwork, plus the high energy efficiency of this method of heating and cooling, combine to produce a total system that is often less expensive than typical building infrastructure systems. The high flexibility comes about through the ease of changing cabling and wiring under the raised floor to service new or changed locations, and also because of the integral outlet boxes and air diffusers built into the 24" X 24" floor panels. To move either a data or power outlet location, the floor panel is simply moved to the desired location. Similarly, if air supply is required in a new location, a floor panel with a built-in air diffuser can be placed there and the pressurised plenum below causes air to be delivered at the design air conditions.

The architectural benefit of the raised floor plenum system is that the ceiling area above can be clear of wires, conduit and air ducts, eliminating the need for conventional ceilings and allowing the use of glare-free indirect lighting and higher spaces.

WIRELESS ALTERNATIVES FOR DATA APPLICATIONS

The increase in the use of laptop computers and the change in work and study practices have fuelled the demand for wireless networks. These wireless networks are a natural complement to fixed wired systems in most libraries, allowing "un-tethered" access to library and Internet resources.

A wireless LAN (WLAN) is just like a wired LAN, with the cable replaced by a radio signal. It allows a patron to have access to networks and "real-time" information while roaming around the library. Wireless networks are evolving rapidly, as are the standards that govern transmission over these networks. These standards and the associated technology evolution have significant impact on the design and deployment of WLAN's within a library building.

Deployment Topology

Wireless networks require the deployment of Wireless Access Points (WAPs) throughout the desired coverage area. The WAPs are connected to a local IDF via a standard data cable (CAT6) facilitating interconnection with the Ethernet switch electronics located within the IDF. All WAPs require power, provided either through the data cable or via an electrical receptacle installed at the WAP location.

This power requirement places further demands on the infrastructure design supporting WLAN technology, since, the exact locations of WAP's are very difficult to determine during the design phase of a project. Each WAP has a specific coverage pattern (or area of coverage) beyond which connection to the network is lost, much like a cell phone. This coverage area is a 150 foot radius from the WAP location.

However, the actual coverage may be significantly less than this 150-foot maximum due to interference from physical building construction and/or other electronic devices that may be transmitting in the same frequency spectrum as that of the WLAN (2.4 GHz, typically). A good rule-of-thumb is to plan for access deployment using a practical 50-foot radius coverage range from the WAP location.

However, final placement of WAP's should be determined in conjunction with a radio frequency spectrum study completed on site when the building construction has been substantially completed. Whenever possible, it is desirable to deploy WAP technology that utilises power over the data cable, in lieu of installing an electrical receptacle at the WAP location. When considering *Power over Ethernet* (POE) it is important to allocate additional power within the distribution facilities (MDF and IDFs) since, the network equipment that provides power to the WAPs over the connecting data cable will contain much larger power supplies. It is not unusual for the POE-capable network equipment to require dual 30A, 208V, single-phase circuits.

Advantages

A wireless LAN within a building or campus allows rapid deployment and support for mobile personnel. The mobility that wireless networks allow also eases management requirements because stations can be deployed where the data is generated. Wireless LANs can be cost effective when compared to fully wired networks, and can often reduce cost by eliminating the need for installed outlet hardware.

Disadvantages

The major disadvantage is restricted bandwidth when compared to traditional wired networks. Technology utilisation that is dependent on *wire speed* network connectivity (*e.g.*, streaming video, high-end graphics applications, etc.) cannot be effectively supported over a WLAN at this time.

However, research and development activity is expected to produce wider bandwidth capability in the near future. The WLAN can also be difficult to integrate seamlessly with wired technologies and is not as scalable or as secure as the wired networks.

WIRING AND TERMINATIONS

COMMUNICATIONS CABLING—GENERAL

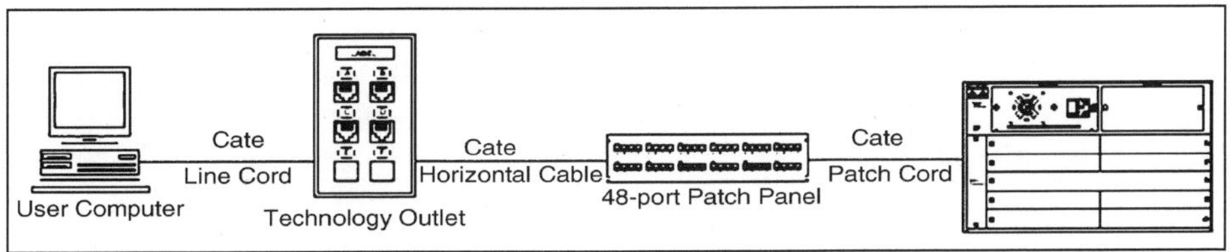

Fig. Communications Cabling Diagram from Workstation to Patch Panel.

Figure shows the end-to-end connectivity of a structured cabling system. From left to right, the work area cord (line cord) connects the phone or computer to the workstation outlet (faceplate). The workstation outlet is connected back to the distribution room over horizontal cable (remember, this can be no longer the 290 feet!). In the distribution room the horizontal cable is terminated on the back of a patch panel, and the network equipment is connected to the front of the patch panel with a patch cord.

A structured cabling system should be installed in the building so that each communications faceplate can accommodate either voice (telephone) or data (computer) applications. This provides a significant amount of flexibility in the system because the application can be changed from voice to data by simply adding a jumper cable in the distribution closet rather than installing a new cable from the closet to the workstation.

TYPES OF WIRE

Copper Cabling

Copper cable supports both voice and data applications. In the backbone the voice is carried over multiple pairs of low performance voice grade cable. This cable can contain from 25 pairs up to 300 pairs on a single cable. Data applications require higher performance with LANs running at speeds up to 1000 megabits per second (gigabit). This performance has generated the development of better cable such as Category 5, Enhanced Category 5, and Category 6.

Category 5 is now rarely used because of the risk of obsolescence. Enhanced Category 5 is the *state-of-the-industry* cable and will support LAN speeds of 100Mbps. Some Enhanced Category 5 cable will support 1.2 gigabits per second; however, the industry trend is to install Category 6 cable to ensure the best performance and future proof the cabling system.

Optical Fibre

Optical fibre is typically used in the backbone connecting the network equipment in the distribution rooms back to the network equipment in the MDF. Although more high end users are connecting fibre to the desktop, in a typical library setting this level of performance would not be required.

TERMINATION DEVICES (FACEPLATES)

Standard wall-mounted faceplates house communications connectors. These should be positioned at the same height and in proximity to the power outlets. Cable is routed to the outlet location through conduit running from the cable tray through the ceiling and down the wall to the outlet location.

A double-gang back box is fitted in the wall with a single gang mud-ring. The communications outlet can house a variation of services including voice, data, CATV and optical fibre connections.

Fig. Wall-mounted Technology Faceplate.

Raceway Terminations

Perimeter raceway systems consist of sections of raceway fixed to permanent walls or partitions at 18" above finished floor or at desk or (counter) height. They contain individual compart-ments, separated by a shielded barrier, for telephone, data and power to eliminate disruption and to reduce interference between systems. Flush-mounted outlets are provided at regular intervals to house cable terminations (jacks) and outlets (receptacles).

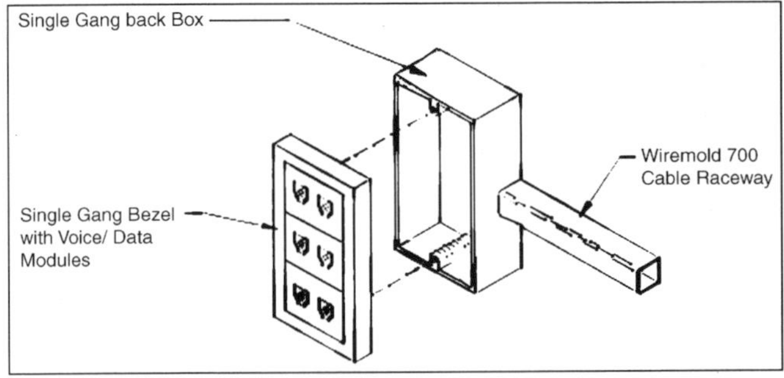

Fig. Termination at Single Compartment Raceway.

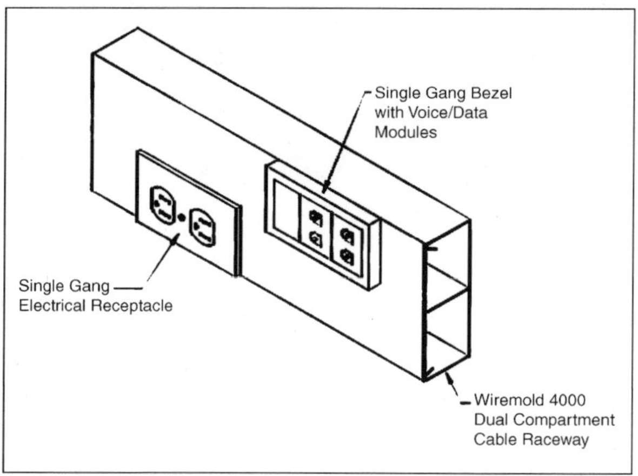

Fig. Termination at Dual Compartment Raceway.

Care must be taken when sizing the individual compartments to ensure that sufficient space is provided for the quantity of cabling that is to be installed and that future expansion needs are considered. Perimeter raceway is a good solution for bringing power and data to a perimeter wall in a renovation project at a relatively low cost. The use of a perimeter raceway cable distribution system requires that all offices, workstations and user locations have continuous access to a fixed wall or partition upon which the raceway can be mounted. Open plan workstations and desks with no connection to a fixed wall or partition cannot be served by a perimeter raceway system.

Power Poles to Workstations

Power poles can be used as a cost-effective solution to add power and data in remodeled buildings. Power and data are routed down from the ceiling through poles that have separate compartments for each service. Systems such as a low-profile raised floor system would be preferable aesthetically, though higher cost would be incurred. Power pole systems introduce visual clutter in open spaces. They are flexible since, the "drops" can be located anywhere below the usual suspended ceiling grid above.

Terminations at Floor Boxes Cast into the Structural Floor

Floor boxes are used for access to communications services that are integral with structural floor slabs. A series of conduits are cut or cast into the structural floor slab. The floor boxes can then be flush mounted or a raised box. The power and communications cabling runs in individual conduits to shared floor boxes. Plenum (fire-rated) cabling is not required provided it is enclosed in conduit its entire length to the IDFs. Care must again be taken when sizing the individual compartments to ensure that sufficient space is provided for the quantity of cabling that is to be installed initially and in the future.

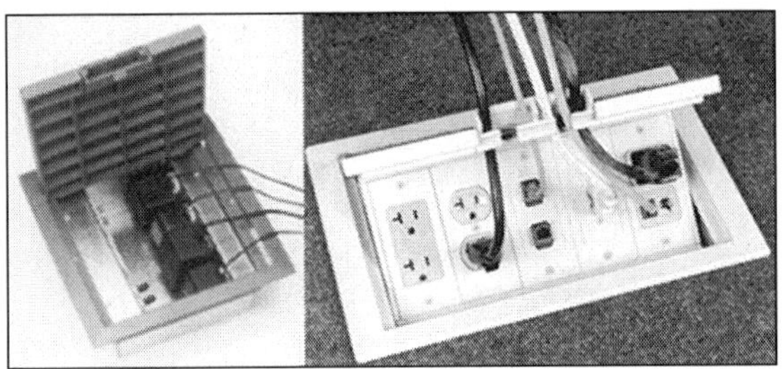

Fig. Typical Floor Boxes Cast into Structural Floor Slabs.

The major advantage of the floor box system is that it provides some flexibility to a furniture layout, although the furniture must be located at the permanently positioned floor boxes. The floor box system can service users in open-plan and enclosed office environments and allows a variety of office configurations, providing that the system has been designed with floor boxes at regular intervals. This is generally not a cost effective approach, particularly in the renovation of an older building. In many cases the costs of trenching or coring through the concrete slab, installation of conduit and boxes, and patch and repair would be cost prohibitive. A low-profile raised floor system would be preferable in these applications.

Terminations at Poke-Through Devices in Structural Floors

A *poke-through* system consists of a series of penetrations that are cored into the building structural floor slab at the time of construction, allowing conduits and cables to pass through the concrete slab from the floor below. The cable tray or conduit is run in a ceiling plenum below to the *poke-through* unit locations, which are located at regular intervals. The floorside penetration of each unit can be fitted with a surface or flush-mounted floor box to house cable terminations and outlets.

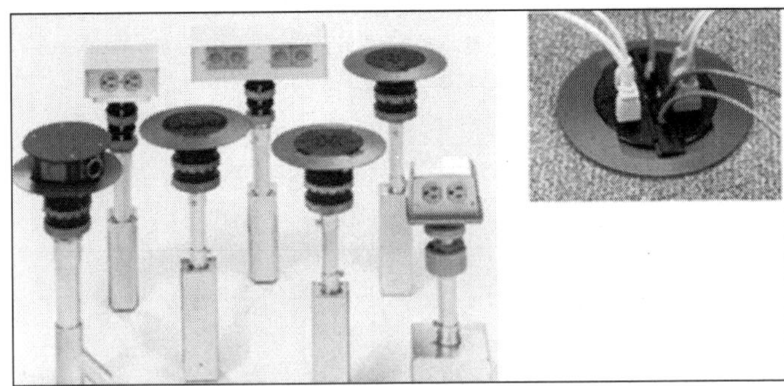

Fig. (Left) Various Types of Poke-Through Devices: (Right) Outlets and Receptacles share Flush-Mounted Device.

Plenum (fire-rated) cabling is required if the communications cables are exposed and the ceiling space is used as a return air plenum. Care must be taken when sizing the individual *poke-through* compartments at the point where they pass through the slab to ensure that sufficient space is provided for the quantity of cabling that is to be installed. Additional cables to be installed in the future should also be taken into account.

The advantage of the *poke-through* system is that it provides a level of flexibility for openplan areas at a relatively low associated cost. The poke-through system can service users in open-plan and enclosed office environments, although the flexibility is limited in that users must ensure that they are located at a poke-through point. The number of poke-through units can be a major issue, since, the use of them can compromise the structural strength of the floor slab and they are also limited by fire regulations.

Terminations at Raised Floor Systems

The terminations at raised floor systems are very similar to the floor boxes that are cast into structural floor slabs, except that they are flush-mounted and integral to the 24" X 24" floor panel.

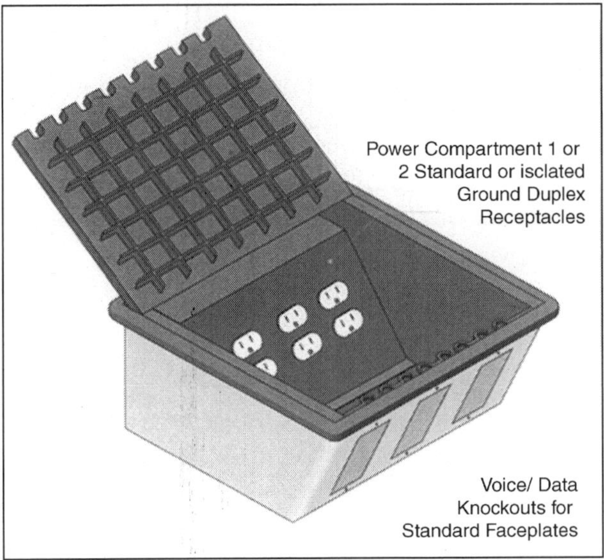

Fig. Typical Floor Box in Standard Raised Acces Floor.

Cables are run in the space below the raised floor, using shallow cable trays in the case of a high raised floor system, and individual cable lines are run to the floor box terminations from there. The access floor panels are easily relocated, making this the most flexible approach.

Electrical conduits are also run beneath the access floor panel system, and electrical wiring is connected to receptacles located in the same floor box as the data outlets. When combined with the HVAC (heating, ventilating and air-conditioning) system, the raised access floor system proves to be very cost effective as a total building system.

Table. Termination Cost Comparison: New Construction.

	Wall Faceplates	Raceway	Power Poles	Floor Boxes	Poke-Through	Access Floor
Overall Flexibility	Low	Medium	Medium	Low	Lowest	Highest
Cost	$	$$	$$$	$$$$$	$$$$	$$[1]
Impact on Structural system	None	None	None	Most	Moderate	None[2]
Impact on Partition locations	None	None	Some	Some	Some	Minimal[3]
Ease of installation of additional cables	Moderate	Easy	Moderate	Difficult	Difficult	Easy
Ability to cope with moves and changes	Limited	Medium	Medium	Limited	Limited	Highest

Notes:

[1]When used as part of an underfloor air system, which may not be feasible in some cases. If only a low-profileaccess floor is possible, then the Cost will be relatively high ($$$$).

[2]When using low-profile access floor, there is no impact on the existing structural system. No low-profile access floor would be located in bookstack areas. However, in the case of a renovated building that can use the high access floor as an air plenum, bookstacks must be located on the access floor system so that air can be provided. More extensive seismic bracing of the pedestal system is required in this case (bolted to structural slab rather than simply glued). Also, the seismic bracing of the bookstacks themselves must be installed through the access floor system to the structural slab below. Thus, use of a high access floor system in bookstack areas will have some additional cost related to structural requirements. In open reading areas, however, there is essentially no structural impact.

[3]Partitions, like bookstacks, can be attached directly to access floor panels. Fire-rated partitions must be attacheddirectly to structural floor below.

Table. Termination Cost Comparison: Renovated Facility.

	Wall Faceplates	Raceway	Power Poles	Floor Boxes	Poke-Through	Access Floor
Overall feasibility for renovation	Medium	High	Medium	Low	High	High
Cost	$$	$	$$$	$$$$$	$$$$	$$[1]
Impact on building design	Some	Little	Some	Most	Some	Some
Impact on structural system	None	None	None	Most	Some	None[2]
Impact on partition	None	None	Some	Most	Some	Minimal[3]
Ease of installation of additional cables	Moderate	Easy	Moderate	Difficult	Difficult	Easy
Ability to cope with moves and changes	Limited	Medium	Medium	Limited	Limited	Highest

Notes:

[1]When used as part of an underfloor air system, which may not be feasible in some cases. If only a low-profile access floor is possible, then the Cost will be relatively high ($$$$).

[2]When using low-profile access floor, there is no impact on the existing structural system. No low-profile access floor would be located in bookstack areas. However, in the case of a renovated building that can use the high access floor as an air plenum, bookstacks must be located on the access floor system so that air can be provided. More extensive seismic bracing of the pedestal system is required in this case (bolted to structural slab rather than simply glued). Also, the seismic bracing of the bookstacks themselves must be installed through the access floor system to the structural slab below. Thus, use of a high access floor system in bookstack areas will have some additional cost related to structural requirements. In open reading areas, however, there is essentially no structural impact.

[3]Partitions, like bookstacks, can be attached directly to access floor panels. Fire-rated partitions must be attached directly to structural floor below.

FURNITURE AND EQUIPMENT INTERFACE

Coordination Issues

Coordination issues pertaining to library furniture and technology should be addressed from the beginning of a project. Furniture plans will be generated by the architect or interior designer during the design phases to make sure that all required elements fit the architectural plans as they develop and to coordinate power and technology interface requirements with furniture and workstations.

These furniture/equipment plans are used as backgrounds for the design engineers to locate the power and technology outlets and distribution systems throughout the project.

It is important that librarians review these design documents carefully for both functional and aesthetic reasons. Exact dimensions of outlets or stub-ups in furniture or millwork should be noted where their location is critical to the placement of these items, both for functional and aesthetic reasons. Careful attention at this time will prevent wiring from intruding into knee spaces when it can easily be routed into cabinets or adjacent to end panels and table legs. Additionally, discussions among the architect, interior designer, technology consultant and electrical engineer should focus on the types of connections to be made to the furniture so that appropriate receptacles will be provided during construction.

As part of the furniture layout in the early design phases, the location of technology equipment should be discussed in order to assure that the correct number of circuits and power load have been provided to each furniture item or cluster. The total quantities of equipment should already be part of the Technology Plan, including allowances for future equipment needs

Furniture Design Issues

Most major library furniture vendors can equip a manufactured product with electrical components and cable management devices so that they are ready to be connected to the building power and communications systems when installed.

This is often the most straightforward approach to take with library furniture design and selection. Custom furniture is another option when a unique look is desired or the space plan demands non-standard sizes or shapes of furniture items. Provision for cable raceways or modular electrical components, cable management, outlets, and so forth, must all be designed into the furniture. When electrical components are installed within the furniture, the components must be *UL-listed,* which means that Underwriters Laboratory (UL) has officially tested and approved these components. Modular systems furniture is sometimes used as an alternative to standard or custom-made library furniture, and is typically used for many staff workroom and office functions. These furniture systems have been used in office space for many years and can be adapted to serve for many library functions.

The panels contain easily accessible horizontal channels at the base, and sometimes at work surface height and the top of the panel, for electrical and communications systems. Vertical panel chases are a fairly recent addition in the effort to bring cable and wiring up from the floor. Outlets and other accessories are also specified with and installed in the panels, so that they are ready to be hard-wired to the building power by the electrician when in place. Depending upon the equipment/power load required, a number of modular workstations may be linked together with only one building power connection. All types of furniture must ultimately be connected to the terminations provided as part of one of the various distribution systems, whether in wall, floor or ceiling.

These connections can be the *plug-in* type, which allows the furniture to be easily relocated and reconnected, or the *hard-wire* type, which requires an electrician to disconnect and reconnect at a new location. The current design direction is towards more plug-in installations for its flexibility of use and low operational cost. In addition to the design of the furniture-to-building connection, the design approach to the equipment-to-furniture connection should be carefully considered. Typically, *UL-listed* modular electrical and communication components will provide outlets and cable management features.

The outlets may be located at the base of the furniture, or just below or just above the work surface. If outlets are in the base, vertical wire management should be provided so that cords do not lie free below the work surface. If outlets are located just below the work surface, a horizontal tray or channel can manage the wires, with grommets or a cord drop in the work surface.

Outlets located just above the work surface are easiest to access and this approach is the correct choice for user laptop locations. Depending on the design, a cord drop and horizontal tray or channel may still be required so that the cords do not lie on top of the work surface. Finally, for a clean and organised installation, well-designed wire management features in the furniture design are essential. The use of grommets or continuous cord drops in the work surface, as well as horizontal and vertical wire management channels under the work surface will assure that the plethora of cords will be organised and out of sight.

5

Succession Planning and Development

Having the right people in the right place and at the right times to do the right things—this happens only when the library has engaged in an ongoing process of identifying, assessing, and developing talent to ensure leadership and management continuity throughout the organisation. It is more than *replacement planning,* although finding backups to fill key vacancies, especially for senior-level positions, is certainly a part of the process. *Succession planning* goes further and is broader. It is about developing talent, so that individuals have the capacity to assume greater responsibilities, do their jobs better, and take on an expanded management or leadership role in their work. Every time a manager makes a work assignment, she is preparing the employee for the future by building on her ability.

Work experience builds competence, and different kinds of work experiences build different kinds of competence. The library with a succession planning process understands this and continually works to build its bench strength by developing staff at all levels. Succession planning is defined as a systematic effort by the library to ensure continuity in key positions, retain and develop intellectual and knowledge capital for the future, and encourage individual advancement. It is designed to be ongoing, owned by leadership.

It encourages a focus on aligning staff and leadership with the library's strategic goals and objectives. We read the stories in newspapers and the business press: an organisation with tremendous influence and clout goes from leading edge to leaderless in one horrible stroke of fate. Not too long ago, McDonald's Corporation announced the sudden death of its chairman and CEO, Jim Cantalupo.

Yet the company continued, hardly skipping a beat, announcing just twenty-four hours after the tragedy a new chairman and CEO. Investors barely responded to the news, and the $40 billion multinational purveyor of Big Macs and super size fries survives better than most of our waistlines. Or consider these organisations with iconic leaders: Dave Thomas of Wendy's, Sam Walton of Walmart, or Habitat for Humanity founder Millard Fuller. Each of these organisations lost a founder who was its public face, yet each manages to live on without missing a beat, and even thrive.

Though you might be hard pressed to name their current CEOs (in the case of Walmart, Mike Duke is the *third* CEO to follow Sam Walton), Wendy's, Walmart, and Habitat for Humanity all worked hard to ensure that new leadership would be ready. In addition, they developed and prepared new leaders who would not be carbon copies of those they succeeded—rather, they would have the talent, understanding, and skills to help their organisations progress through the unique challenges the future would present. How did these companies make such smooth transitions? What can libraries learn from them? The saving grace for each one was succession planning.

They were prepared for a leadership change and could handle a crisis if, and when, one occurred. Succession planning is a common programme in most large corporations. Leaders of these organisations understand that they are obliged to stakeholders to ensure a successful transition. Without plans for replacing top leadership talent, whether the departure is sudden or not, the organisation will suffer.

DO THE RIGHT THING

Many library leaders understand that they, too, have enormous responsibilities to stakeholders—the members of the public who rely on their libraries for education, Internet, story time, research, enrichment, and enjoyment—as well as to the library's employees. Libraries have adopted what William J. Rothwell calls comprehensive succession planning, which anticipates changes in management and creates a strategic plan that puts "the right people... in the right place... at the right times to do the right things." These libraries are prepared for whatever comes down the road. Succession planning is more than planning for contingencies like the proverbial Mack truck wiping out your management team (God forbid).

It means assessing the *key positions* (not just top management positions, but all specialties and areas of expertise) that could become vacant in the near future and providing training, mentoring, special assignments, and other developmental opportunities so that staff members are ready to move into them when the time comes.

This development of "bench strength" (skilled backups for key positions at all levels) is important in small and large libraries alike. Forward-thinking libraries are doing just this. At the root of the issue is the appreciation that the library's most important, most valuable asset is its people. With the large cohort of baby boomers on the cusp of retirement, most perceptive managers understand that there is not a huge cadre of trained, skilled workers ready to step into their places.

Other factors are also shrinking the available labour market for libraries, particularly in some areas of the country. Populations continue to shift to the Sunbelt for better weather, to the southern states for a lower cost of living, or west for the Promised Land, where at the time of this writing housing is more affordable than ever even though state and local governments are struggling financially. Traditional sources of labour—new college and library school graduates—will be highly sought as their cohort shrinks. The labour market is becoming more ethnically diverse, with more individuals for whom English is a second language. All of this means that libraries have to redefine the attributes of their top candidates, learning to value multiculturalism, older part-time workers, employee attributes other than advanced education, and employees who value their leisure time to the extent that they refuse to work more than forty hours a week. As your library tries to address people issues, talent supply, and succession, there are several trends you can count on.

A Checklist of Trends to Count On:

- Aging. The average age of employees will continue to rise, and the workforce will become more multi-generational. Proportionately, mature workers are the fastest-growing age segment, and large employers can expect to double their percentage of workers over 55 during the next five to ten years.
- More ethnic diversity. By demographic standards, the racial and ethnic mix is changing very rapidly, with minorities now accounting for one-third of younger workers. But fewer and fewer are going to library school as other opportunities have opened up for people of colour, people who speak other languages, and so on.
- Increasing lifestyle/life-stage variety. People are no longer "acting their age." Their life plans are no longer linear and predictable. They differ wildly in how they integrate work and other pursuits into their lives.
- Tightening labour markets. As the rate of labour force growth plummets to 2 to 3 per cent per decade, labour markets will tighten and competition for talented people will intensify. Of course, this competition for the best and the brightest will affect not only libraries. There will be a lot of competition for government workers at all levels, as well as workers in the business world, education, non-profits—anywhere that talent and skills are needed.
- Shortages of skills and experience. As the baby boom generation reaches retirement age, organisations face a potentially debilitating brain drain of skills and experience.
- Shortages of workers. Overall demand for workers is already beginning to exceed supply. The gap is projected to grow to millions, perhaps tens of millions, of workers, with potentially profound effects on economic output and standard of living. The current economic climate, with its high unemployment rate, will slow this demand in the short term. But the overall shortfall is inevitable as the population ages.
- Shortages of educated candidates. Despite continuing progress in

average educational achievement, colleges will graduate too few candidates to fill the technical, information-intensive, judgement-intensive jobs five years from now.

- Pressure on training and development. Employers must not only encourage employees' continuing education but also provide that education directly to maintain needed skills levels.
- Tension around HR policies and practices. The whole range of management practices— compensation, benefits, and especially work arrangements—must appeal to the new workforce and accommodate the expanding variety of workers' needs and preferences.
- Strain on organisational coherence. As the workforce diversifies and disperses—adopting flexible schedules, telework, and other technology-enabled arrangements—leaders must find new ways to cultivate and nourish organisational culture and identify.

The public sector, where many of our public, academic, and school libraries live, has additional burdens that private employers may resolve by requiring management degrees. In private industry most managers possess MBAs and formal management training, but in the library world managers come from the ranks of librarianship. Although this situation is changing, library managers rarely receive formal instruction on how to develop strategic plans and achieve goals, negotiate effectively, motivate staff, prepare budgets, manage buildings, or maximize employees' potential.

Even in a tight economy, library managers are usually paid less than those in the private sector and often receive promotions to management positions in lieu of higher pay, bonuses, or other perks simply not available to their library bosses as ways to award their achievements. What do the numbers say? The demographics tell us that in the United States there are about 72 million baby boomers, born between 1946 and 1965. The Department of Labour, 11,000 Americans turn 50 every day, and projections based on the U.S., Census indicate that an average of 4.6 adults turn 65 each minute. This older population will increase dramatically from 1995 until 2025, a period in which members of the populations ages 35–44 and 45–54 actually decrease, especially the former.

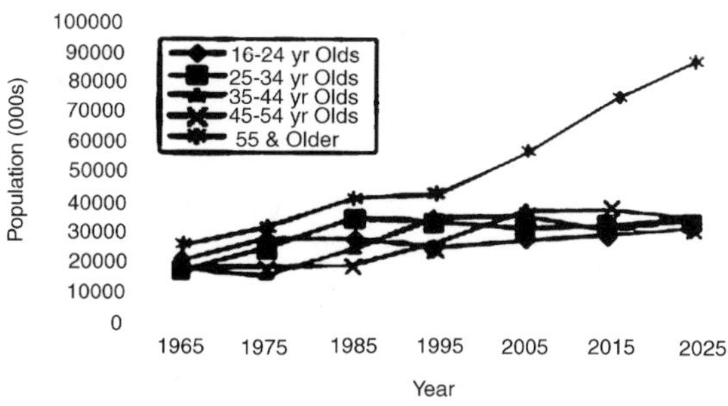

Fig. U.S. Population By Age. 1965-2025.

In the years between 2005 and 2020, this younger population actually decreases by 15 per cent.

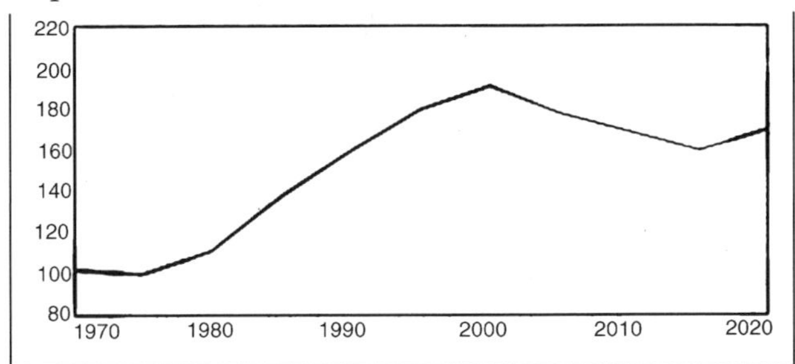

Fig. Shrinking of Traditional Ladership Pools.
35- to 44- year-olds in the United States.

The talent pool following the baby boomers is a shrinking traditional leadership pool. Such numbers are sobreing for those of us working in and with libraries. In landmark research conducted using 1990 census data, the ALA Office for Research and Statistics estimated that 40 per cent of all U.S., librarians would be eligible to retire at age 65 with their baby boomer colleagues by the end of 2014. Recently, using updated census data, Mary Jo Lynch and others found that these numbers have shifted and provide a brief reprieve—but *only* a brief one. These findings indicate that retirements are likely to peak between 2015 and 2020, when more than 45 per cent of librarians will reach retirement age. It is now expected that "the greatest estimated retirement wave will occur between 2010 and 2020, creating a potential deficit of library and information science graduates between 2015 and 2019."

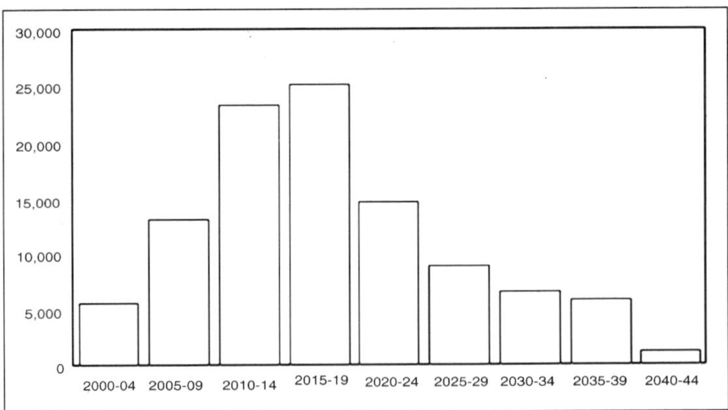

Fig. Number of Librarians Reaching Age 65 (2000 Census Base).

Lynch and her colleagues also pointed out a related trend: between 1990 and 2000 the number of working credentialed librarians grew by 22 per cent. Much of this growth came from people who entered the field as a second career or who had delayed entry into the workforce—most often women in their late thirties or early forties, who will soon approach retirement age. Because library workers are disproportionately middle-age and older, the percentage of younger workers, in their twenties and early thirties, is comparatively quite small. In 1999, ALA estimated that only 7 per cent of the library workforce was ages 20–29.

The 2000 census data show that the smallest cohort of librarians will reach age 65 between 2040 and 2044; these are the people born between 1975 and 1979, who at this writing are 30 or under. "Young talent" is not entering the library workforce in great numbers. As if that weren't frightening enough, ALA's "Diversity Counts" study points to the difficulty of retaining library workers *at all levels* under the age of 45. This includes those who entered the library workforce as career changers in their thirties or forties. Attrition rates for both credentialed MLS librarians and library support staff are so high that they suggest a lack of opportunities and structure for staff who might be recruited into professional practice or promoted into more responsible positions within libraries.

The study points to a

- revolving door effect where individuals are compelled by competing workforce opportunities or by delayed access to managerial leadership to leave the library for greener pastures elsewhere. More so than a matter of not having enough individuals in the pipeline to fill... positions, these numbers point to what can be foreseen in the LIS field as a crisis of leadership.

There will be even more data coming with completion of "The Future of Librarians in the Workforce" study conducted by Dr. José-Marie Griffiths and funded by the Institute of Museum and Library Services. One of the study's goals is to identify the nature of anticipated labour shortages in the library and information science field that may result from retirement of current workers over the next decade. Libraries are experiencing labour shortages now, and many have for several years. But as these charts show, the severest deficit is yet to come. Libraries must accelerate their planning and consideration of how they will deal with this reality. Even though the recession's impact may force some older workers to delay retirement in the short term, the long-term shift in population is inevitable.

Before moving away from the numbers, we want to mention that this material is pertinent to our colleagues across the border in Canada as well as halfway around the world in Australia. The Canadian Library Association's 8Rs 2003 study, "The Future of Human Resources in Canadian Libraries" reports that 50 per cent of Canadian library professionals were over the age of 45 and that, after 2006, there would be double the number of librarians turning 65 than there had been in the previous two years. Jenny McCarthy, in "Planning Future Workforce: An Australian Perspective," writes that 53 per cent of Australian librarians are over age 45 and 20 per cent over 55, whereas only 12.2 per cent of the total Australian workforce is over 55. In her own library, the Queensland University of Technology Library, the average age of staff is 43, with 34 per cent of them over 50. Of staff holding senior management roles, 80 per cent are over 50, and a large portion of supervisory staff are also over 50. It is no surprise that the profession worldwide is asking, Who will run the libraries when this talent leaves? Who will run the library? Individuals identified by current staff and managers as qualified and trainable, and who are given the right opportunities to develop into next-generation library leadership, will run the library.

Planning for an orderly succession is the right thing, ensuring continuity for all constituents, including members of the community who rely on library programmes and services. A rigourous system of succession planning provides a source of strong in-house candidates who can compete effectively for the key positions that become available.

Providing high-potential employees with developmental challenges helps retain them. And it does even more: it also prepares them to step into new challenges and future leadership positions. Succession planning also provides for the orderly transfer of knowledge from the skilled, highly experienced employees to the new generation of leadership and others in key positions without the loss of critical information. Ultimately, succession planning is a plus for any organisation.

Lost productivity and lost expertise are minimized. Costs are controlled because internal talent with in-depth knowledge of the institution can be developed rather than recruited from the outside. It can also be useful for recruitment. A library with a visible succession planning and development programme is more attractive to external candidates. And when the process recognises talent from non-traditional candidates, diversity can be celebrated and leveraged to the library's advantage.

Succession planning is proactive. You do not wait for the talent and those in key positions to leave; you are ahead of the curve, anticipating, developing, and ensuring that the key work is accomplished by topflight staff, and that knowledge is shared and transferred in a healthy, collaborative way. Succession planning is a vital tool for implementing your library's strategic plan. Are you convinced yet? What else do you need to make a case that embarking on succession planning is a good use of your time and energy? What are the arguments you need to make to your library director or board?

Here are some additional ideas; use those that fit your situation.

- As has been written and said so often, succession planning is not an end in itself. It is a means to an end. Succession planning is an important step to achieving your library's goals and strategic plan. It is a way to ensure that you have the right people, in the right place, at the right time, doing the right work. Having a human resources plan that supports the library's strategic plan (along with facilities, technology, budget, and other supporting plans) is a way to ensure that this happens.

- Succession planning and development help you systematically identify and develop employees with high potential for key positions. From traveling the country talking to clients and colleagues, we know that one outcome of budget cuts, new technology, streamlined work processes, and empowered staff is fewer middle managers in libraries. Until recently, these members of the workforce were the ranks from which leadership came. Thus it becomes increasingly important to identify, reward, and develop high potential staff—at every key level for every key job.
- Baby boomers who leave us take with them a tremendous store of organisational knowledge and history. It is important to transfer that intellectual capital, because once it disappears it cannot be recovered.
- Recruitment is not going to be as easy as it once was. Librarians have more choices of jobs to take in far more lucrative positions and industries. As the economy recovers, it will be become evident that we are facing a seller's market. Employees are increasingly selective about where they go to work. This holds true even for library directors and other senior members of leadership. Not only is competition stiff for the wellqualified candidates in these roles, many of them are also quite content where they are. How can you keep yours, grow yours, *and* plan in case/when your key leadership says good-bye?
- Not only is it important to develop staff to meet the difficulties of replacing employees in key positions, but, as good stewards of public funds, we must also consider the cost of turnover, which is a cost you should be able to avoid in many cases. The cost of turnover can easily add up to as much as twice the salary and benefits of the person leaving. First is the staffing cost—that is, the actual cost to hire. This can include fees for a search firm or advertisements and the cost of time to screen résumés, identify and train interview panels, serve on a panel, and so forth. But these are not the only costs. There is also the lost productivity created by a vacancy, the training costs to prepare a new employee, and "acting pay" if your union contract or HR policies require that you pay the employee filling a higher-level position additional salary. You also need to consider the costs of work actually not getting done: projects unfinished, priorities not met, and the actual money spent on substitutes and temporary employees whose value added is limited to keeping the doors open and desks covered rather than moving library strategy and projects forward. And there is, of course, the

impact on colleagues who often are asked to pick up extra work (or just do it because it is the right thing, although it too takes its toll). Finally, there are the training costs of time in orientation and bringing the new employee up to speed—the new hire's time along with the time of her supervisors, colleagues, and subordinates. This is the time required to get her up to speed on the technical aspects of the job and what is happening at your library, as well as on the library's culture and how things are done in the new environment.

- Regardless of your attention to succession planning at the leadership level, you will still be stymied without a succession planning programme that incorporates talent development at all levels, including the creation of a culture that fosters employee development and retention. Look around your library. How many, or what percentage, have been employees in your institution for more than twenty years? fifteen years? ten years? You won't be seeing such high numbers in the next decade. There has been a significant change in the psychological contract between an organisation and the members of its workforce—any organisation, any workforce, not just libraries. Loyalty, for the most part, is a thing of the past. Staff members in generations X and Y have more loyalty to their profession than to their employer (and even more to their family, friends, and other activities). The rewards, opportunities for growth and challenge, and team leadership roles that come with succession planning also help keep your high-potential, high-performing employees in place.

BRINGING IT ALL BACK HOME

What do your numbers tell you? If these arguments in the previous part do not make the case, pull out the data and take a look at your own demographics. Most library directors and boards respond to hard data. Start by taking a snapshot of your workforce by age.

Table. Workforce Snaspshot Example.

	Age Range									
Position	**20-24**	**25-29**	**30-34**	**35-39**	**40-44**	**45-49**	**50-54**	**55-59**	**60-64**	**65+**
Clerk I	10	12	10	5	5	6	5	4	2	1
Clerk II				3	5	2	1	1		
Clerical Manager						8	1	1	2	
Paraprof I		2	10	12	10	6	5			
Paraprof II		3	6	5	12	10	1			
Librarian I			2	6	6	2	2			
Librarian II				4	4	3	5			
Branch Mgr					1	2	3	5	1	
Division Mgr								2	1	1
Asst. Director								2	1	
Director									1	

Table provides an example of what it might look like. Then take it further. An important new step in this research is to look at who is eligible for retirement. This isn't too hard to do and the information, whatever HR/payroll system you are using, should be readily available. Look at the age of each member of the library's workforce.

Do it for a rolling three year period. Then look at this information with a focus on different positions and levels. For example, conduct such an analysis for those in the position of librarian, branch manager, and departmental leader for each branch and your central facility, plus other key positions in your library.

(Needless to say, you will have to adjust these numbers as you learn of retirements and review your employee turnover statistics.) Showing your library director or board of trustees this information just might do the trick.

EVERY PICTURE TELLS A STORY

We worked with a large East Coast urban library that realised it was time to begin a succession planning process. The first thing we did was analyse the status at the time. This is what we found:

Leadership (Director and Deputies, Department and Assistant Department Heads)

Total: 24	
Ages 55+	10 (42%)
Ages 50-54	5 (21%)

These demographics included public service as well as all other members of leadership (*e.g.*, finance, HR, marketing, IT). Of the nine remaining members of leadership under the age of 50, none were in public services. That raised a red flag: it meant that all fifteen members of the senior leadership over the age of 50 were in public services—vital areas, of course, to meeting community needs.

What about the next level down, the talent pool to follow? How did this client fare when it looked at its branch and division managers? Would there be ready replacements from this group for the members of senior leadership? No, these demographics were even worse:

Branch and Division Managers

Total: 63	
Ages 55+	29 (46%)
Ages 50-54	16 (16%)

Even if this client were doing a perfect job of preparing branch and division managers to step up, many of them might retire with—or before—the senior leadership group. Would the talent pool at the next level down be ready to move up to senior leadership? In most organisations, this is not very likely. And it is scary when you think about the impact of recruiting for so many key positions on the commitment you make every day to your stakeholders. What would Habitat for Humanity or Wendy's be thinking about if it seemed likely that 45 per cent of their key leaders and managers would be able to retire within five years? Certainly they would be looking at ways to keep their organisations viable.

In addition to looking at the demographics of your library, ask the following questions to see if your library needs to worry about talent:

- Do key positions have weak bench strength, that is, are only a few employees *ready now* to assume the positions? Do managers complain that they have trouble finding employees ready or willing to take a promotion as vacancies occur?
- Has your library experienced a long-term vacancy in a key leadership position in the past year? Did you have to go outside to fill the position? What was the cost to the library?
- Are key positions filled—but with less than full confidence? Has the library had to compromise on experience or leadership quality to fit certain positions?
- What percentage of your leaders would be selected if they were applying today for their current positions?
- What does turnover look like at your library? Do employees at all levels leave the library to advance professionally or to meet their personal or career goals? How many people who are ready or being groomed for promotion *at any level* typically leave the library before they get that promotion?
- Is *critical turnover* high? Critical turnover is the percentage or number of high-potential workers who leave the library as compared to average or fully successful employees. Does your library have a plan to retain high-performing and key employees?
- Have the business challenges faced by your managers and leaders changed significantly during the past five to ten years? Does your library have the bench strength to staff its strategic and other plans for the changes that will come in the next five to ten years?
- Is the time to fill positions too long, or perceived by managers to be too long?
- Do employees or managers complain that decisions about who to promote or transfer are made on criteria other than best qualified, such as friendship and favouritism?
- Is there a process to respond quickly to sudden, surprise losses of key talent? How long would it take to replace a key member of your workforce who resigned, retired, or died?

If the answers to these questions make you nervous, or if you do not know the answers, it is time for management, and in some cases (pertaining only to the position of library director) your board of trustees, to become increasingly invested in this topic. Do you have any "horror stories?" For example, are you staffing some key positions with retirees from other libraries because your bench strength is weak— the result of a training and development hiatus for too many years? Did you have such a difficult time recruiting a deputy director that you had to promote from several levels down to fill the gap? If a large branch or regional manager left next week, could you quickly think of at least three employees ready to take her place, and three others ready to take the place of the one promoted into the new job? One of our clients *is* this fortunate

This client has been working on leadership development and succession planning for several years. Her library has developed employees via leadership classes, webinars, community exposure, committee experiences, and job rotation. She is not only lucky but smart. Her investment in planning has paid off. Think about the situations in your library, your own best practices and horror stories.

These will also help you make a case to library leadership about moving the agenda for succession planning and development forward. The future is around the corner. As the builders of great library systems, you have invested heavily in creating lasting organisations. What you do now ensures the viability of your organisation going forward.

Table. Reasons to Develop a Succession Planning Programme.

Reason	Significant Impact/Notes for Our Library?
Provide source of in-house replacements	
Retain key talent	
Prepare individuals for future challenges	
Increase library's human capital by providing for critical/timely knowledge transfer	
Accelerate development of key individuals	
Provide challenging, growth-oriented, and rewarding career opportunities	
Ensure continuity of management culture	
Avoid lost productivity (new person's learning curve)	
Control costs—developing internal talent is less expensive than hiring from the outside	
Make organization more attractive to job candidates	
Support diversity goals	

Which are the most pressing to you? Now that you have assessed your needs, take some time to think through your answers to the following questions:

- What are our library's particular goals in developing a succession management programme?
- How does our programme contribute to helping the library achieve its mission and strategic plan?
- What outcomes and results will we measure to assess success?
- What shall we name the programme?

SUCCESSION PLANNING AND DEVELOPMENT PROCESS

PHASE I: IDENTIFYING AND ASSESSING TALENT

One of the key aspects of any succession management and development process is talent identification. In this phase of the process, you identify employees with the potential (often called "high potentials") for success in filling key roles, including leadership, and develop a talent profile for each. This process is completed by a succession planning committee—the leadership team or a subset of it convened for this purpose—and should always include the library director and HR director.

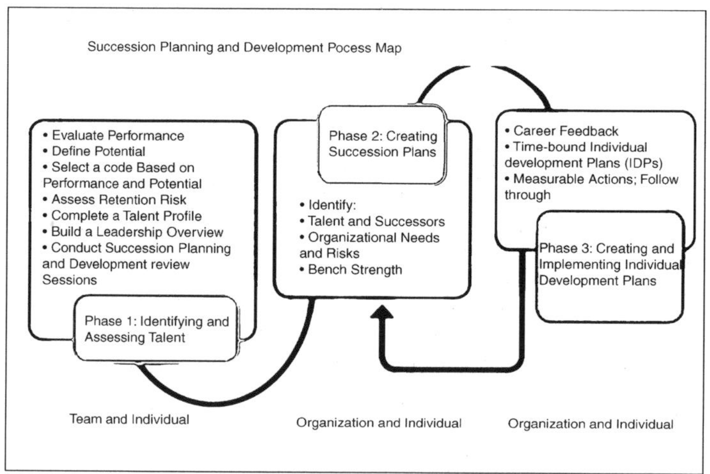

Fig. Succession Planning and Development Process Map.

There are several ways for the library to proceed as it assesses talent:

- The first choice point involves scope. Will identification and assessment be made of all library employees? Will talent profiles be created for all? In the alternative, will it be limited to target groups of employees by level (*e.g.*, all first-line managers)? Will the talent review focus only on leadership and star employees brought to the committee by HR, a library manager, or leader? Successful talent reviews have been conducted in all of these ways. Choosing the first or second option helps ensure that no one falls through the cracks because they are not visible or have a personality difference with their boss. Regardless of which method you chose, it is advisable that you begin the talent review process with senior leadership and other key positions, because these positions are usually hardest to fill and are staffed with employees most likely to retire in the shortest time frame.

- The second choice point pertains to who completes this first level of talent review; that is, who (specifically) compiles the information to create the individual talent profile. Should it be done by the employee's manager or supervisor and then brought to the succession planning committee for review? In the alternative, should the committee as a whole review staff under consideration and complete the profile together? In large library systems where leadership is not likely to be aware of the abilities and potential of most staff members, it is suggested that managers conduct the first level of review and bring their completed talent profiles to the succession planning committee. If the library is small enough that most members of the succession planning committee have a picture of the staff, even if it is just the top layers of staff, you will benefit from having the input of all. Numerous perspectives are likely to broaden the picture painted of the individual.
- The third choice point involves the composition of the committee that performs the second level of review—the succession planning committee. This group should always include the library director, the HR director (if the library is large enough to have one), and a group of senior leaders. They are responsible for the activities in phases 1 and 2 of the succession planning and development process and work from a focused agenda to complete their work. The HR director typically chairs the process and ensures that pre-session work (such as first-level talent reviews, if done by managers) is completed.

Once these choices have been made, leaders complete the following steps for each employee under review, producing a completed talent profile for each employee.

EVALUATE PERFORMANCE

The first step of assessing talent requires an accurate, completed performance appraisal for each employee. It would be shortsighted to build a talent profile on potential alone; performance ratings/profiles must be included as well. You should easily be able to translate the following definitions to your own form and process.

If you do not have an appraisal form, you may wish to consider employees as high, medium, and low performers in terms of the following definitions (and then develop a form and a process):

- *High-performing employees* are rated "exceeds expectations." They consistently meet and often exceed goals, consistently meet and often go beyond expectations defined in competencies, and are viewed as outstanding performers.
- *Medium performers* are often rated as "fully meets expectations." Most of the members of your workforce are likely to fall into this category: employees who fully meet expectations, consistently meet most goals, consistently perform at a satisfactory level in most areas, and may exceed expectations in some. These employees perform all aspects of the job with minimal errors and exhibit most of the competency behaviours. Others rely on these employees to perform all aspects of their jobs with a high degree of proficiency. These performers do have some room for performance growth.
- *Low performers* do not meet the expectations of the job. Though these employees may perform some aspects of the job well, they need improvement.

In this process, each employee is identified as a low, medium, or high performer. This rating will be combined with a rating of potential in the next step before it is entered into the individual talent profile.

DEFINE POTENTIAL

In this next step the library determines the ability and motivation of individual staff members to take on new or more senior roles in the short and long terms. According to many library directors, this is one of the most difficult aspects of the process. But by conducting this review systematically and globally (*i.e.,* throughout the library system), leadership can obtain a picture of its entire workforce and examine employees' potential and possibilities for development, change, lateral transfer, or promotion. During this step, leadership and HR are able to focus on the individual's key talent and ability for growth and increased contributions within the library system. Leadership should be keyed into looking for high-potential employees. But what is, who is, a "high-potential employee"? Employees with high potential are the library's future leaders and holders of key positions.

Broadly, they are the members of your workforce who are able and willing to advance two or more levels in the library, are possible candidates for key positions, or have not yet reached a plateau in their career. High potentials are not the same as stars. Although being rated as a star or as exceeding expectations (or whatever language the library uses to identify those in the top performance category) in the employee's current job is usually a prerequisite to identification as a high potential, not all stars are necessarily high potentials; advancement and leadership potential involve criteria other than current performance, not the least of which are ability, aspiration, and engagement.

Every library identifies its own key positions, yet experience shows us that many are at a loss about defining "high potential." What follows is a way for library leadership to view the differences between low-, growth-, and high-potential performers based on ability, aspiration, and engagement. Start with these definitions and view them as a draft. Feel free to alter and add, so that you create criteria and a narrative that fit your culture. You may find criteria more applicable than ability, aspiration, and engagement, or your culture may suggest different definitions or language for them. Some possibilities include prior leadership experience, education, learning agility, assessment against competencies (often reviewed in the performance management process), leadership ability based on the library's leadership competencies, risk-taking ability, and project management experience. The definitions below can help you assess the potential of each employee in terms of ability, employee aspiration, and how engaged each is in her job and with the library.

But first, before you review employees, here are some tips:

- Be objective.
- Be future oriented; do not focus on the past year.
- *Ask*: Is this employee capable of moving to the next level (*e.g.*, branch manager if presently a librarian, youth coordinator, or subject specialist) or to a leadership or department head role?
- Does this employee consistently demonstrate competencies at the next level (high potential), sometimes demonstrate the next level of competencies (growth potential), or not demonstrate competencies at the next level (low potential)?
- Ensure that you hold no biases, like recency (basing an opinion of most recent performance) or halo-or-horns effects stemming from a positive or negative experience potentially from years ago. There are other biases you might have about individual employees as well. Maybe she is not like you in temperament, personality, or style. Maybe she comes from a different culture; reminds you of your mom, dad, or child; is of a different generation, nationality, gender, level of ability, or sexual orientation—or doesn't laugh at your jokes. We tend to want to hire, promote, and work with people who are like us—but such an approach seriously limits the candidate pool (and, of course, can be illegal). Reflect on your thoughts and feelings about the individuals you are reviewing for potential. Separate feelings from facts about performance and potential as a star employee, high potential, or upcoming library leader. Talking with a trusted colleague or HR about employees has helped many reviewers separate potential biases from employees' actual ability and performance.

- *The leadership team should ask*: Does the employee demonstrate competencies, knowledge, skills, and abilities at that next level? How do you know this? Do performance evaluations document it? What about performance as a member of a key team or committee? Do her projects come in on time and within budget? Does she have a role as an informal leader in the library? How does she use that influence? Do other employees ask her to be assigned to their committees or projects? What comments on the performance appraisal, about actual situations, are indicative of the competencies needed to move to additional challenges in your organisation?
- Finally (and especially where there are gaps), do not rely only on anecdotal evidence. Many of the shelf objective and job-related assessments are available for evaluating the potential of individual employees. Results provide the library, as well as the individual, with important feedback as well as input into a development plan.

After reflection, leaders determine each employee's potential for growth or expanded roles within the library as low, growth, or high (L, G, H), using the following definitions (or something like them):

- Low-potential employee:
  - *Ability.* May be a solid performer with consistent execution but has not demonstrated the capacity for growth in terms of a larger volume (*e.g.*, larger branch) or role (*e.g.*, reference librarian to adult services supervisor).
  - *Aspiration.* May not have the motivation or interest to advance or transfer laterally into other positions; does not actively seek and may not be open to development, feedback, and opportunities.
  - *Engagement.* May not appear to be happy with the library system or its future plans, or infrequently goes above and beyond.
- Growth-potential employee:
  - *Ability.* Has solid competencies in current job; occasionally exhibits the knowledge, skills, and competencies needed for the next level or another job; is smart; exhibits high emotional intelligence (*e.g.*, self-awareness, self-regulation, empathy) as well as strong social and interpersonal skills.
  - *Aspiration.* Conveys the motivation and ability for development and advancement; insightful about own ability and seeks feedback from others.
  - *Engagement.* Is committed to the library, excited about challenges and new directions, often goes above and beyond.
- High-potential employee:
  - *Ability.* Has a track record of results and leadership that is clearly superior to peers; demonstrates the knowledge, skills,

abilities, and competencies of the next level; is smart, analytical, thinks systemically and critically; possesses a high degree of emotional intelligence and social and interpersonal skills.

- *Aspiration.* Demonstrates the motivation, drive, and ambition to rise in the library; aware of own strengths and limitations, actively seeks development.
- *Engagement.* Values and enjoys being part of the library; is excited to be involved in projects; often goes above and beyond.

SELECT CODE BASED ON EMPLOYEE'S PERFORMANCE AND POTENTIAL

At this point you have determined a rating for performance (low, medium, or high) and one for potential (low, growth, or high). Now it is time to determine a code that takes both ratings into account. Coding makes it much more likely that staff are evaluated consistently and on the same terms.

		Potential			
		Low		Growth	High
Performance	High	Key Contributor–KC		Emerging Talent–ET	Promotable–P
	Medium	Key Contributor–KC		Key Contributor–KC	Emerging Talent–ET
	Low	New Hire–NH	Action Required–AR	Improvement Required–IR	Improvement Required–IR

Fig. Charting Performance and Potential.

To complete this matrix, simply identify an employee's performance (low/ medium/high) and potential (low/growth/high) and then choose the category where performance meets potential. You can use the code definitions to confirm alignment with your view of the staff member's talent and potential with the library.

Each box on the matrix has a code that acts as a kind of shorthand to describe the employee's performance and potential:

- *Promotable (P)*: Excellent performer; has a history of high performance ratings and consistently exceeds expectations; high-potential employee; has taken on more responsibility; is ready for next level position; seeks a promotion.
- *Emerging Talent (ET)*: Excellent performer; typically given high performance ratings by manager or supervisor; shows growth potential; can take on more responsibility; promotable within 12–24 months; lateral transfer within 8–12 months.
- *Key Contributor (KC)*: Consistent performer and well placed in

current position; management should provide individual with committee or other assignments to see how employee responds. Manager should value the person in this position and support her efforts.

- *Improvement Required (IR)*: Inconsistent performer; may lack knowledge, skills, abilities, competencies, or motivation in one or more areas; could become a concern requiring action if performance does not improve; not promotable; performance improvement plan should be in place.
- *Action Required (AR)*: Poor performer in current role; transfer if appropriate position in library system can be found or ask to leave; time line for action is required.
- *New Hire (NH)*: Too new to rate; usually less than six months in current position.

Now you are ready to transfer the code that identifies the employee in terms of performance and potential onto the talent profile form. There is no box labeled NH for new hires, since, they are considered too new for leaders to assess performance and potential accurately.

You might also want to use the table matrix, or some variation of it, to get a picture of all members of a unit or classification of employees at once. For example, you might place all librarians, or all staff from one unit, on the matrix to get a picture of emerging and potential leadership. This approach circumvents the possibility of staff with potential falling through the cracks, since, everyone is considered systematically. You will be surprised at how many quiet shining stars emerge through this methodical exercise.

Current Performance			
	High	Steady Producers Strategy: Keep Turn Over Low, Keep Them Motivated and Productive where they are,	Stars Strategy : Keep Turnover Low Accelerate Development.
	Low	Deadwood Strategy: Convert to Steady Producers. Terminate them If they can't be Salvaged	Question Marks Strategy: Convert to Steady Producers Terminate them if they can't be Salvaged.
		LOW	High
		Future Potential	

Fig. Charting Performance and Potential Alternate Grid.

Another way to classify employees by performance and potential is through use of a performance/potential grid using the following definitions: *Stars* are the "exceed expectations" performers who are perceived to have high potential for future advancement.

They are a key source to replace incumbents in key positions:

- *Steady Producers* also exceed expectations in their performance in the current position, but they are not identified as having strong potential to fill key positions at the library. Since, they are still highly productive, the strategy is to capitalise on their skills and knowledge and keep them productive and motivated.

- *Question Marks* are poor performers in their current position, but they might have potential in another position or in the future. The best strategy for working with these employees is to focus on improving their performance, ideally to turn them into stars. Consider coaching, mentoring, or job rotation to help improve performance and productivity.
- *Deadwood* are poor performers seen as having little potential for growth at the library. Because of retirements, layoffs, limited expansions, and budget cuts, fewer of these performers are left in most libraries. Where they do exist, supervisors should be coached to help them improve productivity or to ease them out.

ASSESS RETENTION RISK

Now that talent has been identified, there are still a few steps remaining. One is to assess the degree of risk that the staff person might leave the library in the next year. It is suggested that you identify the level of risk as high, medium, or low (H, M, L) and enter it on the individual talent profile.

High risk implies that the manager or others believe the person will not be in her current job for the next year, medium that she may not be, and low that she likely will remain in her current position for the next twelve months. Your reason for selecting a high/medium/low risk factor can be based on knowledge you have or on your intuition. Some examples of risk based on knowledge include these: employee might be promoted or given a lateral position or developmental position; might make known that she is seeking to leave the library, or is interviewing elsewhere; is having performance problems; spouse is relocating. Examples of risk factors based on intuition are the managers' (or employees') perception of readiness for the next level; leaders' perception of risk or fit; perceived satisfaction with direction in which the library is going; and satisfaction with current job, peer group, or supervisor. The risk factor selected, along with the rationale for it, should be discussed at the succession planning committee meeting.

Examples of other factors, which may or may not be based on knowledge and yet should be considered, are dissatisfaction with compensation or benefits; recently passed over for a promotion; personal or family issues; dissatisfaction with job rotation assignment (*e.g.,* to branch farther from home); does not feel included by peer group or recognised by manager; dissatisfied with potential for career growth or communications flow; does not agree with the direction in which the library is heading based on its recent planning process; feels lacking in the information or training needed to be successful; does not feel challenged and empowered to make a meaningful contribution to the library; does not feel recognised and appreciated for contribution to the success of work group or the library; does not feel part of an effective, diverse, and winning team; and, most important, does not have a good, mutually respectful relationship with supervisor.

COMPLETE THE TALENT PROFILE

The next step is to complete the talent profile forms to create in-depth, individualised profiles. You have already entered results from the assessments you have completed to date regarding performance, potential, and risk. Now be sure you have collected information from prior performance reviews and the individual's résumé. The completed profile serves as basis for discussion in the succession planning committee meeting.

BUILD LEADERSHIP OVERVIEW

The next step is to create a talent summary of the library's leadership team or any group under consideration (*e.g.*, all branches, all librarians). You can create the overview from the information listed in the individual talent profiles. The resulting overview provides a comprehensive, high-level view of top talent and the multiple leadership opportunities available.

CONDUCT SUCCESSION PLANNING AND DEVELOPMENT REVIEW SESSIONS

The succession planning committee meets to review employees with an eye towards growing leaders and providing development opportunities to maximize their potential at the library. At the review sessions, the committee uses the completed individual talent profiles and leadership overviews to move into phase 2 of the process—creating succession pans.

PHASE II: CREATING SUCCESSION PLANS

Leaders create succession plans on the basis of organisational needs, goals, and priorities as well as individuals' performance, potential, ability, and motivation. To accomplish this, they utilise the documents completed in phase 1 to prioritise needs and potential candidates to fulfill these needs. Leadership evaluates library needs in the future through the risk assessments and anticipated retirements to identify bench strength and internal candidates for positions.

At this point, leadership has already identified key positions, including those in leadership. From their risk and retirement analysis, they know which positions may become vacant. High-potential employees are identified, and developmental needs are at least identified. Now is the time to identify successor candidates. When considering successor candidates, start by asking the following questions: How would this position further develop the employee being considered? Would the employee be interested in this opportunity? Table is a sample of a succession planning report summary for leadership positions. It builds on the leadership overview prepared for the review sessions.

Employee	**Position/Title**	**Location**	**Talent Code**	**Development Needs**	**Recommended Next Position**	**Timing**	**Notes**
Jenny Fir	Deputy Director	Central	KC	Current position:managing four generations			
Jane Tree	Director, Public Services	Central	P	Executive coaching to Improve understanding of impact of Behaviour on individuals and groups	Deputy Director	12 Months	
John Oak	Manager, Central and Outreach	Central	ET	Experience with Building projects And facilities management	Director, Public Services	9-12 months	
Harry Maple	Director, Research and Strategy	Central	KC	Excellent in Current role:does not seek Promotions Does not hold an MLS		Not at this time	
Annie Pea	Manager, Community Branches	Central	ET	Leadership development presentation skills	Manager, Central and Outreach	18+ months	

One easy way to assess bench strength, to see if the library can fill vacancies from within with relative ease, is through replacement charting or planning. Replacement charting was the original goal of succession planning before it broadened out to include talent development and building a pipeline of employees ready to fill vacancies. Replacement charting indicates one or more successors for key positions and also helps to create a management inventory for the library. Smaller libraries may not need this at all, but larger libraries will find it useful.

Table. Replacement Charting Using a Demand Forcast.

Table. A

Key Leadership Position or Knowledge Base until	Primary Skills and Knowledge Required	Approx. Months Needed
Central Library Director	• Knowledge of librarianship • Well-developed leadership/coaching skills • Networking within community	60

Table. B

Three potential Successors, in order Of Readliness	Rate Successors' Readlines Level[a]	Strengths	Developmental Experiences Needed
• Central Director Knowledge of • Librarianship Well-developed • Leadership/coaching skills • Networking within community			
Anni Reference	1	Strong leadership skills Strong reference skills	Community networking
John smith	3	Good reference skills	Community Networking Leadership/coaching skills
Jerri Frank	4	Good communicator, Networker	Leadership/coaching skills

Table is one format for a replacement chart. It lists the positions in the hierarchy. Successors are identified under each position with a notation as to readiness to take on the higher-level job. The number "1" identifies those ready for the promotion immediately, number "2" those ready in six months, and so on. Those identified as successors should be both stars and high potentials, or those with a talent profile coded Promotable and Emerging Talent. If they are not, review why the selected code was assigned; is the identified successor truly a successor or just a fill-in in the event of vacancy? In either event, plan to create a robust individual development plan for those identified as replacements (unless there is indication of interest being limited to filling the position only until a replacement is located internally or externally).

PHASE III: CREATING AND IMPLEMENTING INDIVIDUAL DEVELOPMENT PLANS

TALENT DEVELOPMENT

A good understanding of where employees fall in the matrix is not where developing talent stops—it is actually where it begins. The critical work comes from providing feedback and developing staff. Although each employee is different, each more or less fits into one of the nine matrix categories according to performance and potential. Still, it is not sufficient merely to identify an employee by category; providing useful and insightful feedback is key to talent development. How managers and leaders approach each employee and their individual situations requires thought. It calls for honest feedback of potential along with a meaningful conversation about the individual's career growth and development.

Here are some things to think about, tips for development, and talking points for managers and leaders to reflect upon when giving feedback to:

- Promotable/high-potential employees,
- Emerging talent,
- Fully successful key contributors, and
- Employees requiring performance improvement.

Do not forget that every employee, regardless of category, is different; it is the manager's role to consider the needs and motivations of each employee, how they receive and internalise feedback, and to act accordingly.

Promotable/High- Potential Employees

Key Considerations

The primary challenge in working with high-potential employees is to communicate that they are valued without prematurely raising expectations about promotions.

These employees often want to see that they are making measurable progress towards their career goals. As a result, they actively seek additional responsibilities that broaden skills or offer new challenges. They may need help from you to modify their sense of urgency for promotion.

Here are several ideas for working with them:

- Give frequent reassurance that you and the library regard them highly.
  - Do not make promises about promotions or next assignments unless the situation is very clear.
  - Most libraries are unable to provide compensation increases that align with this level of performance. But, to the extent you can, provide salary increases, incentives, and awards commensurate with performance. In addition to or in lieu of monetary recognition, provide recognition to such employees in the manner they want to receive it.
  - Make sure the employee understands the competitive nature of promotion decisions when there are others equally or better skilled. In other words, there are no assurances; no employee is anointed to fill the position of another.

- Assess retention risks and develop a specific plan if appropriate and allowable within civil service or other rules.

Tips for Development

- Help the employee create and implement a vigourous individual development plan.
- Establish frequent one-on-one sessions to discuss career goals and progress in meeting IDP goals. Openly discuss concerns the employee may have about the future. This is particularly important to members of generations X and Y.
- Develop "stretch assignments" by delegating projects or responsibilities you are currently doing (in the important, not mundane, areas).
- Look for opportunities for the employee to get broader visibility and "showcase" her talents (*e.g.*, task force assignments, presentations to library leadership or the board of trustees).
- Allow the employee to stand in for you at meetings or provide backup when you are out of the office or on vacation.
- Encourage the employee to present at state and national library conferences and to get involved in these (and other) organisations to develop talents, learn new skills, get exposed to other ideas, and take on leadership roles in a non-work environment. Encourage volunteer work with local non-profit groups of any type as well as participation in Rotary, chamber of commerce, or other business associations.
- Identify cross-functional developmental (lateral) moves or rotational assignments.
- Arrange a mentoring relationship with a well regarded, successful internal or external leader who can assist in targeted developmental needs.
- Ask the employee to participate in 360-degree feedback or other developmental assessments to gain more insight into career strengths and developmental needs.
- Partner with a coach for targeted developmental needs or prepare for the role in a promotional assignment.

Suggested Talking Points

- It is important to spend some time with you specifically to have a conversation about your career goals and aspirations.
- You are highly regarded by me and other leaders throughout the library. You continue to be an excellent performer—always delivering results in a manner that is congruent with our library's goals, mission, and values. For example (insert appropriate examples). You continue

to expand the scope of your responsibilities, and your work is consistently high quality (again, insert examples—be they the quality of responses to reference questions, helping a page team leader work out schedules, forming a partnership with the local day care center, etc.). These are exactly the types of characteristics we look for in our future professionals/ leaders (as appropriate). (It is critical to use specific examples of the employee's observed behaviour so that she understands exactly what you value.)

- Based on your performance, it is appropriate to begin considering other opportunities for you to enhance your career within our library. Just to check, is that something you want? If so, let's talk about what those possibilities might look like (and really listen to what is being said).
- Now let's discuss how to align your IDP properly with where you would like to see your career heading.
- Please keep in mind that your performance (both results and behaviours as articulated in the competencies—the what and the how) in your current position is one of the most important factors in determining future advancement. We encourage you to continue providing the exceptional performance you have been demonstrating.
- It is also important for us to ensure that we have a qualified individual who is ready to move into your position. Let's talk about who may be a potential successor for you and what we need to do to get her ready (if appropriate).
- What other questions do you have for me? How can I support you in your development? What else could I be doing to help make your work more satisfying and for you to feel that you are learning and growing?
- We will continue to have this type of dialogue on a (insert frequency) basis as a part of our regular meetings. I look forward to our future discussions.

What is it like to be identified and developed as key talent? Succession planning has been a key initiative at OCLC for more than ten years. George Needham is vice president of Global and Regional Councils at OCLC. He went through the first and more recent talent management and succession planning programmes at OCLC and is also someone who identifies and manages others. We asked him to remember being identified as someone with high potential and being invited to participate in the first programme.

He paused for a few seconds to reflect, and I could hear the feeling in his voice: "It was an honour to learn that my boss feels that way. It was a heady feeling." Very appreciative of the opportunities, he said that it made him feel valued and very loyal. He worked harder, stayed longer, and now gives back by developing others.

Emerging Talent

Key Considerations

The primary challenge in working with emerging talent is to convey that they are valued without prematurely raising expectations about growth opportunities.

Development plans for these staff members should include activities that help clarify their growth or performance potential:

- Give frequent reassurance that you and the library hold them in high regard.
- Avoid absolute promises about promotions or next assignments unless the situation is very clear.
- Most libraries are unable to provide compensation increases that align with this level of performance. But, to the extent you can, provide salary increases, incentives, and awards commensurate with the performance. In addition to or in lieu of monetary recognition, provide recognition to this employee in the manner she wants to receive it.
- Make sure the employee understands the competitive nature of promotion decisions when there are others equally or better skilled. Create teams of highly talented peers to accelerate growth and elevate the level of performance.
- Consistently assess retention risks and develop specific plans, if appropriate.

Tips for Development

- Ensure that a vigourous IDP exists and is being implemented.
- Establish frequent one-on-one meetings to discuss career goals and progress in meeting those goals. Openly discuss concerns the employee may have about her future.
- Develop "stretch assignments" by delegating projects or responsibilities you are currently doing (in important, not mundane, areas).
- Look for opportunities for the staff member to get broader visibility and "showcase" her talents (*e.g.*, task force assignments, presentations to library leadership or the board of trustees).
- Allow the employee to stand in for you at meetings or provide backup when you are out of the office or on vacation.
- Identify cross-functional and other developmental assignments.
- Arrange a mentoring relationship with a highly regarded, successful internal or external leader who can assist in targeted developmental needs.
- Ask the employee to participate in 360-degree feedback or other

developmental assessments to gain more insight into career strengths and developmental needs.

Suggested Talking Points

- It is important to spend some time to have a discussion with you regarding your career.
- You know that you are well regarded by library leadership and me. You continue to be a very strong performer—consistently delivering results in a manner that is consistent with library values (insert appropriate examples of observable behaviour). You demonstrate the desire and capacity for further development and growth. Just to check, is that something you want?
- Let's talk for a moment about your career interests.
- Now let's discuss how to align your IDP properly with where you would like to see your career go.
- Please keep in mind that your performance (both results and behaviours) in your current position is one of the most important factors in determining future advancement. We encourage you to continue providing the high level of performance you have been demonstrating.
- What other questions do you have for me? How can I support you in your development? What else could I be doing to help make your work more satisfying and for you to feel that you are learning and growing?
- We will continue to have this type of dialogue on a (insert frequency) basis as a part of our regular communication. I look forward to our future discussions.

Key Contributor

Everyone eventually reaches a level beyond which promotion would be ill advised (for both the individual and the library). This limitation does not imply poor performance in the current position.

Typical types of key contributor:

- Strong individual contributor who may be well placed in her current assignment, whether cataloger, circulation clerk, or department head.
- Employee who prefers to remain in her current role. Not everyone wants to rise in the library hierarchy; sometimes overachiever leaders forget that.
- Staff member with limited experience in broader, more strategic, or big-picture roles or tasks and little or no desire to gain more.
- Staff member with limited ability, or desire, to supervise or manage others.
- Employee who is simply not as qualified as others in the position in the library.

Key Considerations

Regardless of the scenario, your conclusion is that for the time being the present position is the one for which the individual is best suited. Your role is to manage the employee's career expectations constructively.

Here are several ideas on how to provide feedback to these members of the workforce (most employees are likely to fall into this category):

- Regularly recognise contributions the employee is making (especially directly following the initial career discussion).
- Gain a clear understanding of the real reasons behind the employee's desire (if any) for career advancement. Is the motivation income growth, a position or title of "importance," professional recognition, the need for continued challenge and growth, or something else? Acknowledge these needs and develop an understanding that they may not be met immediately or that an alternative way of meeting them may need to be determined. This is critical because these are good, solid employees who are contributing a great deal to the library and are successful in their roles. There are likely many opportunities to meet all but the desire for increased income. Point out opportunities for expansion of current responsibilities and the room for growth in compensation without a promotion.

Tips for Development

- Ensure that an appropriate IDP exists and is being implemented.
- Establish regular time to discuss career goals and progress in meeting those goals.
- Openly discuss concerns the employee may have about her future.
- Identify what the employee is "best at" and leverage that skill in other parts of the library.
- Provide opportunities for the staff member to "showcase" her skills.
- Assign special projects or "stretch assignments" that provide challenge and visibility both functionally and cross-functionally.
- Use the employee to help train new staff in her classification or below.
- Allow the employee to stand in for you at meetings or provide backup when you are out of the office or on vacation.
- Consider a job rotation to provide appropriate technical skill or leadership experiences.

Suggested Talking Points

- I want to have a discussion regarding your performance and career growth.
- As you know from our past performance discussions, you have

made numerous important and significant contributions in your position as (insert job title). You are a solid, highly successful performer with consistent execution (or insert applicable comments and applicable examples of observed behaviour).

- We believe it is in your best interest—and the library's—to continue to challenge you to develop your skills and competencies in your current position.
- I am committed to helping you continue to grow and develop in the direction that best suits you and the library. I look forward to working through the details with you as part of your IDP.

Employees Who Require Improvement

Key Considerations

Employees who require improvement may fall into this area for several different reasons. In general, this employee is either not meeting expectations from a performance standpoint or is exhibiting low growth potential in terms of ability or motivation to succeed. The main point of focus is to discuss the sustained improvements required to remain in the position and with the library. In some cases, a lateral move into another position may be the appropriate solution. If so, keep in mind that at some point this employee was likely seen as having potential and good job performance. She may even have been promoted at some point. You need to reassure her of your commitment to work with her to improve performance. You should also assess factors that could cause this individual to lose motivation and leave the library rather than improve performance and stay.

Tips for Development

- Develop and implement a healthy performance improvement plan. The plan should be time bound with specific measurable actions.
- Establish check-in meetings to discuss career goals and performance progress.
- Openly discuss concerns the employee may have about her future.
- Identify what the employee is "best at" and leverage that skill.
- Provide structured on-the-job training with a trainer, peer, or supervisor.
- Engage the employee in appropriate education- based programmes.

Suggested Talking Points

- I want to respond to your questions about your potential for career growth here at the library.
- As you know from our past discussions, I have several concerns regarding your performance. Specifically, you are not demonstrating (insert appropriate skills, observable behaviour, etc).
- Your most concentrated effort right now needs to be focused on

improving and sustaining your performance in the areas I just mentioned.

- I sincerely want to see you turn this situation around. Therefore, I will work with you to create a targeted plan that incorporates (insert appropriate tactics).
- We will meet on a biweekly basis to discuss your performance plan objectives and progress. As your performance improves, we can talk more specifically about your career growth.
- Aside from the steps that I have mentioned, how else can I support you in your development? What do you specifically need from me?

FEEDBACK STYLES

In the context of career development discussions and feedback, it is important to know the person to whom feedback is being given and to account for personal style, needs, and motivations when planning these conversations. The literature and anecdotal evidence point to the ways members of different generations view and seek feedback.

INDIVIDUAL DEVELOPMENT PLANS

Development plans are based on thoughtful feedback, the individual's career interests, and organisational needs. A time-bound development plan assists in closing the skill and competency gaps between an employee's current role and her next position, be it a lateral or promotional opportunity. By creating an IDP, managers are able to identify specific activities and opportunities for each individual on their staff. Once you have assessed the employee's potential and performance, consider what key experiences would most benefit them in reaching their career goals. These experiences serve as the framework for the IDP and must include the what, how, and when of activities to ensure that the employee is making progress towards her next position. An IDP is essentially a learning contract that conveys what learning gap is being filled (*e.g.*, what competency or skills are acquired), what the employee will learn, how she will learn it, and how this learning is to be demonstrated.

A few tips:

- It is critical that managers understand staff members' needs and desires, as well as the needs of the library, when identifying activities for the development plan. Employees own their development plan, so you should work with them on a regular basis to foster their development and prepare them for career growth.
- To create IDPs, managers and employees must conduct the following two activities: First, determine a lateral career move or the next-level position on the basis of career goals. Then, jointly identify the gaps in the employee's current role to the skills, knowledge, abilities, and competencies needed in the next-level

position or to enhance performance in the current position. It is possible that the employee's next career move will not be within your organisation, perhaps because you do not have an opportunity for her when she is ready. Yet IDPs are for everyone, whether they are "growing in place" or preparing to move up or move on.

- We suggest that, once the areas of development to focus on have been determined, development activities should be structured to include a variety of approaches, including on-the-job experiences (70 per cent), relationships (20 per cent), and education (10 per cent).

Identify and schedule specific time-bound (*i.e.*, six to eighteen months) activities that provide the employee with an opportunity to demonstrate competence or to work to close the gap between her current position and the next (lateral or promotional) position. Activities and time line should be captured in the employee's development plan. Do not just assume that, once it is completed, you and the employee can check off the IDP box. Rather, managers and employees should schedule regular conversations to check progress, reevaluate activities, and provide feedback, support, and recognition.

Progress towards completing the IDP should be a regular component of each performance review. IDPs are useful for staff at all levels, independent of whether they have been identified as candidates for a succession planning programme. OCLC is a good example of an organisation with both a strong succession planning programme and a strong focus on individual career development for *all* employees. At the County of Los Angeles Public Library, every librarian (levels 1–5) is interviewed by her boss in July of each year.

They discuss the librarian's career goals and how the library, and the manager, can help the librarian reach them. These discussions are separate from and in addition to the performance management process and conversations surrounding it. The assistant director of public services reads all plans. Margaret Donnellan Todd, the county librarian, reports several additional outcomes to this method of development planning. First, managers get to know the librarians, even all new level 1s. They are able to discuss how realistic or inconsistent with performance an employee's goals are, then use this occasion to reinforce any changes in performance needed for the librarian to proceed with her career goals.

This is not always a matter of poor performance or attitude. Todd shared a story about a manager who told a librarian that she could not be promoted or developed unless some changes were made. However, this librarian is creative with an artistic (rather than managerial) temperament. She decided to alter her career goals rather than change.

6

Strategies for Developing Staff

GROW YOUR OWN WORKFORCE

There are many ways to provide support for employees seeking a bachelor's degree or MLS. Give employees who are working full-time while attending college or library school tuition assistance (any little bit helps) as well as some time off to study every week. Just an hour or two makes a huge difference to a working student. If you cannot afford tuition assistance or paid time to study—or even if you can—support students in developing practical projects for their course work, and use those projects to benefit customers. A student who can point to her project being used by the library can see the value of her education *and* see how the library values her contribution. Support may also be more formal. For example, the Fresno County Public Library has a librarian trainee programme in which an MLS student may be selected to work under the direction of a librarian and receive mentoring along with pre-professional training and work experience.

PROMOTE MLS STUDENTS TO AN INTERIM GRADE LEVEL

After a student has successfully completed one-half of the degree, reclassify her job from library associate to librarian trainee or another title. Award a grade increase as well as a salary increase. The employee will value your appreciation and show it in her work as well as in her loyalty and decision to remain after graduation.

Taking this approach can also have a downside. It is one thing to encourage someone with great potential to go to school; it is another thing entirely to promote anyone who completes a degree, whether or not she is someone you would hire to fill an MLS position. The disadvantage of paying for education rather than for job responsibilities is that you may find yourself paying for an MLS when the incumbent is not doing MLS-level work, or eventually paying someone an MLS salary when she is not someone you would have promoted into an MLS position.

Another option is to encourage staff with demonstrated potential to apply for available MLS jobs even before they finish their coursework. Promote them and hire them at a provisional rate, giving them salary increases at milestones to degree completion. This is a useful practice when it is hard to recruit qualified MLS librarians and results in loyalty, too.

Encouraging people to apply even if they have not completed the qualification helps them demonstrate their interest in advancement and gain skill in interviewing. You may discover previously hidden potential and then provide coaching or mentoring to help your students become stronger candidates for promotion.

The Carroll County Public Library has used this model to promote several MLS students into MLS jobs, with great success. Over the years they found that they were not seeing the quality of external candidates they wanted to fill entry-level MLS positions, yet they had several experienced bachelor's-prepared staff that demonstrated the library's core competencies (*e.g.*, customer service and teamwork) and were interested in developing themselves. The library supported some staff in pursuit of MLS degrees in order to "grow their own" librarians, but there were not enough students graduating quickly enough to compete for vacancies coming available.

So the library began to advertise to staff that students enrolled in an MLS programme would be considered for some (clearly identified) MLS jobs. Students began to apply for these jobs, and one or two staff members even enrolled in MLS programmes after seeing such job postings. Though it is never a given that an MLS student will be promoted, internal candidates who have demonstrated their interest have the advantage of having their work seen over time.

Successful candidates have had several things in common:

- Relevant experience (such as supervisory experience) acquired from previous jobs
- Demonstrated competencies in the library's core areas, such as customer service or teamwork, and good progress in learning the technical competencies of their jobs (and sometimes of the jobs a level above theirs)
- Enough employment history with the library to have been identified (even informally) as Promotable or Emerging Talent

These librarians would be the first to admit that taking on a new and higher-level position while completing graduate school is not easy. Several of them have talked about "running to keep up" with all the competing demands on their time. Despite this, they have brought to the system a new energy level as their new ideas and new skills are put to use. It is important to note that not every MLS student gets a promotion, even after completing the degree. They must compete for vacant positions, sometimes against external candidates who already have an MLS. But even when a student is not promoted, the library gets a return on its investment, because it finds that students are engaged in learning and in applying what they learn to their work.

DEVELOP A PROGRAMME OF JOB ROTATION AND CROSS-TRAINING

Have staff swap jobs for three to six months. All will return with increased job knowledge, vitality, perspective, and appreciation of the library, its work, and the workforce. Do this as part of a structured programme in which staff members keep a journal or record questions they encounter and discuss their key learnings with their peers, a coach, or both. Alternately, job rotation can be less extensive. You can rotate library associates assigned to the central facility into a branch for a week or rotate employees among branches, if you have more than one building.

Cross-train public service, technical services, and business office employees. Not only do such assignments develop the individuals involved, they provide the library with a more flexible and capable workforce, reducing work stoppages or backlogs when vacation is taken or someone is out on extended sick leave. Employees undertaking a job rotation should develop an IDP that clarifies developmental goals for taking or seeking the assignment. The person is expected acquire new knowledge, skills, and abilities as an outcome of the job rotation. "It's like springtime renewal when a person takes over a new area," says Patrick Losinski, executive director of Columbus Metropolitan Library. Columbus Metro also "switches deck chairs" around (as Losinski calls it), rotating or combining jobs. In one recent example, collection development staff and technical services staff were supervised by the marketing department. This is one way to help someone see the bigger picture, in this case to support centralised collections. Losinski was able to report seeing new ways of thinking within three weeks.

Switching deck chairs was also mandatory for five branch managers in order to provide lateral transfers, new challenges, and new ways of thinking. Many of the branch managers in Cuyahoga County Public Library were reassigned when this twenty-eight-branch library system reorganised. The reorganisation resulted in a rotational move for all branch managers with less than three years of tenure in their branch. Yes, there were some tears and some opposition; a few branch managers even retired a little sooner than planned.

Despite some short-term pain, library director Sari Feldman and her mover-and-shaker deputy Tracey Strobel report that the move was energising overall. They see branch managers as pivotal to making the library's mission a reality, and according to Strobel this move "ramped everything up" across the system. The "jolt" reenergised the whole system, with staff rising to work with (and impress) their new bosses, managers looking at their new location and staff with fresh eyes, and all facing and growing from new challenges. New branch teams initiated many changes; more than a few of these resulted in higher efficiencies, improvement to effectiveness, increased circulation, higher door counts, and more.

TAKE ADVANTAGE OF TASK FORCES AND INTERIM JOB ASSIGNMENTS

Do not repeatedly ask the same people to serve on task forces or committees. For each new task force or job assignment, seek out a promising person who has not been given an opportunity to participate. Ask her to serve. If she agrees, provide support and watch her blossom.

Fast teams are frequently used for problem solving and employee development at Santa Clara County Library. A fast team provides an intensive focus to an issue or problem facing the library. There are few people on fast teams, three to five, from targeted organisational units. Teams usually meet for no more than four weeks. The team decides who will chair it, how many meetings are needed, and how communications up, down, and sideways will take place. One fast team rolled out chat reference. Another was tasked to provide the community with help getting connected with the library. Charters for fast teams have a reasonable scope, and staff members provide their best thinking and research.

The library has seen people rise to the challenge, and Melinda Cervantes, the library's executive director and county librarian, celebrates their success along with them. Shared leadership models such as task groups and committees are frequently used to develop employees at Fresno County Public Library. A combination of employees having subject knowledge, those new to librarianship, and long-term staff participate on the same committee. For example, a task force was created to plan the events around the library's hundred-year anniversary as a county library. Fresno County Public Library also capitalises on staff development under civil service regulations, even though they are often seen as limiting options.

For example, a special salary upgrade for up to nine months can be offered to an employee filling a temporary vacancy. In this manner, a Librarian II who might have the years of experience to qualify as a Librarian III (supervisor) could work in a higher classification during a vacancy or leave. This not only helps the library provide continuous services but provides the librarian with the range of experiences needed to compete for promotion opportunities. County librarian Karen Bosch Cobb and training librarian Camille Turner have used this approach to create opportunities for all, resulting in staff with more competencies, trained and available for promotion.

ACTION LEARNING

Learning through action serves to help employees develop critical competencies by completing important library work. An action learning team tackles a strategic issue and makes recommendations to library leadership. Action learning has also been used to select, assess, and develop stars and high-potential employees to new levels of knowledge, skills, experience, and competencies.

The characteristics of action learning are as follows:

- It is a team-based approach to learning.
- The team works on real-world problems or business challenges that are often for high stakes.
- There is often a training component such as team functioning or problem solving built in.
- The real-world challenge is a stretch assignment that extends beyond members' experience. Thus, teams are challenged and put into a stressful situation while knowing their work will be reviewed and supported by leadership.

Action learning is a prime source of development at the County of Los Angeles Public Library, reports county librarian Margaret Donnellan Todd. When Todd took on the director's role in 2001, she found a gap in candidates for potential leadership positions and few employees between the ages of 40 and 50. She was not too surprised; the library, like many in California, had faced several waves of financial problems, resulting in hiring freezes and talented employees moving on. She realised that she had to promote sooner than she might have wanted in order to fill vacancies, from employees who had the tools but not the experience; she likened it to skipping a grade in school.

Action learning became her way to fill the gap. The library began this strategy after one of its librarians attended an Urban Libraries Council Executive Leadership Institute (ELI) programme. The library's action learning teams do not include senior managers and are limited to librarians early in their career. A chair is appointed and a charter provided. Management helps shape the scope of work and then steps out of the picture. Action learning teams engage in real work, often advancing strategic initiatives of the library. Teams have engaged in practical as well as theoretical (policy) work, including providing services to seniors, studying the future of electronic services, and creating a model for warehousing lesser used books. Todd reports that the system has seen many librarians rise to the occasion, acquire new skills and confidence, and flourish as leaders.

IMPLEMENT A 360-DEGREE FEEDBACK PROGRAMME

In a 360-degree feedback programme, performance data are obtained from peers, subordinates, and the supervisor in order to provide an assessment of an employee's performance up, down, and sideways in the organisation. It provides full circle, or 360-degree, feedback. This type of evaluation process offers employees a learning tool and feedback mechanism to promote growth and development. There are a variety of ways to conduct a 360-degree feedback programme, and not all are expensive. As with other approaches to employee performance evaluation, it is essential that everyone involved understand the purposes of the evaluation and receive thorough training in applying the process.

CREATE A DUAL CAREER LADDER SYSTEM FOR LIBRARIANS

Career ladders allow employees to focus on their expertise as, for example, an individual contributor (*e.g.*, children's librarian) without having to take on a management role to earn more. In this scenario, an employee might advance from Librarian I to II by taking on more responsibility in collection development, conducting research, or designing new programmes in early childhood learning. Other options might include the Librarian I moving up by becoming a specialist in literacy, readers' advisory, information technology, or training.

Some libraries, such as Queens Borough (N.Y.) Public Library, have career ladders that extend through supervisory and management levels in order to prepare even senior managers to fill anticipated vacancies due to upcoming retirements. There are many ways to acknowledge and reward your staff for increasing their responsibility and value to the library outside advancement to a management position. Though the library may ultimately place the employee in a higher grade level and pay a higher salary, that amount will be far less than the cost of replacing her if she goes elsewhere or the cost of low morale and mistakes if she takes a management job she does not really desire, just to earn more.

OFFER COACHING TO MANAGERS AND LEADERS

Most employees are not ready to take on management/ leadership roles when first promoted to them. And why would they be? It is an entirely new role they were not taught in library school or as individual contributors. There are job content and process coaches. As the name implies, a job content coach helps the leader learn what the job entails. A process coach, on the other hand, focuses attention on how the leader affects others, creates roles and boundaries, creates an agenda, and works with a group to achieve results. The coach especially works with the leader to gain an awareness of the special competencies needed at the new organisational level.

Where do you find a coach? A staff member who is already experienced in that job, especially if her experience includes supervisory coaching for staff, can do most job content coaching. Process coaching requires some different skills, including the ability to maintain objectivity. Some HR departments provide process coaching. For some top leadership positions, the library may be willing to pay for an experienced process coach from outside the organisation. There may be someone in your library that already has the right skills or is interested in developing them to fill a unique and valuable role; providing training for a "designated coach"—or a coaching team—may be a worthwhile investment. An excellent resource on coaching is Ruth Metz's *coaching in the Library*. The County of Los Angeles Public Library provides an external coach to its action learning teams, team leaders, and management. The coach helps members through sticky situations and covers team effectiveness, presentation skills, and problem solving. Observing the teams allows the coach to see people in action, showing her who the high achievers are and who needs to develop which strengths; who talks a good game but has little substance; who is quiet but very capable. The process brings valuable input to management to augment the talent assessment process. The library's action learning teams typically work on their own once they are chartered; the executive team does not get involved unless asked.

The coach, however, may suggest that a team or team member call the county librarian, for example, to ascertain direction or understand the politics of a course of action. Often teams' members say they "do not want to bother her," but of course they are missing a valuable resource and opportunity. An important learning experience results in either case.

ASSIGN MENTORS TO NEW AND LONGER-TERM EMPLOYEES

Mentoring can be a powerful tool in employee development, especially when an employee is promoted or assumes a new role. An effective mentoring process takes some thought and planning. It is important to match the mentor and the men tee carefully. Their personal styles and interests should be compatible. Allow a trial period for the relationship to settle in, and if there are problems make needed adjustments. Expectations for the mentoring relationship should be identified clearly. Define the results you expect and discuss responsibilities, roles, and expectations with both mentor and men tee. Provide training for mentors.

Monitor and evaluate progress, and reset expectations as the relationship grows and changes. The formal mentor/ men tee relationship is not intended to be permanent. The final phase of the formal relationship should encourage independence at the appropriate time. Lois Zachary's *Mentor's Guide* is a wonderful resource for developing a mentoring programme or relationship. Both mentor and men tee learn from each other and build relationships that allow both to understand what happens in other parts of the organisation as well.

The "Build the Bench" programme at the Public Library of Charlotte and Mecklenburg County (N.C.) created an "intimate type of learning environment" for high-potential managers. Rick Ricker, HR deputy director, told us that six high-potential managers were identified and paired with six senior managers, who were tasked to provide mentoring and one-on-one development as well as exposure to different management styles. All twelve were provided with mentor/men tee training to help set goals and expectations. The programme offered collaborative project work and development over an eight-week period. Feedback was provided to the men tee managers and the executive leadership team about the potential for success and development needs of each participant.

Participants also worked on an action learning project: small groups were responsible for creating a section of a disaster recovery plan for the library and then cohesively working (inter group or across teams) to develop an effective plan. One manager from this group has since, been promoted. All have created IDPs that will help them acquire the necessary knowledge, skills, and experiences to move towards their career goals. Mentoring is an ongoing activity at Santa Clara County Library. There is no formal programme, but mentoring is institutionalised and has helped many employees.

Sarah Flowers is one:

- I was hired as a programme librarian at the Morgan Hill Library. I had a very good mentor in Catharine Fouts, who was the community librarian then. She spent a lot of time with me, talking about her own under standing of the system and her own philosophy of management. She was tremendously influential in my own development as a leader. Beyond that, though, probably the best thing she did for me was to take at least one four- to six-week vacation every year, leaving me in charge. After three years, she transferred to Los Altos and I was promoted to community librarian. I continued to call on her as a resource on how to do my new job, until she retired a couple of years later. Probably one of the biggest opportunities I was given during the time I was a community librarian was to be on the negotiating team for the SEIU contract negotiations. It was very helpful to have that background when I applied for the deputy county librarian job. I was asked to work out-of-class as deputy county librarian for six or eight weeks. That was a big help in preparing me too. I realised later that of course Julie knew she was leaving and wanted to start training someone for her job.

Nancy Howe is currently the deputy county librarian and has spent most of her library career with Santa Clara County. She has moved to a new position or been promoted six times during her fourteen-year tenure.

Howe says that she has found ample opportunities for new challenges within the Santa Clara County Library:

- I spent most of my career working in the not-for-profit sector, and only came to the library when I was staying home raising my family. I started working as a substitute librarian, almost as a hobby, but quickly decided that my personal ambition was to bring my community and managerial experiences from my previous career to the library. Santa Clara County Library is large enough to have lots of movement and I always have been quick to raise my hand to take on a project, often that no one else wanted to do. I told my supervisors that I wanted to advance and I received lots of encouragement. In taking the deputy position, I really am stretching myself by managing the technology side of the library. I am grateful to Melinda as well as other people who have sensed my passion and believed in my abilities. From working as a substitute librarian in every one of our libraries, to a supervising librarian, adult services manager, staff development librarian, community librarian and now as deputy, I have a breadth and depth of experience that I can apply to future positions, either inside this system or elsewhere. I love the Santa Clara County Library for its values and am proud to be a part of it throughout my library career. It's my turn now to mentor many of our new hires, and one of my proudest accomplishments was having a hand in creating our intern programme that provides library school students with practical experience, often ending up with them working for us as librarians.

OFFER ON-THE-JOB TRAINING

Both formal and informal on-the-job training can be offered. The informal situation is like shadowing. It requires matching a high-potential employee with a star performer and permitting observation and dialogue about the work, situations encountered, how they were handled in the manner they were, and why. Formal on-the-job training is more akin to reference or the training offered on databases or a new integrated library system. In this approach a training plan is developed, usually following a tell/show/do/follow up format of instruction. Formal on-the-job training is a popular approach to staff development. All of the following programmes have a leadership or management curriculum as their cornerstone, but most use more than one strategy—not only classroom learning or on-the-job training—to help staff grow.

BALTIMORE COUNTY PUBLIC LIBRARY

- Did you know that twenty per cent of our top management team (Branch Managers, AO Department Heads, and Executive Leadership) are eligible to retire today? We are in the midst of the "graying of the profession" and must position ourselves to be ready for inevitable staff retirements in the near future. That is where you enter the picture. This memo describes three different succession management initiatives for FY-2009 designed for staff members that:
  - Wish to improve upon management and leadership skills to be more effective in their current role; or
  - Aspire to move into higher-level supervisory and management

positions within BCPL. Please note that while these programmes serve to strengthen your skills in leadership, supervision, and management, participation does not guarantee promotion into future management vacancies.

This is how Jean Mantegna, HR manager of Baltimore County Public Library (BCPL), opens the invitation sent to all staff to participate in the library's succession management initiatives. She then goes on to describe the three succession management initiatives: Leadership Development Programme, Supervisory Skills for New Supervisors, and the Effective Managing Series. BCPL's philosophy is one of creating a pipeline—a pool of viable candidates ready to fill management vacancies when, as Mantegna puts it, "the baby boomers bust out to retirement." Individual staff members are not selected for grooming into targeted positions, and it is acknowledged that leadership competencies are desired at every level in the organisation.

Leadership Development Programme

In its third year, the Leadership Development Programme is intended "to provide learning opportunities around qualities of leadership for staff members that aspire to future management roles." The programme is both theoretical and practical (mostly the later) and very experiential. Increasing competencies around self-awareness and learning by doing are critical components. Mantegna and Jim Fish, the library's director, partnered with the Community Colleges of Baltimore County to design the programme.

Sessions take place in half- to full-day sessions on a college campus covering the following topics: communications, team building, project management, problem solving, conflict resolution, and managing change. Participants learn how to work as a member of a cross-functional team with other leaders at varying levels of the organisation. They are also developing their leadership competencies from the list of twenty selected by the system. Phase two of the programme begins six months into the programme, after participants learn how to function as a team. They begin to work on a team project—a project of key importance to the library, one that drives its work plan forward.

The most recent project is to develop virtual new staff orientation. Prior projects include service to new populations; self-check evaluation and recommendations for improvement; service to teens; and improving the telephone system. Each project has a sponsor (a seasoned manager within the library system), and seasoned managers provide developmental coaching throughout the experience as an aid to the learning process. Continuing education units are provided for the full-day programmes with the college. Peer feedback is provided to and by all (a skill also practiced in the programme). At project completion, presentations are made to the administrative council. Feedback is unfailingly followed by a well-deserved celebration. BCPL, always a learning organisation, has made some recent changes to the programme.

The current class is limited to seven participants, and the length of the programme has increased from nine to sixteen months. Feedback from the first year demonstrated that the class size of twenty-one was too large and the nine month time line too short. To date, thirty-four employees have completed the programme with excellent results. Seven participants have been promoted into managerial positions, and several learned that management is not for them. A few left BCPL, taking their newly acquired leadership skills to another library system. Regardless of whether anyone is actually promoted, there are many positive outcomes. Programme graduates are more self-aware, have a better sense of what they want their career to look like, have acquired project management skills, have learned new skills and competencies, and, most important, are leaders in their position.

Supervisory Skills for New Managers

BCPL offers Supervisory Skills for New Managers in a blended learning environment (face-to-face, independent, and group) as a way to introduce supervisory skills to employees new to their role or aspiring to supervisory positions. The curriculum is broadly shaped around the topics of communications, leadership, management, personal development, and team building. The Division of Library Development and Services of the Maryland State Department of Education purchased the license to online business skills courses provided by Skill soft, a provider of on-demand e-learning training programmes of both business and technical topics.

Participants complete three courses selected by BCPL. The schedule alternates, with participants completing a self-paced course individually one month and meeting as a group to debrief it the following month. During the debriefing, in a highly interactive way, supervisors share their learning and discuss how it applies to supervising staff at BCPL. The first three topics of independent learning taken over a six-month period are "Becoming a Manager— Responsibilities and Fears," "Communicating as a Leader," and "Leading through Change." Starting in month seven of this ten-month class and twice in alternating months, teams of two are formed to review the course catalog, select a topic that addresses a specific area of skill development, and present their learning to the group.

They share key points, along with a review of the course, noting what they liked and disliked about it. Individual learning is not limited to the classes or topics. All learners have access to the full catalog of programmes until the site license expires.

Effective Managing Series

The third BCPL succession management initiative is the Effective

Managing Series. As outlined in the course description, the purpose of this series "is to provide an opportunity for less-seasoned supervisors and managers to come together as a learning community to explore and develop their unique management styles in the context of BCPL's culture and philosophy of effective management." This programme runs for ten months.

With a little bit of theory but mostly lively discussion and practical application, it covers the following topics:

- Managing oneself.
- Planning and evaluation.
- Organising oneself/time management.
- Delegating.
- Managing change.
- Managing challenges, conflicts, and crises.
- Managing one's boss/managing others.
- Communication.
- Decision making.
- To be determined (as selected by the group).

These classes are facilitated by Mantegna, Fish, and experienced managers, who view it as an opportunity to give back, to model different managerial styles to participants, and to transfer their institutional knowledge to the next generation of BCPL leaders.

COLUMBUS METROPOLITAN LIBRARY

Though it is known for creating and even selling strong training and development programmes, Columbus Metropolitan Library did not have a standard curriculum to support managers and leaders or those aspiring to move up.

Patrick Losinski, the library's executive director, and his staff went on a search for a programme of study and selected Business of People leadership training, based in Columbus.

The programme focuses on how one uses oneself to develop the core foundational skills of leadership, acknowledging that each person is the most powerful force for change in her organisation.

The curriculum includes:

- Great people skills: contact skills (two sessions).
- Commitment to the ongoing enhancement of the managed group.
- Wearing two hats effectively: representing your people to leadership and leadership to your people.
- Working with accountability as a personal development process; reviews, monitoring employee growth over the year.
- Understanding the managed group.
- The skills of raising and maintaining high morale.
- Commitment to your own training beyond the training.
- Getting good buy-in, giving direction, dealing with spot problems,

expecting response, and having a framework for dealing with lack of follow-through.

- Integration of Business of People skills.

In the first year, one hundred of the library's managers, in ten groups of ten, went through ten five-hour sessions each month. In the second year, fifty more managers will go through the programme—this time run by library staff who completed a train-the-trainer programme in partnership with trainers from Business of People.

Outcomes, from Losinski's perspective, have been very positive: "It's the best thing we've ever done." In addition, all managers now have a common language and shared experiences. "Staff," Losinski notes, "are dealing with resistance and change far more effectively; they are also more empathetic and results-oriented as managers; their listening skills have been fine-tuned; they understand how to get buy-in from staff, give and accept feedback; and hold staff accountable. Trust has gone up and managers are feeling good about system wide decisions that are made. Staff are using the training, and using the language."

CUYAHOGA COUNTY PUBLIC LIBRARY

Sometimes events or circumstances signal that it is time to do something differently. Cuyahoga County Public Library (CCPL) was at just such a point when the system lost five branch managers over a short period of time. The jobs were posted, but leadership did not see the calibre of candidates they expected. Applicants simply did not have the knowledge, experience, or understanding of the job. CCPL recruited branch managers externally, but library director Sari Feldman and deputy director Tracey Strobel thought the library system had not adequately developed internal candidates. They then put their heads together and, working with a consultant, designed the two-day Branch Leadership Academy to expose staff to the roles and expectations of a branch manager. They expected ten to fifteen staff to apply; forty-eight librarians volunteered to attend the learning event. Feldman and Strobel structured it as an opportunity for interested staff to learn the expectations, including competencies, of a branch manager in their system.

Context

Per its strategic plan, CCPL focuses on six priorities: connect with reading; ensure every child enters school ready to learn; help youth to reach maximum potential; put Cuyahoga County back to work; keep seniors healthy, happy, and independent; and connect with new Americans. One way to fulfill these priorities is through community partnerships. Therefore, it is no surprise that CCPL branch managers are expected to know their communities and local players well. Indeed, branch managers are expected to be proactively involved in the community and to be seen as important players at the community level.

For example, library staff and branch managers are expected to have an impact in and on workforce development, serve as a gateway for new immigrants, and take a leadership role in early childhood education. Strobel offered an example of difference in expectations for different levels of library staff: while it is anticipated that the adult librarian will serve as liaison with the senior center twice a month and have a connection with the senior center director, the branch manager is expected to be visible in the community, liaise with mayor and city council members, serve on a chamber of commerce board, and attend Rotary lunches, press briefings, and Kiwanis breakfasts, to name a few. The expectations and competencies flow directly from the library's mission statement.

Leadership Academy Application Process

All public service librarians and subject specialists with more than one year of experience were invited to apply. To be accepted into the Branch Leadership Academy, candidates were required to link their desire to attend with a commitment to, and experience with, CCPL's branch manager competencies (taken directly from the job description of branch manager). The agenda for the Leadership Academy included welcomes by Feldman and Strobel and discussions about the library's new customer service model, trends in libraries, and best practices for bosses. How-to sessions on analysing library metrics and problem solving and risk taking were followed by exercises in which the potential branch managers could put into practice what they had just learned. A panel of senior branch managers shared experiences of connecting with their community, and all engaged in an exercise called "community opportunity scenario."

Later, after sharing information on circulation, holds, and other library data, Strobel described initiatives the library was planning over the next one to three years to create efficiencies and improve customer service. Participants learned about them here first. A few of the initiatives included changes in delivery models, online booking of meeting rooms managed centrally, online programme registration, system wide centralised selection of materials, floating collections, programming with experts, and a rethinking of materials security measures. It was truly added value that forty-eight system leaders were in on the new customer service model and other initiatives and, as a critical mass, could help move these initiatives forward. Evaluations showed that one of the most highly valued discussions took place at the end of the session when Feldman and Strobel, along with two regional managers, shared their expectations of branch managers, took questions, and provided sincere answers about leadership.

Of the forty-eight attendees, five have become branch managers and eleven have received other promotions (nine at CCPL and two elsewhere). Eight or so participants decided either to slow down on the track to management or not to pursue a management position. Strobel speaks of the

Branch Leadership Academy as a huge success, one that CCPL plans to offer again in the near future.

HARFORD COUNTY PUBLIC LIBRARY

Harford County Public Library (HCPL) used the changing economic climate to analyse its staff development programme. Library director Audra Caplan and HR director Terri Schell realised that limited funds would compel the library to hire and retain the right people in the right job with the right skills. The components of the library's programme are staff development, competencies, supervisory training, mentoring, and leadership development. Succession planning is one part of HCPL's staff development programme, which is designed "for cultivating knowledgeable and skilled staff, developing strong supervisors, managers, and administrators, and preparing emergent leaders for the libraries of tomorrow."

HCPL begins its focus on staff development from an employee's first day on the job, indeed during the recruitment process. Retention starts at orientation, and development is about continuous learning. HCPL builds staff knowledge and skills through both in-house and external efforts, using a variety of learning modalities.

Mentoring is an opportunity provided to new supervisors, managers, administrators, and other professional staff. In 2000, HCPL developed a competency-based performance management system. Working with a committee and consultant, the system identified and defined seven core and four managerial competencies. The core competencies, on which all employees are assessed, are sensitivity to internal and external customer service; communications skills; team player; dependability; efficient management of job responsibilities; knowledgeable of policies, procedures, and technology; and problem solver. Successful managers are expected to mentor and cross-train employees, recognise and reward employee performance, demonstrate leadership, and serve as an employee/system liaison. Staff are recruited and promoted on the basis of these competencies, and training is offered regularly.

An HCPL-specific refresher course, "Concepts and Culture," is offered to incumbents twice per year. Also offered regularly are classes on innovation, a key organisational value articulated in the library's strategic plan. Caplan and Schell know that, for HCPL to remain a thriving twenty-first-century library, staff need to be developed into successful leaders—and that leadership occurs not just at the top but throughout the organisation. The library system created and HR offers a basic supervision course for all supervisors and those considering a supervisory position. This course is offered as self-study and in the classroom. Learners are provided with a video and new supervisor toolbox consisting of eight DVDs and a workbook. They are expected to review this material in advance and be prepared for classroom study by the time training begins.

One advantage of this programme is that all supervisors go through it, thus enhancing consistency in practice, application, and language. An unanticipated outcome has been that some employees, peeking through the window of what is really involved in supervision, choose to opt out before making what might be a poor career choice. Many participants express a new appreciation of what a supervisor—their supervisor— actually does. This look into the backroom work of supervision, if nothing else, shows the library as a system leaving participants with a bigger picture of the library world. To support the transition into supervision and leadership, the library created a mentoring programme.

The programme received very positive feedback from its first group of thirteen mentoring pairs and helped acculturate leaders into their new roles. Succession planning is HCPL's most recent addition to staff development. The succession planning programme was purposefully developed as a proactive means to "prepare staff for promotional opportunities, allow for organisational education, manage anticipated personnel shortages in key positions, identify staff who have potential to become successful supervisors, managers, administrators and leadership, and develop individualised development plans to strengthen necessary skills."

In thinking holistically about succession planning, HCPL realised that it did not really know how many employees were interested in staying in their current positions and how many aspired to a leadership role. To learn more about staff wishes, they conducted a needs assessment and asked. To their surprise, findings indicated that many employees sought new responsibilities, including leadership roles. The next step for HR was to take supervisory training to the leadership and executive level. A leadership programme offering advanced information for senior staff to gain more experience was custom designed to meet HCPL's culture and strategic needs.

It is a blended programme offered through print, online, and face-to-face meetings. It is designed for participants to L.E.A.D.: learn, experience, apply, and develop. Skills to be acquired include project management, facilitator training, and advanced leadership skills. Still in development, the programme offers nineteen topics to choose from, including public speaking, the Public Information Act, intellectual freedom, strategic planning, seeing the big picture, and completing ALA's Certified Public Library Administrator course. Mentoring by a senior library administrator is a key component of leadership development at HCPL, where leaders are expected to take a global approach, engaging in big-picture and systems thinking.

To help them acquire this perspective, HCPL plans to structure rotational assignments for leaders to spend a month or more in other departments to learn what really happens throughout the system at the senior level. HCPL's philosophy and approach are to develop all people and provide everyone the same opportunity to move to the next level. Until budget costs became prohibitive, HCPL provided tuition reimbursement for employees attending library school. At one time, graduates were automatically promoted to librarians; now, graduates compete for professional-level positions in order to ensure that the library is promoting those with the most leadership potential. Caplan and Schell realise that there will not be enough leadership positions for all employees ready, willing, and able to take the mantle, but they too are thinking globally—globally for all public libraries, knowing that talented employees might leave for another system. If they do, Caplan and Schell are proud of their contribution to leadership at other libraries.

PUBLIC LIBRARY OF CHARLOTTE AND MECKLENBURG COUNTY

The Public Library of Charlotte and Mecklenburg County (PLCMC) has engaged in three efforts to date that involve leadership development and succession planning: manager training, a leadership learning initiative for new supervisors and managers, and the "Build the Bench" mentoring programme described earlier. The manager curriculum was designed internally for all managers, is mandatory, and must be completed within eighteen months. The curriculum consists of nine courses designed to build the competencies of integrity, customer service, communication, individual leadership/influencing, teamwork and collaboration, planning, organising and work management, visionary leadership, analysis/problem assessment, and maximizing performance.

Most courses are taught by internal staff—senior members of the HR department. Managers can register easily on a PeopleSoft module at their desk. Each course is scheduled for between two hours and one day. The curriculum includes these courses: New Employee Orientation; Communicating and Listening; Sexual Harassment: A Manager's Responsibility; Salary Administration; Ethics for Supervisors and Managers; Library Practices and Policies; Essentials of Leadership; Working through Conflict; and Behavioural Interviewing Techniques. The plan going forward for this programme is the creation of virtual classrooms, to save both time and money. The goal of the manager training programme is to improve individual as well as organisational success and to develop future leaders for the organisation. The Leadership Learning Initiative was created for newly hired managers and supervisors throughout the system. Seeking a diversity of candidates, the library invited employees of all levels and with different types of experience to participate.

The initial iteration was a six-month programme built around Rachel Singer Gordon's *The Accidental Library Manager: Who Am I?* The core curriculum also focuses on developing managers in the areas of conflict resolution, building successful teams, and communications—competencies PLCMC finds to be the building blocks all supervisors and managers need to be successful. Multifaceted and multimedia, the curriculum consists of a combination of face-to-face meetings, virtual meetings, in-house speakers, and external community speakers. The pilot programme received rave reviews, and PLCMC plans to implement it again, and on an ongoing basis. The change they will make is to shorten it, keep the class size to twelve participants, offer classes more frequently, and eliminate redundancies that may occur with the manager training programme. New action learning projects pertaining to the system's mission, values, or strategic plan will be identified as the programme continues.

7

Succession Planning for the Library Director

Many library boards and local governments across the country will be going through a search process for a library director over the next five to ten years—some more than once. Some boards and local government officials will be putting their heads in the sand to avoid thinking about this issue; others will peek up slowly, until they willingly engage in the process. It is, after all, their most important function. Why is it so difficult? It is not hard to answer this question. It is about change, it is about real work, it is about risk, challenge, and uncertainly. It is also about evaluation and assessment.

There will be more meetings, more dialogue, and a need to talk honestly and look at yourselves—as leaders—and at your organisation—as an important entity in your community or educational institution. It is hard: change is hard, and costly, and frightening—and it the most important activity the members of a board will undertake. While fraught with challenge, this period is also filled with opportunity if you take the time to pause and reflect before rushing to fill the vacancy.

Our values are reflected in our belief that the board's role is to set policy and that the library director, with staff, is responsible for implementing policy. Further, research and our experience have taught us that trustees should steer far away from micromanaging the library; the most important task of the board is to recruit, retain, evaluate, provide feedback to, engage in dialogue with, and support the library director—as well as to terminate the library director if warranted. There is no more important function. The library board, to support your efforts in director succession planning. If your library does not have a governing board—if, for example, a university search committee or city or county hires the director—many of the principles that follow still hold true.

We hope you are reading this before you have to hire a new library director, because the most effective boards are thinking and planning ahead in order to stay ahead. They are looking at ways to capitalise on the inevitable opportunity they will have to shape the library and search for the new. They may even be working with retiring directors to create new models for succession that could bring the library new benefits and create a win for everyone. There *will* be many retirements in the next five to ten years as baby boomers leave our libraries. It will be a very competitive time. We are not seeing a plethora of members of the Generation X community ready and waiting in the wings, their boards, or other governing bodies plan for the inevitable, be proactive, rise to their fiduciary responsibility, and continue to meet community needs. But if you find yourselves with a hiring emergency. It offers a step-by-step emergency plan for succession that you, your departing director, HR department, and city or county leadership should become very familiar with.

WHY PLAN

The primary purpose of an effective succession plan for a library director is to facilitate a seamless transition to the new director. A commitment from the board of trustees or other governing body to a timely planning process ensures that the library makes this transition most effectively and successfully, so that the transition appears seamless to the library's community stakeholders. There are many decisions to make, prompted by many questions.

These questions are about time lines, responsibilities, and desired outcomes— all of which guide the planning process. To be most effective, the process must be systematic and suited to your library's specific needs. In other words, what follows is *not* in and of itself a succession plan for your library director.

There is no one single cookie-cutter plan. Rather, to be effective, the board of trustees, with staff support, must engage in a dialogue that responds to key questions. There is no one right answer to these very delicate questions. What is important to note is that the *process* is a critical aspect and can make or break a succession. The other crucial and often neglected aspect of a leadership change is that it is a *transition* and needs to be considered holistically, not as a one-day or one-time event. The questions and issues we build into the following outline for succession planning address both of these aspects of recruiting a library director, helping to make the transition a smooth and successful one. Our outlined plan is broken into three major phases: preparation, recruitment, and transition.

PHASE I: PREPARATION (WHEN YOU HAVE TIME TO PLAN)

During this first phase the library has an opportunity to take stock, reflect on the past, anticipate and plan for the future, and identify the competencies needed by the incoming library director. Keep in mind that each library needs different competencies of its director at different points in its life cycle as well as in accordance with changing community, staff, governance, or other needs. Libraries facing a union drive, major fund-raising or bond challenge, building projects or construction difficulties, technology overhaul, political upheaval or contentious board relations, low staff morale, or other challenges require unique skills sets of their director. Be very honest, first to yourselves and then to your candidates, about your needs and the knowledge, skills, abilities, and competencies required of the director entering your system. Do not skip over the preparation aspects of this process.

When a library hears that its director is leaving, it is too easy to just rush into the hiring phase. Do that at your own peril. Remember: sometimes you have to go slow to go fast. The work you do in the preparation phase provides a foundation that enhances the success of the library and its incoming director. If you are open, you will see many opportunities in this time of transition. Not rushing, and taking the time to look forward, will help you hire the right leader, one who has the competencies to bring the library to new phases of growth in line with its strategy.

GETTING STARTED: SHOULD YOU USE A CONSULTANT

In recent times many libraries, large and small, have been engaging search consultants or transition consultants. Some consultants generally focus their attention on helping the library recruit a new director. Some assist the board of trustees to ascertain the needs and expectations of the library or to prepare for the arrival of the new director. Some help the library build internal and board capacity so that it is in stronger shape before welcoming the new director.

Others recommend working through the roles of the board and director so there is an easier transition and both can hit the ground running in an effective and healthy manner (yes, this includes eliminating practices of micromanagement, promoting open communications, creating a performance plan, and other forms of open feedback and dialogue). In a few cases, "houses are cleaned," with ineffective or inattentive staff and board members being retired early or otherwise asked to leave prior to the new director coming on board. There are pros and cons to retaining the services of a consultant.

Why retain a consultant:

- Unlike library staff, the consultant is an expert experienced in the search or transition process. She can also provide an unbiased perspective, and the library is the beneficiary of best practices learned from her research and experience with other organisations. A consultant who specialises in libraries (academic or public) knows, and has connections with, many of the most effective leaders in the country—some of whom may never consider applying for a position advertised in a journal but would respond to a phone call from a respected colleague.
- A consultant can help provide an objective assessment of a library's situation and help identify issues library leadership may not have been able to articulate effectively.
- The board of trustees may desire a fresh look at the library's

strategy, its structure, and the nature and scope of the position of library director.

- You may recognise the need for external help with the transition, because you do not have the time to devote to a search or for other reasons.

Why conduct the search in-house:

- Members of the board of trustees and staff have the expertise and time to conduct the search and design a transition process.
- Consultants are an extra expense.
- Board members may see every candidate fresh by not having relationships with potential candidates.
- Your staff or board members have been active in the state and national library associations and personally know or are aware of potential candidates.
- An external consultant cannot know the details of your situation as well as you do.

PRIMARY TASKS OF THE PREPARATION PHASE

In this phase, you begin looking at yourself and your library. Taking the time to assess the library's strategy, culture, and governance honestly supports and guides the succession planning process. It also helps your library board's capacity building and development process.

Identify Library Vulnerabilities

This is an excellent time to take a realistic look at the state of the library and to design and implement strategies where they are needed. For example, this might be the time to create a position of deputy or assistant director—perhaps a step the director had been avoiding.

Or it might be a good time to create an advisory board for marketing, or fund-raising—if the assessment identifies these as areas of weakness. Ensure that the library's financial and HR systems are in order, so that the library's daily operations can run smoothly during any period of interim leadership.

Solidify the Management Team

This is also a time to think about staffing in light of what is required to achieve the strategic direction. For example, suppose there is a gap in marketing competencies at the staff and leadership levels, and strategies to move the library forward indicate a need for marketing expertise. In that case it would be appropriate to establish a plan to develop these competencies in the senior staff, agree to hire a senior staff person with these competencies, or retain the services of a marketing consultant.

You may realise some salary savings in the turnover of the director position, and now is the time to use whatever financial flexibility is associated with her departure. But whether the changes you need cost money or not, consider what changes should be made in leadership, systems, staffing, or structure to ease the director's transition into your library and her ability to hit the ground running. Also at this time, the board should ensure that there is staff or board backup for key director functions. It is also critical that administrative systems (especially financial and human resources) are in order, so that the library can operate effectively during the transition to a new director, which often involves a period when the library must function with interim leadership.

Assess Staff for Leadership Potential

Whether or not you have a succession plan in place, you should ask:

- Are there current employees who have the potential to fill any given position? Now? After a formal training and development process?
- Are these employees interested and motivated to pursue this growth opportunity?
- Will the succession planning process in which your library is engaging put in place a formal training and development process to cultivate these new leaders?

Identify the Library's Broad Strategic Directions

Where are you in implementing the strategic plan? How are your customers and partners responding? Is the annual performance evaluation for the director tied to progress measured against your strategic initiatives? Is there a process for the new director to provide input to the plan?

Build the Board's Leadership Abilities

Is your board operating at an optimal level? Is there a job description for the trustees? Does the board have trouble making decisions or working through conflict? Is there agreement about the kind of authority you are prepared to give the next director and what kind of accountability mechanisms you should consider to ensure responsible board oversight? Assess board governance practices and organisational health, looking at mission, vision, and strategic and operational planning processes.

This is an ideal time to build the leadership capacity of the board and its members. A board member with organisational or board development skills can do this, although you might prefer to use an objective outsider to help you address these often complex, difficult, and very human issues. Using a consultant to interview the departing director as well as individual board members in confidence can really assist the process of moving ahead quickly. The consultant can use this information to help move the board forward in its thinking about roles, relationships, and how board members can individually and collectively support the library and its director.

Back Up the Library Director's key Relationships

Too often we find that the library director is the only person who knows key elected and appointed government officials, important community leaders, grantors, and executive directors of other partners. This is the time to make sure that staff and board members also know and have connections with these leaders.

Prepare a Communications Plan

This is one of the most important steps. Communications to all key stakeholders (city/county officials, higher education leadership, board of trustees, Friends of the Library, library foundation, community leaders, and staff) should be ongoing, sincere, and transparent. Updates at each step in the process are critical. Connect with stakeholders (internal and in the community); talk to them about their needs and expectations for a new director in your community. Determine by whom and how communication will be handled. Board members may develop the plan or assign communication responsibilities to a board committee or staff member to be coordinated. The communications plan you prepare now will be used regularly and often with staff, board members, and all stakeholders is to keep them up to date on the status of the search and transition. It should utilise all of your library's communication channels, such as your web site and intranet, newsletter, and news releases.

Ultimately, it will:

- Announce why the director is leaving and highlight her many accomplishments.
- Announce the formation of a search committee.
- Invite community input regarding possible attributes for success, candidates, and organisational priorities.
- Circulate the profile and encourage applicants to apply.
- Provide status reports.
- Announce selection of the new director and let the community know how they can meet her.

At every milestone in the process, your communications plan should answer these questions: who needs to know what is happening, and how do we tell them?

Set Financial Parameters

Discuss possible financial and budgetary issues for the succession (hiring costs, severance package costs for the exiting director, training and development and compensation package for the new director, fee for a search or transition consultant if used).

Deal with the Personal and Professional Barriers for the Departing Director

Issues might be the degree to which the director is emotionally and financially prepared for retirement or the best exit strategy to make all parties feel good about the ending. You will want to help make the departing director's transition as easy as possible, especially if she is appreciated throughout the community and has served for a long time. Set a fixed departure date. Everyone needs to be able to move forward, and there is much work to do. Or, you may even decide to continue some new kind of working arrangement with the departing director, redefining what retirement means. In that case, all parties want and need clarity about what the new arrangements and roles are—and are not. Make plans now for when and how you will say good-bye, publicly and graciously, to the departing director. Celebrate her successes and contributions.

PHASE II: RECRUITMENT AND SELECTION

PRIMARY TASKS OF THE RECRUITMENT AND SELECTION PHASE

As soon as the library director announces her intention to leave the system and sets a date for so doing, the recruitment and selection process begins.

Develop an Up-to-Date Job Description

Although your inclination may be to reach for the departing director's job description, resist the temptation. Instead of looking to the past and what was, focus on the future. Look forward towards the library's aspirations and then shape the job, and job description, around your current and future leadership needs. What are the core values, beliefs, and assumptions about how the library operates that are important for the new director to understand? What are the "nonnegotiable" behaviours that the director should uphold and nurture? What current processes and activities create the most frustration, confusion, or dysfunctional behaviour within the library that the board wants the director to change? Does the new director need to fit the current culture, or is she expected to change it? How? Completing a profile of the ideal candidate helps you update the library director's job description as well as recruitment materials such as job postings.

Craft a profile by answering these questions:

- What are the desired experiences and qualifications of the director?
- How are your library's values and needs matched to the director?
- What is exceptional about your library and why is *this job* a wonderful opportunity?
- What leadership skills and competencies are unique to the library's needs and challenges?
- What are the key attributes needed (*e.g.*, visionary, seasoned manager who provides stability and structure, turnaround expert, transformational change agent, entrepreneur, community builder, strategic thinker/actor)?
- Does the new director have to be a librarian?

- Does she need to be politically astute?
- Does she need to have skills in fund development?
- Does she need to be skilled in working with a union?
- How does the director attend to the board's feelings and needs?
- How does the director envision changes in organisational functioning?
- How does the director communicate and interact with the board?

Appoint a Selection Committee

Such a task force, appointed by the board, might be composed of members of the board as well as key constituents such as county elected or appointed officials, the school system superintendent, the director of the county's literacy group, the head of the United Way, a teenager, and a representative from the chamber of commerce.

The library's HR director staffs the committee process. The charge for this group is very specific: identify and prioritise the key competencies, knowledge, skills, and abilities that the next library director should possess *before* advertising the position. Input from the library's key constituencies is important to this process. Ultimately, the full board will interview the final two or three candidates.

When finalists are brought in for interviews, the selection committee members will attend public presentations or meet and- greet sessions and provide feedback to the board, to help them make a better decision. Should you use staff in the recruitment process? There are differences of opinion about how and to what extent staff should be involved in the leadership selection and transition process.

We believe, again, that staff should be kept informed and that ongoing communication is important to staff at all levels, but that they should not play a deciding role in selection. We strongly support Tom Gilmore's thoughtful perspective: "The only universally wrong step a board can take (and many do) is not to have thought through how the staff will be involved and be kept informed at all stages of the process."

Gilmore suggests that staff should be very involved in assessing the library's strategic challenges and identifying the characteristics needed of the director as well as in recommending candidates and resources for recruitment.

Staff should also be invited to meet the final candidates, often as part of an interview process, and provide their advice and input. However, the final selection should not be made by staff; that is a decision to be made by the board of trustees. In general, we agree that staff should not serve on the search committee. If your library has an HR director, it would be appropriate to ask her to staff the process and work directly with the members of the search committee.

If not working with a search or transition consultant the HR director should, at a minimum, support the search committee by engaging in the following tasks:

- Work closely with the committee chair throughout the process in a support capacity.
- Issue invitations to serve on the search committee, prepare agendas (with committee chair), and arrange for meeting room space, refreshments, and so forth.
- Take notes at meetings; send to committee members.
- After search committee conversations, draft the job description and other collateral public relations materials.
- Help prepare the communications plan for staff and community.
- Advertise the job opening as appropriate, for example, in *Library Journal, Library Hotline.*
- Determine how and when candidates will receive communications throughout the process, and who will communicate with candidates.
- Screen résumés against established criteria.
- Prepare summaries of highly qualified candidates for the search committee.
- Provide sample interview questions and any other preparation needed by interviewers.
- Schedule telephone screening interviews on behalf of the search committee.
- Schedule and arrange interviews for finalists.
- Check references.
- Suggest, based on data, a fair and equitable compensation and benefits package for the person selected. Determine who will handle the offer and salary negotiations.

The HR director must act with the highest integrity and utmost confidentiality throughout this process. You may wonder if another staff member could take on this role. The answer is possibly, and probably not. In our experience, general staff are accustomed to and respect the barrier of silence from HR staff about all personnel issues. They do not have the same expectations of other staff, nor are other staff members accustomed to this level of confidentiality.

Keep in mind that the confidentiality extends beyond your library. Many applying for the position will not make their interest known at their present workplace. Recruiting at this level must be handled delicately and with the utmost confidence. Many high-potential and highly visible candidates working in other libraries will not apply unless confidentially can be guaranteed unless and until they are named as a finalist. There are other considerations as well.

Consider the plight of one system that did not have a full-time HR manager. With the resignation of the library director, the library's four senior managers were asked to function as a team in an "interim director" role. We worked with this team to help them clarify roles, responsibilities, and expectations. The group worked together rather effectively—until a shift in roles occurred. One of the team members was assigned by the board to work with the search consultant and staff the search committee. Although this individual was capable, other team members became jealous and insecure because they were not privy to the same information as their colleague. This made for a less than effective process and also affected the team's longer-term working relationships.

Plan the Search, and Search

Plan a national, or at least regional, search. To assist with this, the board asks the library director and senior staff for a list of five to ten key library leaders to talk with who either might be interested in the job or could recommend other viable candidates. Through conference attendance and journal reading, staff and board members also keep an eye out for current and emerging leaders. The library announces the position vacancy formally, using a variety of communications channels including its web site, statewide and national electronic discussion lists, and professional journals. The library's public relations staff helps by developing a piece that sells the position, the library, and the community to potential applicants. Note the individual responsible for each recruitment step. Add more time, because a search always takes longer than one thinks it will. The board can take advantage of any additional time to plan and prepare adequately.

Identify an Interim Library Director

This should not be a candidate for the permanent position. Establish a separate job description for the interim position that articulates scope, boundaries, duties, and responsibilities. If the interim director is a member of the library's senior staff, the library should provide a salary supplement in the form of a separate check or temporary pay increase (rather than part of base pay).

Communicate

It is critical to begin implementing the communications plan you began to develop in the preparation phase so that all of the library's key stakeholders—both internal and external—are kept informed throughout the process.

PHASE III: TRANSITION

Trustees need to be aware that a leadership transition is a time of stress and anxiety for staff, especially senior staff. They will have many questions that are rarely articulated: What is my role? Will she like me? Will she bring in her own leadership team? Will I have a job here? Will I like and be a part of any changes in direction or strategy? Where will I fit in? Is it time for me to get off the bus? Rumors fly and water cooler chatting increases substantially. Having a schedule, sticking to it, and communicating regularly help to allay the anxiety.

Another thing that reduces staff anxiety is helping the leader get off to a good start—ensuring that she too has a smooth transition. Board members set the tone for that transition and for how they will work with the incoming director. From the time they offer the job and begin negotiating a salary and employment agreement, they are beginning to orient the new director to the culture of the organisation. Thus, they must give some thought to structuring the kind of orientation that serves their board, the library, and the new director well.

Considering these questions can help:

- Who on the board will serve as the director's primary contact for management and coaching? How—and how often—will the board expect to hear from or meet with the director?
- Who on the board can help introduce the director to community partners, university or local government department heads, and other valuable people outside the library? How can the board pave the way for the director to establish her new network of connections?
- What role should senior (or other) staff take in orienting the director?
- What are the performance goals and expectations for and with the newly hired director at three, six, and twelve months? What mechanisms will be used to review performance and share feedback?
- How quickly can the new library director be scheduled to go through the same orientation process that all staff attend?

Remember that your new director will have a list of tasks to undertake shortly after coming on board that will be a part of her orientation to the job, the staff, the community, and the board of trustees. These important activities include (if a public library director) meeting local elected and appointed officials, community leaders, partners, fenders, media representatives, and local and statewide library directors. She will also want to meet all staff quickly, especially those who report directly to her, and visit all branches; spend time reviewing the budget, policies, HR policies, strategic, facilities, marketing, technology, and other important library documents; meet with all board members one-to-one and as a group; and review bylaws, the trustee manual, and other relevant documents.

Be prepared to help your new director into each of these tasks. Finally, don't forget that there is another element to being new in a community. If you have ever moved to take a new job, whether across town or across the country, you know that your orientation to the community is not complete until you find a trustworthy auto mechanic, the best bakery, a good handyman, a great hairdresser, the physicians who take your new health insurance plan, and so on. Your new director will not really feel at home until she knows the territory, so be sure to let her know that, when she needs a local recommendation, you stand ready to help.

EMERGENCY SUCCESSION PLAN

Sometimes a surprise happens: the director lets you know, with little or no warning, that she is leaving the job for another opportunity, family issues, health, or other reasons. In the worst case, she has been struck by a bus or challenged by a major illness, and there is little time to prepare. That is why it is important to have in place, at a minimum, an emergency plan. The trustees of one of our academic library clients made the mistake of not worrying about succession planning since, the library director, who was 60 years old, said that he was planning to stay for another five years, at least until age 65. They did not want to upset the director, whom they valued highly, by raising the issue of succession planning before he was ready for it. And what happened? They were surprised—and so was he! His daughter had triplets, and he and his wife decided to move cross-country to help her.

The moral is clear: every library should have at least an emergency plan for library director succession at all times. An emergency succession plan ensures the continuous coverage of executive and administrative duties critical to the ongoing operations of the library and its services to its customers or patrons and fenders, political officials, and others by outlining policies and procedures for the temporary appointment of an acting executive director. There are several key components to such a plan.

It should identify the priority functions of the library director, both the general functions of a library (or any) leader as well as tasks that are exclusive to your library.

Second, the plan should specify what happens in the event of a short- or long-term absence of the library director. This includes notification of trustees, the process that the board or board president begins once notified, the compensation and authority of an acting director and provisions for recruiting a new director.

Another component of the emergency succession plan should be the identification of one or two senior staff members capable of appointment to the position of acting or interim director. If the board decides to divide the functions of the director, these should be clearly delineated in writing.

If necessary, any provisions for cross-training staff to help them fulfill priority director functions should be made. Such cross-training should begin with the adoption of the plan. Finally, a communications plan and protocol should be outlined, including categories of constituents (*e.g.*, public officials, customers) who should be personally notified, how (in writing, personally, by phone) and by whom (the board, interim director, other), and in what time frame.

If the succession plan has to be implemented in an emergency, the board should ensure that the following are in place:

- Board members who have experience in search/transition.
- Senior staff member(s) or others who can serve as interim director.
- An up-to-date job description for the position of interim or acting library director.
- A key contact list to notify individuals and communicate plans/status.
- Written procedures for conducting a search (with and without a search firm) and for the selection process.
- Identification of a key spokesperson for the library board.

8

Additional Stories of Library Succession Planning and Development Programmes

FRESNO COUNTY PUBLIC LIBRARY

- The Vision of the library is that Fresno County residents of all ages will have free access to library services and materials to enhance the quality of their lives and further life-long learning.

This vision from the mission statement of Fresno County Public Library (FCPL) is to be taken seriously; Fresno's population is expected to experience tremendous growth. To support this increase, most of the county's branch libraries as well as central will need to expand. Libraries will need more materials, computers, and meeting rooms to better serve their communities and experienced, competent staff to support them. Karen Bosch Cobb, county librarian, joined FCPL in 1972 and has served as director since, 2003.

Like so many library directors and county librarians, she looked around at the management team and saw that many could be retiring within close proximity of each other—and perhaps sooner rather than later. The FCPL succession management and talent development experience has been coloured by past good fortune. In 1998 a sales tax measure resulted in amasing growth for the library.

New positions were created, new services and programmes offered. The library grew from 143 to 320 staff members in a relatively short time. Prior to 1998 many of these positions were filled by baby boomers, who are a large group of the library's formal and informal leaders. After 1998 new entry-level librarians filled many new positions.

Bosch Cobb spoke of a variety of strategies the library utilises to develop leaders, including executive training through Info people, the Urban Libraries Council Executive Leadership Institute, and California State Library Eureka Leadership Institute; special salary upgrades during leaves of absences; responsibility charting; serving on task forces and committees; shadowing managers; taking on lead responsibilities; growing its own librarians through the use of librarian trainee classification; participation in community leadership opportunities; one-on-one coaching to help staff seeking a promotion develop a résumé and prepare for interviews; and staff forums.

STAFF DEVELOPMENT

Bosch Cobb believes in committing time, energy, and money to continuous staff development. Opportunities were identified that would develop competencies in FCPL staff, with the California Library Association's (CLA) personal and professional competencies used as a starting point. Training is one of the ways to develop these and other competencies; both internal and external training opportunities are available. FCPL employs a fulltime training coordinator librarian, Camille Turner, who both offers programmes and helps staff find the appropriate learning forums. Turner graduated from Infopeople's Master Trainer Programme, which added skills to her repertoire of facilitating staff development.

Four librarians have completed Urban Libraries Council's (ULC) Executive Leadership Institute (ELI) programme. Their projects included supporting the rural community and working with the business community to create an awareness of how the library can support economic development; developing homework centers; and expanding world language services. Two fellows of the ELI programme are currently members of the library's management team.

In addition, two other librarians attended the Eureka Leadership programme, completing a joint customer service and culture-altering project now called "People First!" Staff members regularly attend workshops and webinars sponsored by the statewide Infopeople library staff training initiative. Over twenty employees participated in Infopeople's Building Leadership series of monthly classes, and many learn from OCLC and ULC conferences, seminars, and materials. ULC provided a grant to allow seven employees to attend library school.

GROWING OUR OWN

One example of growing your own is a librarian trainee programme in which paraprofessionals (library assistants) who have a bachelor's degree are selected to work under the direction of a librarian as they attend library school. Librarian Trainee is a provisional classification and incumbents must complete eligibility requirements for a Librarian I within three years to retain employment with Fresno County. These employees receive pre-professional training, mentoring, and work experience while in the programme. The goal is to promote trainees to the Librarian class when they have successfully completed an MLIS or MLS programme.

The Friends of the Library supports the programme by offering scholarships of up to $2,500 for those attending library school. Fresno also promotes staff development by encouraging involvement with committees and projects in the CLA and ALA as well as attending conferences. Not only does this help build staff members' professional development, the library generally benefits from the knowledge and experiences gained through participation. Bosch Cobb talked about outreach as an important component of the library's mission and sees not one but three libraries: the physical branches, the virtual library, and the library in the community.

Because the library in the community is so vital, staff members are encouraged not only to take library services to the community but to take on leadership positions in local non-profit and other agencies as well as attend local leadership programmes (such as Fresno Leadership). FCPL's tactic for filling promotions is a bit unusual. In this system, by library practice, all vacancies are offered internally first.

Most transfers and promotions are viewed as opportunities for staff to grow. If an employee wants to, the training and development activities are available—as are the vacancies—to make it happen. The ability to move up into leadership positions is touted as a benefit of working at FCPL when recruiting. It has been a successful marketing tool.

A TOOL: RESPONSIBILITY CHARTING

An important tool Fresno began using some years ago that has served to develop leaders is responsibility charting. Bosch Cobb recommends this tool—long used by organisation development practitioners to help clarify roles and responsibilities— to managers and supervisors for major or complex projects throughout the library.

She has found it to be very useful in clarifying who is responsible for what and to what degree. Outcomes of using this tool have been quicker goal attainment, increased accountability of staff, less time wasted in meetings, less duplication of effort, and staff who are clear about responsibilities. For each project all tasks and decisions to be made are listed along the vertical axis and key stakeholders are listed horizontally. Key stakeholders are anyone touched by the project.

In each box one of the following codes should be entered:

- A (approve),
- R (responsible),
- C (consulted),
- I (informed),
- DK (don't know, and need to determine),
- Blank (no relationship to task).

There are several tips useful to completing the chart:

- Define each task and the people involved by both name and title; be very clear.
- Assign one "R" for each task; only one person can be responsible.
- The person assigned the "R" role must understand and accept the

conditions of performance on the task, including accountability for budget, time frame, completion dates, and milestones.

- Only the "R" person and the "Cs" need to meet with regard to the task.

WHERE IS FCPL NOW

Recently the California Library Association and the Fresno County Public Library updated their competencies to include "develop political savvy and awareness," that is, be able to identify and enlist the support of strategic partners to complement strengths and weaknesses of the organisation and to obtain key resources and assistance to support the achievement of mutual goals.

To gain knowledge in this arena as well as to promote big-picture thinking, a variety of new experiences were suggested. These include attending Fresno and Clovis business conferences, board of supervisor and city council meetings, the State of the County breakfast, and the California Library Association's legislative day; in-house training on how to get items on the board of supervisor's agenda and on the best and worst experiences in the political sphere; attendance at San Joaquin Valley Library System committee meetings as an orientation to local library governing; obtaining experience with elements of urban planning; attending Friends of the Library board, council, and oversight committee meetings; and visiting branches and obtaining an overview of service areas and goals. I ended my conversations with Bosch Cobb and Turner with two questions: "Is it working?" and "Given budget cuts and hiring freezes, will you continue succession planning and staff development?" Bosch Cobb provided positive answers to both.

Many employees (seventeen) have been promoted, and vacancies are successfully filled rather quickly without having to worry about new employees learning their staff, culture, organisation, county, software, and so forth. Newly promoted employees are ready to go on day one. "We will continue carrying some things forward that are time tested and make changes as well," Bosch Cobb said. The programme is reviewed and updated every twelve to eighteen months, to ensure that it is relevant and meeting the library's needs. Examples of recent changes are the opportunities to increase political awareness and savvy and a move towards e-learning. Continue? "Yes," said Bosch Cobb. "You can't stop. If we are going to move ahead, there is always a need to engage in staff development."

JOHNSON COUNTY LIBRARY

Johnson County Library (JCL) is a busy metropolitan library, as of 2009 serving 370,000 residents via thirteen facilities, supported by 365 employees. For some years, JCL administrators experienced a shortage of qualified candidates for midlevel and senior management positions. Recognising in addition impending retirements from baby boomers and projections for fewer new graduates from MLS programmes, the library decided to develop an internal leadership development programme to grow its own leaders and create its own recruitment pool. Then deputy and now library director Donna Lauffer and her leadership team identified the need on two levels.

First, there was a need for leadership at every level in making decisions and leading projects to make the library more stable and simultaneously more nimble. In addition, managers and senior leaders interested in advancement needed to build skills in creating, leading, and managing system wide projects. The library aspired to change—both individual and organisational change—resulting in a culture of leadership development that naturally generated leaders and succession rather than a series of programmes or initiatives.

Here is how the programme was described in a nomination for the National Association of Counties Achievement Award *it won* in 2009 (prepared by Pat Hassan and modified). The library created a leadership development steering committee that conceived a two-tiered, two-year programme to address the two levels of need, utilising consultants only for the design of the Tier 2 curriculum. Piloting Tier 1 in 2007 and Tier 2 in 2008 was a learning experience that would guide Cycle 2, which began with the second Tier 1 group in January 2009.

FIRST CYCLE, TIER 1

After nearly two years of planning that included obtaining partial funding, partners, and a curriculum design, the leadership development steering committee launched Tier 1 in January 2007.

Tier 1 was open to all staff, and its twenty-seven participants included a cross section of staff:

- Pages,
- Clerks,
- Paraprofessional and professional librarians,
- Supervisors, and
- Managers.

Tier 1 focused on developing behaviours rather than technical skills. Seven identified behavioural competencies served as the basis for all learning: personal accountability, listening and responding, teamwork and cooperation, initiative, flexibility, customer service orientation, and genuineness. (These same behaviours had been identified in prior years as behavioural competencies that supported the library's values, but because the steering committee members felt that these were not extensive enough for full leadership development, Tier 2 was required.)

Over eleven months, each participant was expected to spend 240 hours in four components:

1. Classroom learning including four-hour monthly sessions about library governance, public governance, and the behavioural competencies.

2. Independent study initiated with a 360-degree feedback evaluation on the seven behavioural competencies, developing an individual development plan, followed by evaluations.
3. Project teamwork (using a Project Runway format but without voting anyone off the show) based on real library needs from the strategic plan, utilising a budget and parameters within which to work.
4. Mentoring by the leadership development steering committee, whose members were trained by external specialists.

Because the partial funding obtained was dedicated to Tier 2, no paid instructors could be used. Instead, former staff development coordinator Tiffany Hentschel and other library managers taught sessions. University of Missouri–Columbia professors and public administration budget experts provided some in-kind support. In addition, the library could not afford to hire substitutes to cover off-desk time that participants spent in the programme. Almost immediately, time constraints forced changes to the programme. The first casualty was individual development plans, in favour of the project teamwork that required more immediate attention, team interaction, and revolving deadlines—in addition to tangible results. Lack of off-desk time and uneven support by some managers were added factors.

Mentoring was also uneven, working well with some assigned pairs but not with others. The project teams, however, provided high-impact change to the library and the highest sense of satisfaction among participants. One of the projects, the "Art in the Stacks" public exhibits programme, received a new name, logo, and contact list.

FIRST CYCLE, TIER 2

To design the curriculum for Tier 2, the library hired Paula Singer and Christi A. Olson as consultants. The intention was that the first Tier 2 graduates would teach Tier 2 in ensuing years, with no further use of consultants.

The consultants envisioned that Tier 2 participants would develop helpful and relevant conceptual frameworks, build leadership skills, and learn how to focus on achieving results for strategic initiatives and complex projects. Tier 2 focused on four key leadership competencies: leads change, influences people, achieves results, and fosters communications..

The consultants designed a programme consisting of eight modules, weekly online sessions, and three consultant-led face-to-face workshops. The three workshops focused on problem diagnosis and resolution, skills development, and group learning. Steering committee members led all other coursework. In addition, participants were expected to spend 1.5 hours per week on reading and written assignments.

Tier 2 also utilised self- assessments and individual development plans. Tier 2 goals included increasing leadership skills in complex project management, organising and managing system wide meetings, resolving problems in a group setting, and facilitating public and community forums. Participants also learned to adapt to and manage change at all levels of organisations. As with Tier 1, the Tier 2 curriculum had to be adjusted midway.

By May, the steering committee had dropped individual written assignments and journaling in favour of concentrating on two chief vehicles for learning:

1. Monthly breakfast discussions (moderated in turn by steering committee members) of concepts in consultant-identified management/leadership books; and
2. Action learning team projects that addressed strategic goals.

Each team was given background, a budget, and parameters with which to work intensively over ten months to produce recommendations for solutions to specific issues on materials handling, internal communication, organisational culture, and a new way of thinking. These were already on the library's work agenda, and Tier 2 participants invited other staff members to assist them in intensive investigation and problem solving.

Criteria of success:

- Create a culture of *ad hoc* work teams that come to life and bring everyone's best work forward.
- Bring ideas into the organisation and have a "spirit of innovation" on a daily basis.
- Stop saying and acting "You can't do that" and "It's always been done that way."
- Be forward thinking, carry a forward-looking attitude.
- Produce better integration across projects.
- New leaders emerge and are encouraged and mentored.
- Participants develop or hone key competencies required for successful change and growth of themselves and JCL.

Programme goals:

- Prepare people for library leadership in a complex environment.
- Engage more people in the organisation to work actively on strategic initiatives and community needs.
- Fill the identified leadership gap.
- Foster better communication among a broader group of leaders.
- Create management depth and opportunities to practice skills.
- Increase skills in complex project management, organising and managing system wide meetings, resolving problems in a group setting, and facilitating public and community forums.
- Adapt to and manage change at all levels of organisation.

The first Tier 2's thirteen graduates included five senior managers, two members of the leadership development steering committee, and six Tier 1 graduates. Tier 2 concluded with a celebratory luncheon at which library board members heard presentations on the team projects.

SECOND CYCLE, TIER 1

As the second two-year cycle began in January 2009, the steering committee made the following adjustments to the existing Tier 1 plan, based on input from the first Tier 1 class and initial feedback from participants in the second Tier 1:

- All work time for Tier 1 was scheduled in advance and relayed to both participants and their supervisors; this helped supervisors understand the commitment up front and plan schedules.
- The number of projects was decreased.
- Reading materials for upcoming lectures are to be provided in advance.
- All presenters will incorporate more interaction into presentations.
- More field trips will be part of the agenda. Mentoring will be retained as part of the programme.

RESULTS/SUCCESS OF THE PROGRAMME

The retirement crunch did hit the Johnson County Library in 2007 with eleven retirements, in addition to normal turnover, and Tier 1 resulted almost immediately in movement among staff: seven Tier 1 participants were promoted or transferred during the course of the programme, including three to management positions.

Many expressed that they applied for jobs they would not have considered prior to the programme, as even partway through the programme they had gained new confidence and had a better understanding of the organisation. By the same token, managers began to notice a better appreciation for the complexity of decision-making processes in the library. Four members of Tier 2 have been promoted to date. An unintended consequence of Tier 1 was that the library's biennial staff engagement survey at the end of 2007 reflected improved scores of more than 7 per cent in two areas—satisfaction, loyalty, and growth and development.

TIER 2

The Tier 2 pilot included members of the steering committee, members of the leadership team, and several others. It was a tumultuous time. The library director retired, the staff development coordinator resigned to take a promotion with the county, and the committee chair resigned. Time was limited, workloads high, and reflection less valued by participants than the consultants. With one exception, all participants felt that the correct goals for success were identified.

Regarding programme success, participants' evaluations revealed that 83 per cent felt that the programme resulted in creating an organisational culture of *ad hoc* work teams that bring everyone's best work forward; 66 per cent felt that new ideas were brought into the organisation with a "spirit of organisation" on a daily basis; 85 per cent felt that they were empowered to find a new way of doing things; 83 per cent felt that they were free to be forward thinking; 59 per cent felt that there was better integration across projects; 67 per cent felt that new leaders emerged from the process; and 67 per cent felt that they developed or honed key competencies for successful change and continued personal and organisational growth.

Regarding overall effectiveness of Tier 2, 83 per cent of participants felt that they had increased their leadership skills, 75 per cent felt that their new knowledge would be valuable in performing their current jobs, and 75 per cent felt that what they learned would be valuable in new senior positions. After evaluating their experiences with the first cycle of Tier 1 and Tier 2 and their outcomes, library administrators believe the leadership development programme has been extremely beneficial for the organisation as a whole. So important is this effort to the library's long-term success that administrators asked the entire library staff to support the effort by backfilling for frontline participants' time spent in the programme—not for just one year but ongoing since, 2007. The entire organisation has stretched to ensure the success of this programme.

ONLINE COMPUTER LIBRARY CENTER

Based in Dublin, Ohio, the Online Computer Library Center (OCLC) is a non-profit, membership, computer library service and research organisation dedicated to the public purposes of furthering access to the world's information and reducing information costs. More than 71,000 libraries in 112 countries and territories around the world use OCLC services to locate, acquire, catalog, lend, and preserve library materials. We include the OCLC story because most libraries are members, the organisation knows libraries at a deep level, with 1,250 employees OCLC is larger than most library systems, and OCLC is committed to leadership and career development.

It also has a formal succession planning programme. I spent some time talking with George Needham, OCLC vice president, Global and Regional Councils, to learn about that programme. Motivated by the graying of vice presidents and directors, succession planning has been a key initiative of OCLC for almost eleven years, since, president and CEO Robert L. "Jay" Jordan first joined the organisation. Since, that time, the talent management and succession planning programme has evolved and remains a key senior leadership initiative. Top-level commitment to the programme is vital, as is the strong support of HR.

The first iteration of succession planning focused on leadership development, mostly in terms of providing technical business expertise. Sixty or so vice presidents, directors, and others from around the world were invited to attend a programme designed for this purpose by Ohio State University's Center for Leadership Development. Focused on business operations, the programme was dubbed "Business School in a Box." It was a two-week programme, offered one week at a time separated by six months. Topics included how to read spreadsheets and financial reports, mergers and acquisitions, and conducting due diligence. There were also self-assessments designed to identify strengths and weaknesses and build on strengths. In truth, the assessment process did not pass the "smell test," and several participants referred to it as "one step away from voodoo." Many positive outcomes resulted from this programme.

Two participants were later promoted to vice president, the commonality of language increased understanding and effectiveness, and the interaction with professors and OCLC staff from all over the world enhanced cohesion and trust, thus improving business outcomes. Talent management and succession planning is now a far more formal programme and includes many of the steps and processes outlined in this book. Leadership reviews key positions and key contributors in the context of OCLC's strategic plan and human resources needs towards talent utilisation and competency development. It includes a 360-degree feedback assessment for learning how one is perceived and where skills might be missing.

The well-respected Birkman Method has replaced the "near voodoo" assessment tool. Managers, directors, and vice presidents identify employees in management positions on the basis of performance and potential. Managers and above can self-nominate.

Anyone wishing to participate in the programme must complete an application, which includes an individual talent development profile of career goals, strengths, and development areas. Development plans are made for and with participants (key talent candidates), who are also invited to attend special training programmes around key leadership competencies with OCLC leadership and participants' managers. A recent programme was "Outcome Thinking— Building Leaders," offered by Impression Management Professionals described as a programme to build on new ways of thinking in order to execute and focus on results as well as on building the plans to achieve them. Offered over two days, the programme series includes Managing Your Message, SMART (strategic mindsets and articulate in real time) Leadership, and Conflict Harmoniser.

MENTORING

Internal, informal mentoring is a strong component of OCLC's succession planning processes. These relationships often cross divisions and are cross-hierarchical, with staff and vice presidents exposed to each other. For example, one of his colleague vice presidents asked Needham to mentor a young creative individual. They meet for lunch once a month and discuss libraries, OCLC culture, management style, and other topics.

Training is provided, including documents and checklists, to help mentors and mentees successfully negotiate and maximize the relationship. In the

OCLC culture, anyone can feel free to ask for mentoring. Outcomes of these relationships include familiarity with the talent in the organisation, exposure to difference styles of management and leadership, safe feedback on issues of importance, a perspective on organisational life and politics, and a breakdown of narrow departmental tunnel vision. Needham notes, "I learned at least as much about online community, breaking technology, and blogging from my mentee as he ever learned about libraries from me!"

INDIVIDUAL AND CAREER DEVELOPMENT PLANS

While OCLC has a strong talent management and succession planning programme, it also has a strong focus on individual career development for *all* employees. It trains managers and employees to develop IDPs and expects every employee to have one.

The organisation ensures that this happens by including employee IDPs as a factor on which all managers are evaluated:

- On its web site one can find that OCLC recognises the importance of continuous development and training to ensure employees have the knowledge and tools to perform their job responsibilities at the highest level and to meet the challenges of a demanding library environment in a rapidly changing information age. OCLC encourages employees to develop their skills through the various programmes and development opportunities provided by the organisation, as well as academic offerings through our tuition reimbursement programme.3

The organisation provides development and training opportunities for employees in the areas of individual development planning, management and leadership development, technology training, individual and team assessments and coaching, office automation, quality control, ethics and compliance training, and workforce harassment training. Through Web Junction, it also offers employees online self-paced learning in a variety of genres.

Tuition reimbursement (to a maximum of $5,250 per year) is also provided to employees for courses that are relevant to their current position or to one to which the employee might reasonably aspire. OCLC also supports library staff in developing their skills and knowledge through a series of awards and scholarships for new librarians, established professionals, researchers, librarians in developing countries, and ALA Spectrum scholars.

PIERCE COUNTY LIBRARY SYSTEM

The Pierce County Library System (PCLS) is headquartered near Tacoma, Washington. Its seventeen branches, two family bookmobiles, and an Explorers' Kids bookmobile bring people together, enrich lives, and provide children and adults with opportunities to learn. The library is an independent junior taxing district. With a 2009 budget of almost $29 million, it serves 534,000 over 1,600 square miles. Led by executive director Neel Parikh since, 1994, PCLS is funded by a separate property tax levy.

County citisens showed their support for the library by reauthorising the library system's levy, to meet the needs of its growing and changing communities—definitely a blessing, and an obligation to the community, that Parikh does not take lightly. PCLS made four levy promises to the community: new materials and faster service, 20 per cent more open hours, additional services for kids and teenagers, and upgraded services and technology for customers by offering more computers with Internet access in libraries for public use and computer classes for adults.

The library's customer focus of giving those who responded positively to the levy, and all members of the communities served, what they want is seen in the following statement of services:

- The Library System's services and resources bring the world of information and imagination to communities. Customers will find helpful, welcoming staff who:
  - Answer questions.
  - Help find good books to read.
  - Assist with using the Library's many resources, including books, magazines, music, movies, audio books, computers and online resources.
- The Library strives to grow and change along with the needs of its customers and constantly reevaluates what and how it offers services.

Parikh and the board of trustees knew that succession planning and the development of leaders would be critical if the system was to grow and change along with the needs of its customers. The board, comprising business executives, requested that a succession plan be developed. The request was supported by PCLS's then new HR director, Holly Gorski, who remarked, "Tumbleweeds will be blowing through this place if we don't do something!" After much study and dialogue, in 2005 Parikh and her executive team decided not to take the route of determining who was going to retire and identifying succession for particular positions. Instead, like others, they chose a multi-pronged approach to develop all staff, improve leadership throughout the organisation, and create a learning organisation. An early step was to evaluate the employee pool to determine who and what percentage of employees could potentially retire within the next ten years (assuming a retirement age of 65).

Their analysis led to identifying three different categories of employees:

1. Top-level leadership: Executive team and leadership team (department heads and managing librarians).
2. Specialty positions: Individuals who do not come from the library profession for whom the library would expect to recruit

replacements outside the organisation. Generally for individuals who lead these departments, PCLS would not expect their replacement to come from within the library.

3. Library professional or clerical: Individuals who develop expertise working in the system and would potentially be eligible for higher-level positions within the organisation. This category divides between MLS librarian career-track and paraprofessional supervisory and specialist positions.

In 2009, Parikh shared the following analysis with the PCLS board:

- We have many positions in the organisation for which we have no trouble recruiting replacements (*e.g.*, library pages, branch assistants, custodians). Some of them may become supervisors or become librarians. I will describe the situation in various tiers.
- Executive Leadership Roles: There are 24 Department Heads and top-level administrators. 37.5 per cent will be eligible to retire in the next 10 years. However, looking more closely at the number, you see a different picture. Of the Executive Team, only 1 out of 6 will be eligible to retire, or 16 per cent. The major impact on the organisation would be the retirement of professional librarians in leadership roles. It is important to note that the library system is becoming nationally known for innovative services. It is likely that high-level positions that become vacant will also attract national attention for applicants. PCLS ideally will look for a balance of internal and external.
- Mid-level Supervisors and Specialists: Of 58 employees 43 per cent will be eligible for retirement in the next 10 years. The majority of that falls in the branch clerical supervisory role. This area is a target for attention for developing leadership skills or leadership opportunities for individuals in the organisations to move into these positions. We are also looking closely at these positions because of the need to expand the number of opportunities for librarians to develop supervisory experience.
- The analysis covers 82 individuals or approximately 23 per cent of the employees in the library. The other 277 employees are generally entry-level positions (such as pages, branch assistants, librarians) or specialty positions (such as Finance Department, custodians, facilities maintenance, graphic designers). There are high retirement rates in some of those categories, but it also easy to recruit for those positions. For instance, nearly half of the page positions are eligible for retirement. We have no problem recruiting for this position. For example, earlier this year over 100 people applied for a single part-time page vacancy. These individuals are an extremely important core to the learning organisation and we will pay

attention to their learning and growth, building potential for leadership roles.

In another memo to the board, Parikh summarises the library's approach to succession planning in the areas of hiring, nurture/growth, and creating opportunities to lead.

All, she wrote, "are an important part of assuring that we are growing people and 'potential successors'":

- *Hiring—Get the Right People on the Bus:* Recruit and hire high potential talent and ensure that we are hiring people that share the library's vision and with potential to grow and contribute to the library. A key element is regular evaluation of the organisational structure and job descriptions to ensure the library can meet future goals. This includes recruiting talented new graduates from library school or individuals from libraries across the country, in addition to talent in professions. As PCLS gains a national reputation, we are able to attract talent nationwide.
- *Nurture/Growth:* Create an environment that fosters and supports learning and growth. We must offer opportunities to learn and actively support individual growth. This includes not only formal training within the library or outside, but also creating an environment that encourages experimentation, risk taking and decision-making. This is the core philosophy that led to the creation of the "Learning Organisation" and the Learning Department.
- *Create Opportunities to Lead:* This element includes not only the opportunity to lead projects, but also ensuring that our organisational structure allows individuals to develop leadership skills in preparation for higher level positions. This also means evaluating our organisational structure to ensure that it supports future goals and creating career-ladder positions that would lead to positions of increased responsibility.

Parikh is definitely taking a systems approach to succession planning. Several projects were begun to support the succession planning initiative. She knew that a culture change was required to create a succession plan, leaders at all levels, and a truly customer-focused library. One leverage point was through defining leadership, and leadership behaviours, at PCLS. The original list of leadership descriptors was drafted by Parikh and deputy director Georgia Lomax and vetted by the executive team, then introduced to the leadership team (which includes all branch managers and department heads). As part of the rollout and training, managers learned to act and then tell what leadership descriptors they were using.

They now ask, and ask themselves, these same questions. In a series of meetings in each branch and five at the main library, Parikh and Lomax introduced them to all staff. The final list of leadership descriptors is found.

"All staff need to be leaders," was the message Parikh sent. Staff responded to one question: "How can we help you become a leader at PCLS?" The responses led to training, coaching, and I2P2, an idea incubator project. Still in pilot stages, I2P2 is designed to encourage ideas and risk taking as well as incubate ideas of potential services and programmes in a safe environment. As in numerous libraries and other organisations, too many employees felt inhibited about putting ideas forward.

Parikh and the executive team knew that, for the library to develop a strong culture of customer focus, all ideas would be needed and all staff would need to be accountable.

The leadership descriptors were further operationalised by core skills and qualities required of all staff members along with behavioural dos and don'ts for each. The nine skills/qualities identified are customer focus, teamwork, professional integrity, leadership, communication, problem solving, change and learning, positive attitude, and diversity. They had started with competencies, but that just did not work for them. The dos and don'ts were simply more effective in this culture.

In rolling out the skills and qualities, HR director Holly Gorski wrote:

- These are the skills and qualities all of us need in order to work together and provide outstanding library service, now and in the future. We are currently working to change the Library System's hiring process to ensure new employees are selected based on these attributes. In 2009 we will be changing the performance appraisals for all positions to focus on these as well.

The learning culture being fostered by PCLS relies heavily on coaching, modeling behaviour, and setting expectations. Training is based on an 80:20 model, with only 20 per cent classroom based. Much of the rest is in-the-moment, just-in-time training and coaching. The newly created Learning Team developed "Foundations of the PCLS Learning Organisation". This document articulates the critical elements for PCLS to be a successful learning organisation. The team also used this document to develop a work plan with strategies for each of the items listed.

Staff members are retooling their perspectives, looking beyond their immediate actions and behaviours to what the implications of their behaviour are regarding internal and external customers alike. Employees are constantly asked, and ask each other, "What is the customer perspective on this action or this policy?" A recent illustration is going beyond making a simple change pertaining to e-mail on the server (good internal customer service) to assessing the implications for staff members working at home or away from the office (great leadership and customer-focused behaviour). I asked Parikh how she would know she was successful.

She responded by saying that there would be leaders ready to fill vacancies, all employees would be taking on the role of leader (at their appropriate level), things would be happening and getting done, expectations would be set, and staff would be stepping up with ideas as well as taking responsibility for their decisions and behaviours. Staff would be asking the right questions, retooling their thinking, constantly modeling customer focus. Staff would be living the leadership descriptors. PCLS is spending a lot of time and money creating a culture and a legacy of staff ready to move into new, different, and higher-level positions.

In some ways it is the hard way to create a succession plan; in others, it is the only way. I asked Parikh about the time and money, especially in this economy. With further developmental plans tied to succession planning, I was curious: was she going to continue this effort?

At their current level of intensity? "Yes," she said, "It's essential: we are investing in our future. Staff salaries and benefits comprise 70 per cent of the library's budget. We must keep developing staff so they are ready, willing, and able to provide customer-focused service—especially when this generation retires." With some realism and a smile she continued, "We are ballot based, as an independent taxing authority—if we are not relevant, we are toast!"

QUEENS BOROUGH PUBLIC LIBRARY

Queens Borough (N.Y.) Public Library (QBPL), *Library Journal*'s 2009 Library of the Year, serves 2.2 million people from sixty-two locations plus seven adult learning centers and two family literacy centers. It circulates the highest number of books and other library materials in the country. The library's budget is $127.5 million. In fiscal year 2009, QBPL circulated 23 million items, opened its doors to 16 million people, and offered 30,000 programmes. It has 6.7 million items in its collections and supports 827,500 active borrowers. Like the County of Los Angeles Public Library, it is a large and diverse library system with many needs, including that for a strong cadre of potential managers and leaders. Succession planning at QBPL, though not formal, is purposeful. What follows are several initiatives described by Tom Galante, CEO and library director.

SUCCESSION PLANNING FOR COMMUNITY BRANCH MANAGERS: MONEY AND EDUCATION

The library recently made some organisational changes to facilitate mid-management development and succession planning. It took money. Many of the forty assistant community branch manager positions were open. Senior librarians did not want to promote into the position, for there was little salary incentive to do so. To fill the vacancies, the library added $3,000 to the salary. That broke the ice. The assistant manager positions are now filled. But that was not enough to prepare for the future. Assistant community branch manager is a key feeder position in the community library system, so the need to provide learning and development opportunities for the incumbents was clear. The library contracted with a library school that created and facilitated a management certification programme for twenty-five employees. Many were assistant branch managers. The curriculum included the topics of management, budget and finance, technology management, human resource management, building management, and general administration. A course with a rigourous curriculum, it was offered on-site, once a week for six months. Homework was required. After completion of five courses over three years, all participants graduated. "The outcome," said Galante, "has been great. These employees, current and prospective library managers, have been networking, sharing their experiences, and learning from each other. They have begun peer coaching and all have a broader view of the organisation.... And," he adds proudly, "there have already been a number of promotions."

DUAL CAREER LADDERS

To support retention of professional librarians, including its library managers, QBPL restructured its compensation structure, including new positions, enhancing its already existing dual career ladders for librarians and managers. To the positions of senior librarian, supervising librarian, and principal librarian a second level was added. For senior librarian positions, a third level was added to support promotions into select assistant manager positions. (The move from Librarian I to Librarian II is relatively automatic.) In both ladders, after six months of satisfactory performance, jobholders are automatically moved to the next level and receive a salary increase.

SUCCESSION PLANNING AT THE SENIOR LEVEL

The library has taken a similar approach to creating a pipeline for system wide management positions. Because the size of the system justifies it, QBPL has seven associate and assistant director positions reporting to public service department heads (directors). Four of those positions are responsible for supervising community library managers. In addition, various support departments include an assistant director position. All in these positions lead major organisational initiatives as part of their development as senior leaders. All are observed, supported, and developed to be able, at a minimum, to serve in an interim capacity in the event of a department head vacancy.

KNOWLEDGE MANAGEMENT AND CAPITALISING ON RETIREES

Galante is concerned about losing good people to early (or regular) retirement. To date, knowledge transfer planning has been minimal. To help the system buy some time, and to appeal to those retiring and looking for more flexibility and free time, two policy changes were made. First, QBPL now provides an opportunity for those interested in retiring to work part-time. Second, the library is offering retirees the ability to work at a lowerlevel position yet keep their seniority when setting the pay rate. For example, if the individual was paid at fifteen-year experience in the salary range of the job she is leaving, her new salary remains at the fifteen-year salary range of the new position. This option has proven attractive to retirees who might have otherwise left the system without transferring their knowledge, mentoring new staff, or supporting programmes.

TRANSFERS AND JOB ROTATION

Similar to other libraries, QBPL has been rotating staff into different community branches and central. With over seventy locations, there are many opportunities for job transfer. Because the demographics of this system vary widely, staff transferring often find themselves in a very different environment serving a different community and customer. "This provides a broader view and creates stronger, flexible, customer-oriented staff." For union-represented positions, the labour agreement provides for internal transfers for similar positions based on seniority if QBPL-specified job requirements are met; for union and non-union supervisory and management positions, interviewing is done to select the best candidate from external and internal applicants. Rotations and transfers extend to the top of the library system as well. In addition to the COO, whose responsibilities include all public services, a dozen department heads report directly to him. With a few exceptions, half of them trade jobs every year.

ON THE LOOKOUT

Galante acknowledged that he is always recruiting, always on the lookout for talent. He knows that not all positions can, or should, be filled from within. He has been networking and searching for a new wave of managers: creative individuals who can support the new service model of delivering to customers what they want and need. He also wants to recruit leaders who can deal with City Hall—not a typical competency, or desire, of many senior library managers.

SANTA CLARA COUNTY LIBRARY

Succession planning at Santa Clara County Library (SCCL) starts at the point of hiring, where a solid job description reflecting the desired skill set and competencies propels the library towards its strategic BHAG (big hairy audacious goal): "Building upon our reputation for service excellence, the Santa Clara County Library will have the highest percentage of library service area cardholders in the nation." The three specific areas the library will focus on in the next five years are convenience, public awareness and marketing, and information literacy. So how does Cervantes find and develop the leadership that will continually propel the library towards meeting its BHAG? She engages in two distinct processes, one external and the other internal.

EXTERNAL VIEW

One way to locate leadership is by investing years actively watching, waiting, and creating a good reputation for the library. Cervantes keeps her eyes and ears open for the up-and-comers in the library community. She goes out of her way to meet them when their paths cross, reads the articles they write, and watches them present at conferences. Cervantes invests her time so she has a front-row seat as talent rises. When the library's deputy county librarian retired last year, and when several community librarians (managers) retired, several librarians nationwide were invited to participate in the county's recruitment process.

INTERNAL FOCUS

Cervantes's most important and intense focus is internal. SCCL really works developing internal staff. "This library system," she said, "seeks to prepare staff for their next job and provides the opportunity to develop leadership within their current job."

Job Rotation

Job rotation is in its first iteration at SCCL. It is designed to help staff acquire big-picture thinking and deliver district wide service while supporting staff to grow, stretch, and explore. One facet of job rotation is moving community library staff into other community libraries and into headquarters jobs as well as ensuring that employees assigned to headquarters have experiences in community libraries. At another level, the library is trying out the rotation of three senior management positions among the incumbents for twelve-month periods: system wide circulation manager, reference librarian (which includes 24/7 virtual reference and assisting with collection development), and services managers (adult, youth).

An opportunity arose when a community librarian took medical leave. To fill the gap, the library interviewed qualified managers to take a temporary assignment at the largest and busiest library in the system (2.5 million annual circulation). This resulted in an experienced community librarian from a much smaller library having the opportunity to take on new challenges, learn, and grow. Consequently, a programme librarian (manager) became the acting community librarian, and a librarian became a programme librarian (adult or youth services manager) for the same period of time.

Cervantes shares two success stories. One shining star in the organisation stepped forward and volunteered on an early version of the library's web page redesign. This star, Allison Parham, is now an electronic resources librarian and leading a formal web redesign project for the library. Paul Sims, formerly an SCCL librarian, is now the technical services manager for Mountain View Public Library. ("Sometimes our succession planning benefits other libraries!") Sims graduated from the San Jose State University MLIS programme and went on to become an adjunct faculty member. Building on his enthusiasm for the SJSU/MLIS programme, Sims asked if he could offer an orientation to potential students from SCCL staff ranks. He developed the presentation, including PowerPoint slides, and promoted the workshop to recent graduates, current MLIS students, and potential librarians. Both Cervantes and Sarah Flowers (former deputy county librarian) were invited to speak about their own career paths and the SCCL opportunities afforded to MLIS graduates.

At least two of the dozen or so who attended this workshop enrolled in the SJSU/MLIS programme, and one or more completed their undergraduate degree requirements with Sims's encouragement. "Succession planning," said Cervantes, "can be viral."

Development beyond Boundaries

This library system goes beyond its own boundaries to develop staff. Staff members at all levels are encouraged to become involved and engaged with the California Library Association, ALA, PLA, and the Urban Libraries Council (and pays institutional membership dues and conference attendance fees). This ensures that the library's name is out there, which results in attracting high-quality candidates when vacancies occur. Of course, library staff and the library gain as well. Involved employees learn from their efforts with CLA and other professional associations, develop technical and leadership skills, and build networks. Because one of its goals is to be involved with the cities and county it serves, SCCL also encourages service on local chambers of commerce, the arts and culture, non-profits, and other key constituent communities.

The library pays the dues of managers and supports involvement and leadership opportunities in local volunteer organisations for all staff. One manager who stands out to Cervantes is Rosanne Macek, Morgan Hill community librarian. Macek joined the SCCL staff as a children's programme librarian in 2001, became community librarian in 2002, completed the Leadership Morgan Hill programme sponsored by the Morgan Hill Rotary Club, and is now working on a master's degree in public administration using the library's tuition reimbursement programme. SCCL has been working actively on succession planning since, 2005. At the time it was facing several retirements among key library managers.

Earlier, deputy county librarian Julie Farnsworth had created a leadership training programme for potential leaders and invited employees to self-identify. Participants in the leadership programme completed nine classes covering all aspects of management and leadership in the SCCL system. More than fifty emerging leaders completed the programme during two series of classes. SCCL places a premium on developing leaders internally and wisely also pays attention to future leaders nationwide. Cervantes showed us the importance of having a variety of smaller, targeted leadership development programmes in addition to formal, large programmes.

SNO-ISLE LIBRARIES

Located in the north Puget Sound region of Washington State, Sno-Isle Libraries, with twenty-one locations in Snohomish County and Island County, serves as a community doorway to reading, resources, and lifelong learning and a center for people, ideas, and culture. Jonalyn Woolf-Ivory is the library director. Pat Olafson, HR director, explained some of the library's efforts in succession planning. Olafson and her colleagues have been thinking quite a bit about succession planning in recent years. Familiar with the literature on the graying of the library workforce, and looking (literally) at the members of the Sno-Isle workforce, they decided to identify potential vacancies and to develop a backup plan towards ensuring stability and continuity in providing excellent library service to the communities served.

The board of trustees was also interested in having bench strength for senior positions in the organisation. The first step was to identify key jobs. Olafson then matched the key positions with the people in them to ascertain the level of risk of retirement each one might be in—that is, she looked at data on each individual holding these jobs to get a deeper understanding of their age and service and a picture of when retirements might take place. She created a schema of employees: at immediate risk (IR), at risk (AR), and at low risk (LR) for retirement. Olafson defined these categories in concrete terms based on the retirement eligibility provisions of the pension plans.

Those in IR are 60 years of age and above today with an anticipated (for the purpose of this exercise) retirement date in the next five years. AR staff in key positions are ages 55–59 or age 50 with at least ten years of service. It is anticipated that these individuals will move into the IR category in the next five years. LR employees do not fall into either of the other categories by age or experience. Another organisation's definitions might differ depending on retirement plan provisions covering its employees. Olafson then linked those in key positions to their risk of retirement. Among those in key positions, she found four IR and three AR staff members holding key positions. Olafson mentioned some examples, starting with the library director, and included herself.

The director, at age 55, has twenty-nine years of pension service credits. She is viewed as AR. Olafson, the HR director, needed to code her own position as IR. At age 63 with more than fifteen years of pension service credits, she is eligible to retire within five years. Over the years, with encouragement from the board, positions have been installed that not only filled a workload need but also were intended as immediate temporary backup in case of a vacancy in some management positions. For example, several of the larger Sno-Isle community libraries have an assistant managing librarian position, and there is an assistant manager in collection development. Incumbents in these positions could step in until a replacement is hired when someone in a key position and IR retires earlier than anticipated. Library leadership took this approach further and realised that some of those designated as "backup until filled" might not take (or even want) the vacant key position or might not be ready to take on the full responsibility long term when the time comes.

With encouragement from the board to develop a deeper bench and to work towards "growing their own," Sno- Isle identified "developmental positions" (designated "Dev" on the chart; defined as a position, not a person) that could be a step towards a key position. Here Olafson again looked at service and age, this time for individuals currently holding positions categorised as developmental to determine who might retire and create an opening in one of those jobs. They too were coded as IR, AR, and LR.

This analysis indicated that several developmental positions could be open in the next few years due to retirements. This provided a list of potential developmental opportunities. In addition, Sno-Isle has experimented with creating one developmental position to broaden the experience of those who may be interested in library administration. The facilities manager job was recently created (as a temporary position, for two years only) to provide developmental work experience in facilities management and capital facilities development. The incumbent is acquiring a great deal of experience and exposure working on special assignments such as branch renovation projects and creating a preventive maintenance plan for every building.

She is now the key contact for building issues in each branch. In addition, she attends community and board meetings and meets regularly with the library director. Previously she was a manager of a large building and will have the opportunity to return to this position at the end of two years. Of course, by allowing staff to take a temporary job and return to their original job, Sno-Isle created a whole string of temporary positions, creating developmental opportunities for many across the system. At the end of two years the library leadership, with input from the incumbent, will decide whether to retain the facilities job as a temporary developmental position or make it a regular assignment.

Along with creating development opportunities in a variety of jobs, Karri Matau, director of strategic initiatives, is charged with creating a leadership development programme for the organisation. This programme, which will support succession planning efforts, is still in developmental stages. Many—if not most—libraries find themselves in difficult financial straits because of the recession.

Thinking about this, I asked Olafson a question for which she had an interesting and clear answer. "Pat," I asked, "in the beginning of this conversation, you talked about the budget constraints facing Sno-Isle Libraries. You mentioned the potential of a hiring freeze.

How much leadership development and succession planning do you plan to continue in these tough times?" Olafson's answer was not one I often hear. "We know we need to have leadership development initiatives and succession planning in process even when times are bleak. Strong, skilled employees are a key ingredient to facing tough times and to carrying out our strategic plan. The library district cannot afford to put leadership development on the back burner." Sno-Isle library leadership has made a choice—one that has them working diligently to ensure that knowledge is transferred as long-term employees get ready to move into the next phase of their lives and younger members of the workforce get ready to take the baton and bring the library into the future.

9

Imapcts of Motivation on Library Staff

NATURE OF MOTIVATION

The concept of motivation focuses on explaining what "moves" behaviour. In fact, the term motivation is derived from the Latin word 'movere', referring to movement of activity. Most of our everyday explanation of behaviour is given in terms of motives. Why do you come to the school or college? There may be any number of reasons for this behaviour, such as you want to learn or to make friends, you need a diploma or degree to get a good job, you want to make your parents happy, and so on. Some combination of these reasons and/or others would explain why you choose to go in for higher education. Motives also help in making predictions about behaviour.

A person will work hard in school, in sports, in business, in music, and in many other situations, if s/he has a very strong need for achievement. Hence, motives are the general states that enable us to make predictions about behaviour in many different situations. In other words, motivation is one of the determinants of behaviour. Instincts, drives, needs, goals, and incentives come under the broad cluster of motivation.

The Motivational Cycle

Psychologists now use the concept of need to describe the motivational properties of behaviour. A need is lack or deficit of some necessity. The condition of need leads to drive. A drive is a state of tension or arousal produced by a need. It energises random activity. When one of the random activities leads to a goal, it reduces the drive, and the organism stops being active. The organism returns to a balanced state. Thus, the cycle of motivational events can be presented.

BIOLOGICAL MOTIVES

The biological or physiological approach to explain motivation is the earliest attempt to understand causes of behaviour. Most of the theories, which developed later, carry traces of the influence of the biological approach. The approach adhering to the concept of adaptive act holds that organisms have needs that produce drive, which stimulates behaviour leading to certain actions towards achieving certain goals, which reduce the drive. The earliest explanations of motivation relied on the concept of instinct. The term instinct denotes inborn patterns of behaviour that are biologically determined rather than learned. Some common human instincts include curiosity, flight, repulsion, reproduction, parental care, etc. Instincts are innate tendencies found in all members of a species that direct behaviour in predictable ways. The term instinct most approximately refers to an urge to do something. Instinct has an "impetus" which drives the organism to do something to reduce that impetus. Some of the basic biological needs explained by this approach are hunger, thirst, and sex, which are essential for the sustenance of the individual.

Hunger

When someone is hungry, the need for food dominates everything else. It motivates people to obtain and consume food. Of course we must eat to live. But, what makes you feel hungry? Studies have indicated that many events inside and outside the body may trigger hunger or inhibit it. The stimuli for hunger include stomach contractions, which signify that the stomach is empty, a low concentration of glucose in the blood, a low level of protein and the amount of fats stored in the body. The liver also responds to the lack of bodily fuel by sending nerve impulses to the brain. The aroma, taste or appearance of food may also result in a desire to eat. It may be noted that none of these alone gives you the feeling that you are hungry. All in combination act with external factors to help you understand that you are hungry.

Thus, it can be said that our food intake is regulated by a complex feedingsatiety system located in the hypothalamus, liver, and other parts of the body as well as the external cues available in the environment. Some physiologists hold that changes in the metabolic functions of the liver result in a feeling of hunger. The liver sends a signal to a part of the brain called hypothalamus. The two regions of hypothalamus involved in hunger are - the lateral hypothalamus and the ventro-medial hypothalamus. LH is considered to be the excitatory area. Animals eat when this area is stimulated. When it is damaged, animals stop eating and die of starvation. The VMH is located in the middle of the hypothalamus, which is otherwise known as hunger-controlling area which inhibits the hunger drive. Now can you guess about people who overeat and become obese, and people who eat very little or who are on a diet?

Thirst

What would happen to you, if you were deprived of water for a long time? What makes you feel thirsty? When we are deprived of water for a period of several hours, the mouth and throat become dry, which leads to dehydration of body tissues. Drinking water is necessary to wet a dry mouth. But a dry mouth does not always result in water drinking behaviour. In fact processes within the body itself control thirst and drinking of water. Water must get into the tissues sufficiently to remove the dryness of mouth and throat. Motivation to drink water is mainly triggered by the conditions of the body: loss of water from cells and reduction of blood volume. When water is lost by bodily fluids, water leaves the interior of the cells. The anterior hypothalamus contains nerve cells called 'osmoreceptors', which generate nerve impulses in case of cell dehydration. These nerve impulses act as a signal for thirst and drinking; when thirst is regulated by loss of water from the osmoreceptors, it is called cellular-dehydration thirst. But what mechanisms stop the drinking of water? Some researchers assume that the mechanism which explains the intake of water is also responsible for stopping the intake of water. Others have pointed out that the role of stimuli resulting from the intake of water in the stomach must have something to do with stopping of drinking water. However, the precise physiological mechanisms underlying the thirst drive are yet to be understood.

Sex

One of the most powerful drives in both animals and human beings is the sex drive. Motivation to engage in sexual activity is a very strong factor influencing human behaviour. However, sex is far more than a biological motive.

It is different from other primary motives in many ways like:

- Sexual activity is not necessary for an individual's survival;
- Homeostasis (the tendency of the organism as a whole to maintain constancy or to attempt to restore equilibrium if constancy is disturbed) is not the goal of sexual activity; and
- Sex drive develops with age, etc.

In case of lower animals, it depends on many physiological conditions; in case of human beings, the sex drive is very closely regulated biologically, sometimes it is very difficult to classify sex purely as a biological drive. Physiologists suggest that intensity of the sexual urge is dependent upon chemical substances circulating in the blood, known as sex hormones. Studies on animals as well as human beings have mentioned that sex hormones secreted by gonads, *i.e.*, testes in males and the ovaries in females are responsible for sexual motivation. Sexual motivation is also influenced by other endocrine glands, such as adrenal and pituitary glands. Sexual drive in human beings is primarily stimulated by external stimuli and its expression depends upon cultural learning.

SOCIAL MOTIVES

Social motives are when people do or give things because they feel they have a sense of responsibility to their community. People with social motives may have endured racial discrimination, poverty or may want to live in a selfless way:

- Social motives manifest themselves in different ways. There are people who work in soup kitchens because they were homeless at one time. Another person may focus on citisen advocacy because he experienced unfair treatment from law enforcement.
- Having a social motive for doing or giving is beneficial because it allows a person to be less self-centered and more focused on the needs of others. For example, if one grew up with a bias towards single mothers, social motives can gradually turn the bias into compassion.
- Some famous people are well-known for their social motives to help to the less fortunate in society. For example, Oprah Winfrey built a school for disadvantaged girls in South Africa so they can have quality education. Michael Jackson was a philanthropist throughout his career.
- If you're a person that seeks to advance the causes of the less fortunate, you can contribute even in small ways. Some ideas include donating items to the local food bank, visiting a battered women's shelter, bringing school supplies to a foster home or assisting the unemployed in a job search.
- A lot of good has been done in the U.S., because of people with social motives. For example, abolitionists crusaded for the end of slavery and female suffragists made it possible for women to vote.

PSYCHOSOCIAL MOTIVES

Social motives are mostly learned or acquired. Social groups such as family, neighbourhood, friends, and relatives do contribute a lot in acquiring social motives. These are complex forms of motives mainly resulting from the individual's interaction with her/his social environment.

Curiosity and Exploration

Often people engage in activities without a clear goal or purpose but they derive some kind of pleasure out of it. It is a motivational tendency to act without any specific identifiable goal. The tendency to seek for a novel experience, gain pleasure by obtaining information, etc., are signs of curiosity. Hence, curiosity describes behaviour whose primary motive appears to remain in the activities themselves. What will happen if the sky falls on us? Questions of this kind stimulate intellectuals to find answers. Studies show that this curiosity behaviour is not only limited to human beings, animals too show the same kind of behaviour. We are driven to explore the environment by our curiosity and our need for sensory stimulation. The need for varied types of sensory stimulations is closely related to curiosity. It is the basic motive, and exploration and curiosity are the expressions of it.

Our ignorance about a number of things around us becomes a powerful motivator to explore the world. We get easily bored with repetitive experiences. So we look for something new. In the case of infants and small children, this motive is very dominant. They get satisfaction from being allowed to explore, which is reflected in their smiling and babbling. Children become easily distressed, when the motive to explore is discouraged.

ACHIEVEMENT, AFFILIATION AND POWER [MASLOW'S HIERARCHY]

ACHIEVEMENT

You might have observed some students work very hard and compete with others for good marks/grades in the examination, as good marks/grades will create opportunities for higher studies and better job prospects. It is the achievement motivation, which refers to the desire of a person to meet standards of excellence. Need for achievement, also known as n-Ach, energises and directs behaviour as well as influences the perception of situations. During the formative years of social development, children acquire achievement motivation. The sources from which they learn it, include parents, other role models, and socio-cultural influences. Persons high in achievement motivation tend to prefer tasks that are moderately difficult and challenging. They have stronger-than-average desire for feedback on their performance, that is to know how they are doing, so that they can adjust their goals to meet the challenge.

AFFILIATION

Most of us need company or friend or want to maintain some form of relationship with others. Nobody likes to remain alone all the time. As soon as people see some kinds of similarities among themselves or they like each other, they form a group. Formation of group or collectivity is an important feature of human life. Often people try desperately to get close to other people, to seek their help, and to become members of their group. Seeking other human beings and wanting to be close to them both physically and psychologically is called affiliation. It involves motivation for social contact. Need for affiliation is aroused when individuals feel threatened or helpless and also when they are happy. People high on this need are motivated to seek the company of others and to maintain friendly relationships with other people.

POWER

Need for power is an ability of a person to produce intended effects on the behaviour and emotions of another person. The various goals of power motivation are to influence, control, persuade, lead, and charm others and most importantly to enhance one's own reputation in the eyes of other people. David McClelland described four general ways of expression of the power motive.

First, people do things to gain feeling of power and strength from sources outside themselves by reading stories about sports stars or attaching themselves to a popular figure. Second, power can also be felt from sources within us and may be expressed by building up the body and mastering urges and impulses. Third, people do things as individuals to have an impact on others.

For example, a person argues, or competes with another individual in order to have an impact or influence on that person. Fourth, people do things as members of organisations to have an impact on others as in the case of the leader of a political party; the individual may use the party apparatus to influence others. However, for any individual, one of these ways of expressing power motivation may dominate, but with age and life experiences, it varies.

MASLOW'S HIERARCHY OF NEEDS

Maslow's hierarchy of needs is a theory in psychology, proposed by Abraham Maslow in his 1943 paper 'A Theory of Human Motivation'. Maslow subsequently extended the idea to include his observations of humans' innate curiosity. His theories parallel many other theories of human developmental psychology, all of which focus on describing the stages of growth in humans. Maslow studied what he called exemplary people such as Albert Einstein, Jane Addams, Eleanor Roosevelt, and Frederick Douglass rather than mentally ill or neurotic people, writing that "the study of crippled, stunted, immature, and unhealthy specimens can yield only a cripple psychology and a cripple philosophy." Maslow studied the healthiest 1 per cent of the college student population. Maslow's theory was fully expressed in his 1954 book *Motivation and Personality*.

HIERARCHY

Maslow's hierarchy of needs is often portrayed in the shape of a pyramid, with the largest and most fundamental levels of needs at the bottom, and the need for self-actualisation at the top. The most fundamental and basic four layers of the pyramid contain what Maslow called "deficiency needs" or "d-needs": esteem, friendship and love, security, and physical needs. With the exception of the most fundamental needs, if these "deficiency needs" are not met, the body gives no physical indication but the individual feels anxious and tense.

Maslow's theory suggests that the most basic level of needs must be met before the individual will strongly desire the secondary or higher level needs. Maslow also coined the term Metamotivation to describe the motivation of people who go beyond the scope of the basic needs and strive for constant betterment. Metamotivated people are driven by B-needs, instead of deficiency needs.

Self-actualisation

"What a man can be, he must be?" This forms the basis of the perceived need for self-actualisation. This level of need pertains to what a person's full potential is and realising that potential. Maslow describes this desire as the desire to become more and more what one is, to become everything that one is capable of becoming.

This is a broad definition of the need for self-actualisation, but when applied to individuals the need is specific. For example one individual may have the strong desire to become an ideal parent, in another it may be expressed athletically, and in another it may be expressed in painting, or inventions. In order to reach a clear understanding of this level of need one must first not only achieve the previous needs, physiological, safety, love, and esteem, but master these needs. Maslow's descriptions of a self-actualised person's different needs and personality traits. Maslow also states that even though these are examples of how the quest for knowledge is separate from basic needs he warns that these "two hierarchies are interrelated rather than sharply separated". This means that this level of need, as well as the next and highest level, are not strict, separate levels but closely related to others, and this is possibly the reason that these two levels of need are left out of most textbooks.

Esteem

All humans have a need to be respected and to have self-esteem and self-respect. Also known as the belonging need, esteem presents the normal human desire to be accepted and valued by others. People need to engage themselves to gain recognition and have an activity or activities that give the person a sense of contribution, to feel accepted and self-valued, be it in a profession or hobby. Imbalances at this level can result in low self-esteem or an inferiority complex.

People with low self-esteem need respect from others. They may seek fame or glory, which again depends on others. Note, however, that many people with low self-esteem will not be able to improve their view of themselves simply by receiving fame, respect, and glory externally, but must first accept themselves internally.

Psychological imbalances such as depression can also prevent one from obtaining self-esteem on both levels. Most people have a need for a stable self-respect and self-esteem. Maslow noted two versions of esteem needs, a lower one and a higher one. The lower one is the need for the respect of others, the need for status, recognition, fame, prestige, and attention. The higher one is the need for self-respect, the need for strength, competence, mastery, self-confidence, independence and freedom. The latter one ranks higher because it rests more on inner competence won through experience. Deprivation of these needs can lead to an inferiority complex, weakness and helplessness.

Love and Belonging

After physiological and safety needs are fulfilled, the third layer of human needs are social and involve feelings of belongingness. This aspect of Maslow's hierarchy involves emotionally based relationships in general, such as:

- Friendship.
- Intimacy.
- Family.

Humans need to feel a sense of belonging and acceptance, whether it comes from a large social group, such as clubs, office culture, religious groups, professional organisations, sports teams, gangs, or small social connections. They need to love and be loved by others. In the absence of these elements, many people become susceptible to loneliness, social anxiety, and clinical depression. This need for belonging can often overcome the physiological and security needs, depending on the strength of the peer pressure; an anorexic, for example, may ignore the need to eat and the security of health for a feeling of control and belonging.

Safety Needs

With their physical needs relatively satisfied, the individual's safety needs take precedence and dominate Behaviour. These needs have to do with people's yearning for a predictable orderly world in which perceived unfairness and inconsistency are under control, the familiar frequent and the unfamiliar rare. In the world of work, these safety needs manifest themselves in such things as a preference for job security, grievance procedures for protecting the individual from unilateral authority, savings accounts, insurance policies, reasonable disability accommodations, and the like.

Safety and Security needs include:

- Personal security.
- Financial security.
- Health and well-being.
- Safety net against accidents/illness and their adverse impacts.

Physiological Needs

For the most part, physiological needs are obvious — they are the literal requirements for human survival. If these requirements are not met, the human body simply cannot continue to function.

Physiological needs include:

- Breathing.

- Nutrition.
- Water.
- Sex.
- Sleep.
- Homeostasis.
- Excretion.

Air, water, and food are metabolic requirements for survival in all animals, including humans. Clothing and shelter provide necessary protection from the elements. The intensity of the human sexual instinct is shaped more by sexual competition than maintaining a birth rate adequate to survival of the species.

CRITICISMS

In their extensive review of research based on Maslow's theory, Wahba and Bridgewell found little evidence for the ranking of needs Maslow described, or even for the existence of a definite hierarchy at all. Chilean economist and philosopher Manfred Max-Neef has also argued fundamental human needs are non-hierarchical, and are ontologically universal and invariant in nature—part of the condition of being human; poverty, he argues, may result from any one of these needs being frustrated, denied or unfulfilled. The order in which the hierarchy is arranged has been criticised as being ethnocentric by Geert Hofstede.

Hofstede's criticism of Maslow's pyramid as ethnocentric may stem from the fact that Maslow's hierarchy of needs neglects to illustrate and expand upon the difference between the social and intellectual needs of those raised in individualistic societies and those raised in collectivist societies. Maslow created his hierarchy of needs from an individualistic perspective, being that he was from the United States, a highly individualistic nation. The needs and drives of those in individualistic societies tend to be more self-centred than those in collectivist societies, focusing on improvement of the self, with self-actualisation being the apex of self-improvement. Since, the hierarchy was written from the perspective of an individualist, the order of needs in the hierarchy with self-actualisation at the top is not representative of the needs of those in collectivist cultures. In collectivist societies, the needs of acceptance and community will outweigh the needs for freedom and individuality.

Maslow's hierarchy has also been criticised as being individualistic because of the position and value of sex on the pyramid. Maslow's pyramid puts sex on the bottom rung of physiological needs, along with breathing and food. It views sex from an individualistic and not collectivist perspective: *i.e.,* as an individualistic physiological need that must be satisfied before one moves on to higher pursuits. This view of sex neglects the emotional, familial and evolutionary implications of sex within the community.

ENTREPRENEURIAL MOTIVATION—MEANING

It is often said that a person cannot win a game that they do not play. In the context of entrepreneurship, this statement suggests that success depends on people's willingness to become entrepreneurs. Moreover, because the pursuit of entrepreneurial opportunity is an evolutionary process in which people select out at many steps along the way, decisions made after the discovery of opportunities—to positively evaluate opportunities, to pursue resources, and to design the mechanisms of exploitation—also depend on the willingness of people to "play" the game. In this paper, we argue that human motivations influence these decisions, and that variance across people in these motivations will influence who pursues entrepreneurial opportunities, who assembles resources, and how people undertake the entrepreneurial process. In recent years, entrepreneurship research has focused largely on the environmental characteristics influencing firm foundings and the characteristics of entrepreneurial opportunities.

Although this focus has greatly enhanced our understanding of the entrepreneurial phenomenon, it ignores the role of human agency. Entrepreneurship depends on the decisions that people make about how to undertake that process. We argue that the attributes of people making decisions about the entrepreneurial process influence the decisions that they make. Although previous researchers have rightly criticised much of the existing empirical research on the role of human motivation in entrepreneurship, we argue that inadequate empirical work does not negate the importance of understanding the role of human motivation in the entrepreneurial process. In fact, even sociologists who have argued strongly against the usefulness of trait-based research in entrepreneurship implicitly acknowledge that motivation must matter to this process.

Scholars write, entrepreneurial activity "can be conceptualised as a function of opportunity structures and motivated entrepreneurs with access to resources". We also believe that these criticisms have resulted in insufficient consideration of the role of the human motivation in the entrepreneurial process in recent entrepreneurship research. Consequently, we are left with theories of entrepre-neurship that do not consider variation in the motivations of different people.

We believe that such an omission is problematic because, as Baumol eloquently argued, the study of entrepreneurship that does not explicitly consider entrepreneurs is like the analysis of Shakespeare in which "the Prince of Denmark has been expunged from the discussion of Hamlet." We identify several human motivations that influence the entrepreneurial process. In our arguments, we explicitly assume that all human action is the result of both motivational and cognitive factors, the latter including ability, intelligence, and skills. We also assume that entrepreneurship is not solely the result of human action; external factors also play a role. However, environmental factors being held constant, we argue that human motivation plays a critical role in the entrepreneurial process. To this end, we suggest ways that researchers could develop more realistic explanations for how human motivation influences the entrepreneurial process than is the norm in the literature to date.

We believe that this approach could overcome many of the criticisms of prior research on person-centric explanations for entrepreneurship. Finally, we offer suggestions on how empirical researchers should test these arguments in ways that overcome many of the criticisms of extant research on this topic. We define entrepreneurship and present several arguments for why the study of entrepreneurship in general and consideration of the role of human motivation in the process in particular are important. We discuss opposing views of how opportunities may affect the relationship between motivation and entrepreneurship.

We summarise the major mechanisms by which previous researchers believe motivation influences entrepreneurship. We identify what we believe are the major problems with prior research on motivation and entrepreneurship. We provide some recommendations for researchers conducting empirical research in this area. We offer some tentative conclusions about motivation and entrepreneurship.

WHAT IS ENTREPRENEURSHIP AND WHY STUDY IT FROM THE POINT OF VIEW OF HUMAN MOTIVATION

We believe that the study of the entrepreneurial process is important for several reasons. First, entrepreneurship drives innovation and technical change, and therefore generates economic growth. Second, as the Austrian economists have explained, entrepreneurial action is the process through which supply and demand are equilibrated. Third, entrepreneurship is an important process by which new knowledge is converted into products and services.

Fourth, entrepreneurship has become an important vocation and we need to understand its role in the development of human and intellectual capital. We adopt Shane and Venkataraman's definition of entrepreneurship as the process by which "opportunities to create future goods and services are discovered, evaluated, and exploited." As these authors have explained, this definition does not require viewing entrepreneurs as the founders of new organisations.

An options trader can be an entrepreneur, as can a corporate salesman who discovers and pursues opportunities for the creation of new products. Moreover, this definition shows that entrepreneurship is a creative process. By rearranging resources in a new way, entrepreneurs engage in creative activity. However, the degree of creativity involved in entrepre-neurship varies across the types of resource recombination that occurs. For example, the creation of business to undertake space tourism may be more creative than the creation of a new restaurant in a strip mall. Entrepreneurship involves human agency. The entrepreneurial process occurs because people act to pursue opportunities. People differ in their willingness and abilities to act on these opportunities because they are different from each other. We argue that the variation among people in their willingness and ability to act has important effects on the entrepreneurial process.

Recent research has been relatively accepting of arguments that people vary in their willingness and ability to engage in the entrepreneurial process because of non-motivational individual differences. Researchers have shown that the willingness of people to pursue entrepreneurial opportunities depends on such things as their opportunity cost, their stocks of financial capital, their social ties to investors, and their career experience. We argue that motivational differences also influence the entrepreneurial process.

For example, such things as variation across people in their perceptions of risk and opportunity influence entrepreneurial decisions. People vary in how they view the risk of expending resources before knowing the distribution of outcomes. Similarly, the probability of success at the entrepreneurial process is low, and those people who are willing to proceed despite these odds might be more optimistic or higher in self-efficacy than people deterred by these odds.

We consider the incorporation of this individual-level variation in motivation to be important to the entrepreneurial process. To isolate the effects of entrepreneurial motivation, other factors that could have a causal effect on the process and outcome of entrepreneurship need to be controlled. One category of control variables is the external environment. These would include such things as:

- Political factors (*e.g.*, legal restrictions, quality of law enforcement, political stability, and currency stability);
- Market forces (*e.g.*, structure of the industry, technology regime, potential barriers to entry, market sise, and population demographics); and
- Resources (*e.g.*, availability of investment capital, Labour market including skill availability, transportation infrastructure, and complementary technology).

Most researchers either explicitly or implicitly agree that these categories of factors influence the entrepreneurial process and need to be controlled to measure the effect of motivations on the entrepreneurial process. While it is clear why the above factors need to be controlled if we are to fully understand how motivation is related to entrepreneurship, it is less clear how opportunities affect this relationship.

Because the first two authors were unable to agree on the concept of opportunities, we present two versions of the relationship between opportunities and motivation. First, as suggested, present the view shared by Shane and Collins, then as suggested, present Locke's view.

ENTREPRENEURS, OPPORTUNITIES, AND THE EFFECTS OF MOTIVATION

Opportunities are aspects of the environment that represent potentialities for profit making. We follow Shane and Venkataraman to define entrepreneurial opportunities as "situations in which new goods, services, raw materials, and organising methods can be introduced and sold at greater than the cost of their production." Since, potentialities are not yet actual, measuring them objectively and prospectively at the level of an individual entrepreneur poses daunting challenges. Entrepreneurs can pursue opportunities in any industry at any time.

For example, some entrepreneurs build successful new companies by contributing to the founding of a new industry, such as Robert Swanson in biotechnology. Other entrepreneurs build new companies in old and mature industries such as Sam Walton in retailing. Aggregate statistics show us that the general category of opportunities to which Sam Walton and Bob Swanson responded was not equal. The average value of new businesses created in retail is lower than the average value of new businesses created in biotechnology.

Because human motivations are likely widely distributed across industry categories at the aggregate level, statistically significant differences in the mean value of businesses created in different industry categories suggest that the value of opportunities varies across industry. This does not mean that entrepreneurs cannot successfully pursue opportunities in lowopportunity industries. Rather it means that the opportunities in these industries are simply less attractive to the average person. The value of opportunities also varies within industries. Because the opportunities that entrepreneurs identify and pursue have different economic value, the opportunities themselves influence entrepreneurial Behaviour.

We believe that it is important for Behaviourally oriented entrepreneurship researchers to consider and measure the economic value of these opportunities in research about the motivations of entrepreneurs. For example, in the early 1970s, Butler Lampson and Chuck Thacker, researchers at Xerox Parc, invented the Alto—the first personal computer. However, their design would have cost over US$10,000 to build. When Steve Jobs and Steve Wozniak came up with the design for the Apple computer, their design cost less than US$3000 to build.

Because the number of people who would pay more than US$10,000 for a PC was much smaller than number of people who would pay US$3000, the financial value of the Jobs and Wozniak opportunity was greater than the value of the Xerox opportunity. One would expect that differences in the estimates of the value of the PC opportunity that resulted from the different solutions influenced the decisions of the different parties about their opportunities. Of course, although it is possible that Jobs and Wozniak possessed more of the relevant motives to pursue entrepreneurial opportunities than did Lampson and Thacker, researchers can only estimate the effect of these motives if they account for the differences in the two opportunities.

Although we argue that opportunities influence entrepreneurial behaviour, we do not argue that opportunities fully determine the process. Entrepreneurs are people and may make different decisions when confronted with similar opportunities. In addition to being influenced by the opportunity that Steve Jobs pursued at the time of founding, the development of Apple was likely influenced by Steve Jobs' motivations. Empirically, the objective and subjective parts of opportunity are difficult to separate. The mechanism for actualising an opportunity often initially exists mainly in the entrepreneur's mind, making the entrepreneur's idea for how to exploit the opportunity a personal interpretation of the opportunity. This idea is basically what we would call vision.

Such judgements may be mistaken; entrepreneurs sometimes believe that they have identified valuable opportunities when, in fact, no valuable opportunities actually existed, at least in the form in which they were conceptualised. Also, entrepreneurs may differ in how they interpret opportunities. For example, the development of the Internet has allowed entrepreneurs to develop new organising methods, such as "e-tailing", that were never before possible.

Although a wide variety of entrepreneurs have responded to the opportunities to develop new organising methods that the Internet has generated, these entrepreneurs have developed approaches of different value in response to this organising opportunity. Some entrepreneurs have developed opportunities to compete with established retailers through e-tailing, while others have sought only to design web sites. Even though the way that opportunities are manifested in the entrepreneur's plans for exploitation are personal, the variance in their estimated value likely influences the decisions that people make in the entrepreneurial process and can confound attempts to measure the effects of motivation on this process. This is true even if the value is partially a function of the other decisions that the entrepreneur has made and partially a function of external forces.

MOTIVATION AND ENTREPRENEURSHIP: IMPORTANT MOTIVATIONAL CONCEPTS FROM PRIOR QUANTITATIVE RESEARCH

Previous research has explored several motivations and their effects on entrepreneurship. We discuss several of these concepts. However, we do not provide a complete review of prior empirical research for two reasons. First, the definitions of entrepreneurship used in previous empirical research on motivation and entrepreneurship are inconsistent with our definition, making it impossible to draw direct implications of prior work for research using our definition. Second, prior research has suffered from significant methodological problems that we discuss, making prior findings suggestive rather than conclusive, even for research that employs the same definition of entrepreneurship as was used in those studies. Therefore, we discuss previous empirical research only to illustrate the ways in which motivation can influence different aspects of the entrepreneurial process.

Need for Achievement

Within the research domain of personality traits and entrepreneurship, the concept of need for achievement has received much attention. McClelland argued that individuals who are high in nAch are more likely than those who are low in nAch to engage in activities or tasks that have a high degree of individual responsibility for outcomes, require individual skill and effort, have a moderate degree of risk, and include clear feedback on performance. Further, McClelland argued that entrepreneurial roles are characterised as having a greater degree of these task attributes than other careers; thus, it is likely that people high in nAch will be more likely to pursue entrepreneurial jobs than other types of roles.

Johnson conducted a traditional review of various studies, which varied regarding samples, measurement of nAch, and definitions of entrepreneurship. Based on this group of studies, Johnson concluded that there is a relationship between nAch and entrepreneurial activity—in this case, nAch distinguished firm founders from other members of society. In a similar review of studies, Fineman concluded that both projective and questionnaire measures of nAch significantly predict firm founding. Collins, Locke, and Hanges conducted the first and only meta-analysis of nAch and entrepreneurship studies, examining 63 nAch and entrepreneurship studies.

The overall finding of the meta-analysis is that nAch is significantly related to founding a company. The nAch both differentiated between entrepreneurs and others and predicted the performance of the founders' firms. Further, they found no significant differences in the predictive validity of three different measures of nAch. Moreover, Collins found that the relationship between nAch and entrepreneurial activity was moderated by several factors.

First, nAch was a more robust predictor of group-level effects (*e.g.*, mean differences between firm founders and another profession, mean differences between high-performing and low-performing founders) than individuallevel effects (*e.g.*, predicting the performance of individuals). Second, they found that while nAch is a strong differentiator between firm founders and non-managerial employees, it is not a strong differentiator between firm founders and managers. Based on these results, Collins concluded that nAch is an effective tool for differentiating between firm founders and the general population but less so for differentiating between firm founders and managers. Further, they concluded that nAch might be particularly effective at differentiating between successful and unsuccessful groups of firm founders. Thus, nAch could play a very useful role in explaining entrepreneurial activity.

Risk Taking

Risk-taking propensity is another motivation of interest, which emerged from McClelland's original research on entrepreneurs. McClelland claimed that individuals with high achievement needs would have moderate propensities to take risk. This claim by McClelland is especially interesting for entrepreneurship research because the entrepreneurial process involves acting in the face of uncertainty.

Liles argued that entrepreneurs often must accept uncertainty with respect to financial well-being, psychic well-being, career security, and family relations. Moreover, several theories of entrepreneurship view the entrepreneur as bearing residual uncertainty. Scholar argued that individuals who have higher achievement motivation should prefer activities of intermediate risk because these types of activities will provide a challenge, yet appear to be attainable. On the other hand, individuals who score high on the motive to avoid failure will avoid intermediate risks.

Instead, they will prefer easy and safe under- takings or extremely difficult and risky ones. Following the lead of Atkinson, risk-taking propensity has been defined in the entrepreneurship literature as the willingness to take moderate risks. Despite these theoretical claims, previous research suggests that firm owners do not differ significantly from managers or even the general population in risk taking.

For example, Litsinger failed to find any difference between motel owners and motel managers on risk preference. Kogan and Wallach found that firm founders clustered around the mean risk-taking score of the general population. In comparisons of firm founders and managers, neither Babb and Babb nor Palich and Bagby found significant differences between the two groups in terms of risk-taking propensity. However, none of the studies identified if firm founders were low, moderate, or high risk-takers. Only Brockhaus tested for the actual level of risk taking, and he found that firm founders did prefer moderate risk but did not differ from managers in this regard.

Only one study found a difference between firm founders and managers in this motivation. In a study of 239 New England business executives, Begley found that risk-taking propensity was the only trait on which founders and non-founders differed. Begley failed to identify whether the level of entrepreneurial risk taking was low, moderate, or high. While these empirical findings suggest that risk taking may or may not be an entrepreneurial motivation, self-efficacy may be confounding the findings. Several recent evaluative studies using interviews and expert evaluations showed that firm founders objectively have a higher propensity for risk than do members of the general population, but that firm founders do not perceive their actions as risky.

Similarly, Sarasvathy, Simon, and Lave found that when expert firm founders were asked to evaluate the same entrepreneurial simulations as bankers, the firm founders saw opportunities in information that the bankers thought indicated risk. Thus, the measurement of risk-taking propensity may be confounded with high self-efficacy.

Tolerance for Ambiguity

Schere argued that tolerance for ambiguity is an important trait for entrepreneurs because the challenges and potential for success associated with business start-ups are by nature unpredictable. Budner defined tolerance for ambiguity as the propensity to view situations without clear outcomes as attractive rather than threatening. Because entrepreneurs continually face more uncertainty in their everyday environment than do managers of established organisations, entrepreneurs who remain in their jobs are likely to score high on tests for this trait than would managers. There is mixed support for this prediction.

Begley and Boyd found that firm founders scored significantly higher in tolerance for ambiguity than did managers, defined as non-founders working in business. In smaller sample studies, both Schere and Miller and Drodge found that firm founders were significantly higher in tolerance for ambiguity than were managers. Finally, based on a review of four additional studies, Sexton and Bowman identified tolerance for ambiguity as a distinguishing psychological characteristic between firm founders and managers. However, several studies did not match these findings.

Babb and Babb found no significant difference in tolerance for ambiguity between founders and non-founders of rural businesses in Northern Florida. Similarly, Begley found no significant differences between New England firm founders and managers on their tolerance for ambiguity. This inconsistency in findings and potential methodological problems in the research that provides support for the tolerance of ambiguity proposition suggests that we do not yet know if tolerance of ambiguity is a motivation that affects any part of the entrepreneurial process.

Locus of Control

Another motivational trait that has received attention is locus of control—the belief in the extent to which individuals believe that their actions or personal characteristics affect outcomes. Individuals who have an external locus of control believe that the outcome of an extent is out of their control, whereas individuals with an internal locus of control believe that their personal actions directly affect the outcome of an event. As McClelland discussed earlier, individuals who are high in nAch prefer situations in which they feel that they have direct control over outcomes or in which they feel that they can directly see how their effort affects outcomes of a given event.

This point was extended by Rotter who argued that individuals with an internal locus of control would be likely to seek entrepreneurial roles because they desire positions in which their actions have a direct impact on results. The research on locus of control suggests that firm founders differ from the general population in terms of locus of control. Shapero found that firm founders from Texas and Italy were more "internal" than other groups of professions reported by Rotter.

This same pattern holds with female firm founders versus the general female population and with Black firm founders versus the general Black population. While locus of control orientation differs between firm founders and the general public, most studies have not found a difference between firm founders and managers on locus of control, a result similar to the situation with studies on nAch.

For example, Babb and Babb found no differences in locus of control between founders and managers in small businesses in Northern Florida. Similarly, Brockhaus found that managers and owners of new businesses did not differ on locus of control. In a longitudinal study of students, Hull, Bosley, and Udell found that locus of control did not differentiate between students who went on to work in managerial positions and those who started their own business. Finally, in the studies of New England entrepreneurs, Begley and Begley and Boyd found that locus of control did not distinguish between founders and managers.

We suspect that one reason for the difference between firm founder and the general population, but not between founders and managers, is the similarity between founding a company and managing. Defining entrepreneurial situations as starting a company rather than working for others might not capture the real differences between entrepreneurial and non-entrepreneurial situations. For example, serving as a manager in a rapidly growing high-technology company might demand greater entrepreneurial motivations than starting a corner grocery store.

Self-efficacy

Self-efficacy is the belief in one's ability to muster and implement the necessary personal resources, skills, and competencies to attain a certain level of achievement on a given task. In other words, self-efficacy can be seen as task-specific self-confidence. Self-efficacy for a specific task has been shown to be a robust predictor of an individual's performance in that task and helps to explain why people of equal ability can perform differently. An individual with high self-efficacy for a given task will exert more effort for a greater length of time, persist through set backs, set and accept higher goals, and develop better plans and strategies for the task. A person with high self-efficacy will also take negative feedback in a more positive manner and use that feedback to improve their performance.

These attributes of self-efficacy may be important to the entrepreneurial process because these situations are often ambiguous ones in which effort, persistence, and planning are important. One study directly assessed the effect of self-efficacy on some dimension of the entrepreneurial process. Baum assessed firm founders in the architectural woodworking industry on a number of variables including general traits and motives, specific skills and competencies, situation-specific motivation, vision, and strategic action. In a LISREL model, Baum found that self-efficacy had a strong positive relationship with realised growth. In fact, it was the single best predictor in the entire array of variables.

Goal Setting

Tracy, Locke, and Renard conducted a study of the owners of small printing firms. Both concurrent and longitudinal measures of four aspects of performance were obtained: financial performance, growth, and innovation. The quantitative goals the entrepreneurs had for each outcome were significantly related to their corresponding outcomes, both concurrently and longitudinally. Baum, Locke, and Smith also found that growth goals were significantly related to the subsequent growth of architectural woodworking firms. Although there have been other studies of entrepreneurial goals, to our knowledge, only these two have related quantitative measures of goal difficulty to performance.

PROBLEMS WITH PREVIOUS RESEARCH ON HUMAN MOTIVATION AND ENTREPRENEURSHIP AND SUGGESTED SOLUTIONS TO THESE PROBLEMS

Despite the importance of including individual-level factors in a comprehensive explanation for the entrepreneurial process, previous studies of entrepreneurial motivation have often led to disappointing results. However, we believe that researchers should not conclude from this failure that human motivation is irrelevant to the entrepreneurial process. Rather, we suggest that there are specific reasons for the limited results obtained in previous research.

Controls for Opportunities

Previous research has suffered from a lack of control for the variation in the opportunities that different entrepreneurs pursue. To accurately measure the effects of motivation on entrepreneurial decisions, researchers need to control the effects of opportunities. As Venkataraman argued, a valuable opportunity for an individual is one that generates a level of profit that exceeds the entrepreneur's opportunity cost, a premium for the illiquidity of money, time, and effort expended, and a premium for bearing risk and uncertainty. Because some opportunities will exceed this threshold by a greater amount than will others, the nature of the opportunity will influence entrepreneurial decisions.

Researchers need to know the magnitude of the force exerted by the opportunities themselves to accurately estimate the effect of the individual motivations on entrepreneurial decisions. In the absence of such controls, one cannot know if the effects observed represent the effects of individual motivations or are artifacts of unobserved correlation between the opportunities and the people who pursue them. Prior research has generally failed to control the effect of opportunities by examining entrepreneurs pursuing different opportunities without explicitly modeling the value of the different opportunities pursued.

In addition, prior studies have generally compared managers with firm founders. However, human motivations can influence the tendency of people to engage in entrepreneurial activities only if those activities are possible. If people have not discovered entrepreneurial opportunities or have discovered opportunities but cannot act on those discoveries, it is impossible to determine if their individual motivations make them more or less likely than others to act on entrepreneurial opportunities.

Therefore, one cannot tell from studies that compare managers to firm founders whether certain motivations influence people to make entrepreneurial decisions unless researchers have ensured that the managers have discovered opportunities and have measured the value of those opportunities. Otherwise, researchers might only capture the fact that some managers have all of the right motivations, but no opportunities in which to use them. We offer four suggestions to researchers interested in examining the effect of motivations on entrepreneurial decisions about how to deal with variation in opportunities.

First, researchers could explore settings in which potential entrepreneurs pursue reasonably identical opportunities. For example, every year, many potential entrepreneurs evaluate and pursue opportunities to purchase McDonald's franchises. When a person applies to be a McDonald's franchisee or company-owned outlet manager, one applies only to be part of the system rather than to select a particular outlet. Therefore, the opportunities to which people respond in this setting are identical. By comparing the motivations of a sample of people seek to be McDonald's franchisees with people who seek to be McDonald's company-owned outlet managers, researchers can determine the contributions of particular motivations on the decision to entrepreneur.

Second, as a variety of researchers are beginning to do, scholars could employ experimental designs in which potential entrepreneurs are asked to make a series of entrepreneurial decisions in a controlled simulation. By measuring the motivations of potential entrepreneurs and examining the correlation between the motivations and the decisions made in these simulations, researchers could determine how motivations influence entrepreneurial decisions.

Third, the most obvious means of controlling opportunity are to use a sample of entrepreneurs within the same industry and country and to measure aspects of the environment that might vary within industry and region. We recommend these approaches to limiting other sources of variance than motivations from studies of motivation and entrepreneurship. Fourth, as some researchers are beginning to do, scholars could employ third parties to code the value of potential opportunities.

For example, researchers could explore the propensity of inventors to found companies based on their inventions. Because all inventors are at risk of exploiting their inventions through firm formation, this setting provides a useful context in which to explore the decision to entrepreneur. By partialing out the externally evaluated value of the opportunities, researchers could determine whether motivations influence the decision to entrepreneur, net of the effects of the value of the opportunity.

Entrepreneurship as a Process

Much of the prior research has looked at entrepreneurship as a profession that certain types of people adopt, rather than as a process that occurs over time. This approach is problematic because the appropriate conceptual lens through which to look at entrepreneurship is as a dynamic process. Because entrepreneurship is episodic and much entrepreneurial action is not long lasting, it is unrealistic to model motivation as dividing entrepreneurs and other members of society into two groups.

In fact, relatively little of the motivation research on entrepreneurship has considered the effects of motivation on specific steps in the entrepreneurial process. Most studies on motivation and entrepreneurship adopt static designs that seek to determine if firm founders are different from each other, managers, or the general population at the moment the two groups are measured. This approach makes two problematic assumptions. First, it assumes that a given motivation influences all steps in the entrepreneurial process equally, and that the effects of a given motivation do not select out some people at earlier stages in the process.

Second, it assumes that, at the moment in which the founders are compared to the others, the founders who are still in charge of the organisations that they founded represent the population of people who engage in entrepreneurial activity. Because entrepreneurship is a process, with tremendous selection at each step, we believe that these assumptions are quite faulty. The motivations that allow progression from opportunity recognition to resource assembly might not lead from financial assembly to first sales. For example, to assemble resources, a person might need to be highly confident. Those people lacking sufficient overconfidence to assemble resources are selected out of the entrepreneurial process.

If there is very little variation in over-confidence among the people who have resources and seek to reach first sales, overconfidence will have no effect on achieving first sales. For these reasons, we believe that it may not be possible to examine the direct effects of a lead entrepreneur's motivations on the financial performance of a new company that the individual founds. The effects of motivation might be captured by the intervening variables in any causal model of the effects of motivation on firm performance. For example, those higher in nAch might be more likely to obtain venture capital financing. However, once venture capital financing is measured, there is no effect of nAch on firm performance.

We offer several specific suggestions for how researchers could better think about how motivations influence the entrepreneurial process. First, researchers could incorporate motivations into a dynamic evolutionary perspective on entrepreneurship by using motivations to distinguish those individuals who select out at different steps in the entrepreneurial process. For example, motivations could separate those individuals who positively evaluate opportunities from those who do not, those who obtain outside funding from those who do not, those who continue to pursue opportunities from those who abandon the effort, or those who pursue rapid rather than slow growth.

The pursuit of opportunity provides a good example. As Aldrich and Zimmer explain, "opportunities are irrelevant unless taken advantage of, and people vary widely in their ability to seise opportunities". We agree, but would argue that people also differ widely in their motivation to seise opportunities. It would be interesting to know if certain motivations predispose people to take action in response to the discovery of opportunities. One might argue, for example, that people higher in self-efficacy will be more likely to seek financing to exploit opportunities than will people lower in self-efficacy. Because the process of financing exposes a person's entrepreneurial ideas to the scrutiny of skeptical others, those people willing to expose their ideas to scrutiny might have to be more confident than those who will not. Second, researchers could theorise more deeply about how motivation might impact entrepreneurial decisions.

Rather than falling back on the stock idea that firm founders must be fundamentally different types of people from other members of society, we suggest researchers consider how motivations might influence some people to make different decisions from others in the entrepreneurial process. For example, inventors higher in selfefficacy might found firms to exploit their inventions while inventors lower in self-efficacy might license their technology to others. Similarly, entrepreneurs with a greater need for independence might self-finance new firms, whereas those with a lesser need for independence might seek venture capital. We also suggest that it is not necessarily important for entrepreneurship researchers to show that specific motivations influence the financial performance of new firms.

If financial performance of a new firm is conditional on the ability of an entrepreneur to create the firm, and that act of creation depends heavily on human motivation, then human motivation matters to entrepreneurship even if motivation has no direct effect on the performance of the newly founded firm. In fact, we would expect that the more significant a firm that an entrepreneur founds, the less their motivations influence the firm formation process. For example, the more significant the new firm that an entrepreneur builds, the less influence they will have personally on day-to-day operations, and the less that we would expect the financial performance of the firm to be affected by their personal motivations.

Meta-analysis

The third criticism of previous research is the failure to use meta-analysis. The ability to combine the results of scores or hundreds of individual studies into a single statistic was not always available to researchers. This sometimes led people who conducted narrative reviews to underestimate the effect of the variable being considered; for example, non-significant results in single studies may be due to sampling error rather than invalidity. Although metaanalytic results are not available for all the motivations we discuss, such data, where available, throw new light on some motivations.

Wrong Motives

A fourth criticism of extant research is its tendency to study the wrong motives. Some motives are more relevant to entrepreneurial activity than others. For example, risk-taking propensity as measured by self-perception and tolerance for ambiguity has long been assumed to be an entrepreneurial motive, but the evidence so far is only equivocal. Regarding risk, perhaps the problem has been that people cannot perceive the riskiness of their own actions, or that what is risky to one person is not risky to another. For example, several recent studies using interviews and expert evaluations showed that entrepreneurs objectively have a higher propensity for risk than either entrepreneurs or the general population but that entrepreneurs do not perceive their actions as risky.

Thus, the effects of risk-taking propensity may be confounded with the high self-efficacy of entrepreneurs. We suggest that researchers better define the motives that they think are important and focus on more precise measures of them. One way to do that would be for researchers to go back to the underlying psychological literature and examine how researchers have dealt with the nuances of theorising about and measuring the same motives in other settings.

If psychologists have figured a way around the problems of using self-perceptions in the measurement of risky Behaviour, like drug usage, those same techniques can be brought to bear on the measurement of risky behaviour in entrepreneurial settings. We believe that another important step for research on motivation and entrepreneurship would be for researchers to develop more complete models of the entrepreneurial process before examining the effects of particular motives on particular activities. A fuller understanding of the role of motivations in the overall process would require consideration of factors other than motives. We suggest that researchers develop explanations that include the variety of such influences.

Indirect Effects

A fifth criticism has been the failure to look for indirect effects of motivational traits. Most, though not all, researchers have assumed that traits and motives have direct effects on outcomes and this may be true to some extent.

However, an increasing body of literature is revealing that traits affect action indirectly through other mechanisms. For example, in the general realm of work, conscientiousness is a reliable predictor of performance, but there is considerable evidence that the effects of conscientiousness on work performance are mediated by situation-specific factors such as goal setting and goal commitment. Similarly, Bandura has argued that locus of control is not a strong, direct predictor of performance in a task; and studies have shown that the effects of self-efficacy mediate the effects of locus of control when self-efficacy is added to the equation.

Therefore, locus of control effects reported in the entrepreneurship literature might be proxying unobserved self-efficacy. One recent study to have taken the approach of considering indirect effects of motivation in the setting of entrepreneurial action is that of Baum, who studied the growth of small companies in the architectural woodworking industry. They included variables from five separate domains: traits and motives, skills and abilities, situation-specific motivation, business strategies, and environmental factors.

They combined the measures within each domain into single indexes and related these indexes to each other and to venture growth. All the domains played a role in venture growth but the effects of motives were all indirect. Motives worked through skills, situation-specific motivation, and strategies to affect growth.

Given the indirect effects observed in this study, we suggest that researchers consider such indirect patterns in their explanations for the effect of motivation on entrepreneurial action.

Definitions

A sixth criticism has stemmed from a lack of consistent definitions of entrepreneurship. In general, the definition of what constitutes entrepreneurial activity varies significantly across studies. For example, McClelland viewed managerial positions of certain types such as sales as one that demanded entrepreneurial skills, whereas much of the recent work in the applied field of management has sought to compare entrepreneurs to managers.

Therefore, it is unclear if the samples from these different studies are comparable, or even represent entrepreneurship in a meaningful way. This point, of course, brings us back to the importance of a common definition of entrepreneurship. As we indicated earlier, we advocate the definition proposed by Shane and Venkataraman. Whether researchers adopt this particular definition, however, is less important than the existence of a common definition. Without a common definition, it will not be possible to accumulate findings that are comparable from study to study.

HOW MOTIVATIONS INFLUENCE ENTREPRENEURSHIP

We suggest how human motivations might influence the entrepreneurial process. We offer this example to help future researchers design empirical tests of the role of motivation in entrepreneurship. We begin with the set of human motivations that psychologists have shown to influence many aspects of human Behaviour. These include the motivations that we described earlier in the study, in particular, nAch, locus of control, desire for independence, passion, and drive. We propose that entrepreneurship is a process that begins with the recognition of an entrepreneurial opportunity and is followed by the development of an idea for how to pursue that opportunity, the evaluation of the feasibility of the opportunity, the development of the product or service that will be provided to customers, assembly of human and financial resources, organisational design, and the pursuit of customers.

We suggest that some or all of the motivations influence the transition of individuals from one stage of the entrepreneurial process to another. In some cases, all of the motivations might matter. In other cases, only some of the motivations might matter. The relative magnitudes of how much each motivation matters will likely vary, depending on the part of the process under investigation.

In fact, it is quite plausible that motivations that influence one part of the process have all of their effects at that stage in the process and have no effects on later stages in the process. In this example, motivations are not the only things that influence these transitions. Cognitive factors, including knowledge, skills, and abilities, certainly matter. All action is the result of the combination or integration of motivation and cognition. First, the entrepreneurs need to have some knowledge, especially of the industry and of any relevant technology that is critical to success. They can hire people with certain specialised skills that they lack, but they must possess enough expertise to know that they are doing the right thing. Second, the entrepreneur must have skills. The necessary skills will depend on the circumstances, but they may include such factors as selling and bargaining, leadership, planning, decision-making, problem solving, team building, communication, and conflict management.

Third, the entrepreneur needs to have the requisite abilities, including intelligence. Possessing the necessary KSAs enables the entrepreneurs to develop a viable vision, including a strategy for the organisation and to carry it out successfully. Motivation helps the entrepreneur to acquire such KSAs in the first place and provide the impetus and energy to implement the needed actions. The human capital literature in entrepreneurship has begun to show the effect of certain types of knowledge and skills on the start-up and resource assembly parts of this process.

The opportunities themselves certainly matter. Prior research has shown that such things as the possession of a patented technology make individuals more likely to engage in the entrepreneurial process. One would expect that identification of a large market or a high margin product would do the same. First, opportunities may interact in interesting ways with the attributes of people. Second, as much of the macro-level research has shown, the willingness to engage in entrepreneurial activities depends on such things as the legal system of the country in which the entrepreneur operates, the age of the industry, the availability of capital in the economy, the condition of capital markets, and the state of the overall economy.

We believe that these factors are important, but that it might also be interesting to know whether motivations of particular people lead to different types of entrepreneurial action under different environmental conditions. Motivations might be more or less stronger than these other factors in the degree that they influence particular transition points. In addition, there might be important and interesting interaction effects between motivations and opportunities, KSAs, and environmental factors.

The relative importance of different categories of factors, their independent and combined effects, and their relative importance at different stages of the entrepreneurial process are clearly important theoretical and empirical questions that remain largely unexplored. We hope that researchers will begin to explore them because they appear to us to be central issues in the field of entrepreneurship.

MOTIVATION FACTORS AND THEORIES

MOTIVATION FACTORS

- When we look at the psychology of human Behaviour we can begin to understand certain baseline motivations which draw adults to on line social networks. Abraham Maslow published his theory of human motivation in 1943. Its popularity continues unabated. Like his colleague Carl Rogers, Maslow believed that actualisation was the driving force of human personality, Motivation and Personality. Maslow's great insight was to place actualisation into a hierarchy of motivation. Self-actualisation, as he called it, is the highest drive, but before a person can turn to it, he or she must satisfy other, lower motivations like hunger, safety and belonging. The hierarchy has five levels.

- Physiological (hunger, thirst, shelter, sex, etc.).
- Safety (security, protection from physical and emotional harm).
- Social (affection, belonging, acceptance, friendship)
- Esteem (also called ego). The internal ones are self respect, autonomy, achievement and the external ones are status, recognition, and attention.
- Self-actualisation (doing things).

Maslow points out that the hierarchy is dynamic; the dominant need is always shifting. The hierarchy does not exist by itself, but is affected by the situation and the general culture. Satisfaction is relative. Douglas McGregor makes it the building block for his Theory X and Theory Y. A 1990s example of self actualisation may be surfing the Internet. Empirical research has confirmed the first three levels, but has not done so for the fourth and fifth levels of esteem and self-actualisation. Some have noted that Maslow's hierarchy follows the life cycle. A newborn baby's needs are almost entirely physiological. As the baby grows, it needs safety, then love. Toddlers are eager for social interaction. Teenagers are anxious about social needs; young adults are concerned with esteem and only more mature people transcend the first four levels to spend much time self actualising. Based on the observations across numerous networking platforms and reflect on the past definitions of human motivation we can see that social networks on line provide a primary motivation for adults in the category of self actualisation, or doing things. Maslow defines self actualisation as growth-motivated rather than deficiency-motivated:

- Based on observations and interview as suggested, provide a general categorisation of the factors that enhance individual growth for adults participating in on line social networks. Each of these factors will be defined in greater detail in future articles post.
- With all the hype, craze and media coverage of social networking platforms, *i.e.*, Facebook and Linkedin, many adults are drawn to the medium to learn what the hype is all about.
- Once adults enter networks and learn the "tools of the trade" many are amazed to find the presence of other adults they know and many they don't already engaged with the medium.

- Adults begin to find association with groups, causes, forums, media and other affinities which relate to their interest both personally and professionally.
- The predominant business segment using social networks today is employment recruiters. However, as the medium and adult participation has grown there is an exponential growth of business opportunities that adults are learning to facilitate using social networks as the medium.
- Adults, and their businesses, are applying creative ways to use the technology behind social computing to extend its value to both personal and professional needs.
- When you consider the creative possibilities of social networks adults expect to the formation of some economic and social value to be derived from their participation whether currently or in the future.

The expectation of individual growth and satisfaction is high.These factors combined with the media hype over social networking are the motivating issues which are driving millions of adults to the medium at annual growth rates of 70 per cent and more. The opportunity to capitalise economically is emerging quickly. Word of mouth will fuel growth rates faster than any other technological medium in our past.

THEORIES OF MOTIVATION

Contribution of Robert Owen

Though Owen is considered to be paternalistic in his view, his contribution is of a considerable significance in the theories of motivation. During the early years of the nineteenth century, Owen's textile mill at New Lanark in Scotland was the scene of some novel ways of treating people. His view was that people were similar to machines. A machine that is looked after properly, cared for and maintained well, performs efficiently, reliably and lastingly, similarly people are likely to be more efficient if they are taken care of. Robert Owen practiced what he preached and introduced such things as employee housing and company shop. His ideas on this and other matters were considered to be too revolutionary for that time.

Jeremy Bentham's "The Carrot and the Stick Approach"

Possibly the essence of the traditional view of people at work can be best appreciated by a brief look at the work of this English philosopher, whose ideas were also developed in the early years of the Industrial Revolution, around 1800. Bentham's view was that all people are self-interested and are motivated by the desire to avoid pain and find pleasure. Any worker will work only if the reward is big enough, or the punishment sufficiently unpleasant. This view - the 'carrot and stick' approach - was built into the philosophies of the age and is still to be found, especially in the older, more traditional sectors of industry. The various leading theories of motivation and motivators seldom make reference to the carrot and the stick. This metaphor relates, of course, to the use of rewards and penalties in order to induce desired Behaviour.

It comes from the old story that to make a donkey move, one must put a carrot in front of him or dab him with a stick from behind. Despite all the research on the theories of motivation, reward and punishment are still considered strong motivators. For centuries, however, they were too often thought of as the only forces that could motivate people. At the same time, in all theories of motivation, the inducements of some kind of 'carrot' are recognised. Often this is money in the form of pay or bonuses. Even though money is not the only motivating force, it has been and will continue to be an important one.

The trouble with the money 'carrot' approach is that too often everyone gets a carrot, regardless of performance through such practices as salary increase and promotion by seniority, automatic 'merit' increases, and executive bonuses not based on individual manager performance. It is as simple as this: If a person put a donkey in a pen full of carrots and then stood outside with a carrot, would the donkey be encouraged to come out of the pen ? The 'stick', in the form of fear-fear of loss of job, loss of income, reduction of bonus, demotion, or some other penalty–has been and continues to be a strong motivator.

Yet it is admittedly not the best kind. It often gives rise to defensive or retaliatory Behaviour, such as union organisation, poor-quality work, executive indifference, failure of a manager to take any risks in decision making or even dishonesty. But fear of penalty cannot be overlooked. Whether managers are first-level supervisors or chief executives, the power of their position to give or with hold rewards or impose penalties of various kinds gives them an ability to control, to a very great extent, the economic and social well-being of their subordinates.

Abraham Maslow's "Need Hierarchy Theory"

One of the most widely theories of motivation is the hierarchy of needs theory put forth by psychologist Abraham Maslow. Maslow saw human needs in the form of a hierarchy, ascending from the lowest to the highest, and he concluded that when one set of needs is satisfied, this kind of need ceases to be a motivator. As per his theory this needs are: These are important needs for sustaining the human life.

Food, water, warmth, shelter, sleep, medicine and education are the basic physiological needs which fall in the primary list of need satisfaction. Maslow was of an opinion that until these needs were satisfied to a degree to maintain life, no other motivating factors can work. These are the needs to be free of physical danger and of the fear of losing a job, property, food or shelter. It also includes protection against any emotional harm. Since, people are social beings, they need to belong and be accepted by others. People try to satisfy their need for affection, acceptance and friendship. Once people begin to satisfy their need to belong, they tend to want to be held in esteem both by themselves and by others.

This kind of need produces such satisfaction as power, prestige status and self-confidence. It includes both internal esteem factors like self-respect, autonomy and achievements and external esteem factors such as states, recognition and attention. Maslow regards this as the highest need in his hierarchy. It is the drive to become what one is capable of becoming, it includes growth, achieving one's potential and self-fulfilment. It is to maximise one's potential and to accomplish something.

From the standpoint of motivation, the theory would say that although no need is ever fully gratified, a substantially satisfied need no longer motivates. So if you want to motivate someone, you need to understand what level of the hierarchy that person is on and focus on satisfying those needs or needs above that level. Maslow's need theory has received wide recognition, particularly among practicing managers.

This can be attributed to the theory's intuitive logic and ease of understanding. However, research does not validate these theory. Maslow provided no empirical evidence and other several studies that sought to validate the theory found no support for it.

"Theory X and Theory Y" of Douglas McGregor

McGregor, in his book "The Human side of Enterprise" states that people inside the organisation can be managed in two ways. The first is basically negative, which falls under the category X and the other is basically positive, which falls under the category Y.

After viewing the way in which the manager dealt with employees, McGregor concluded that a manager's view of the nature of human beings is based on a certain grouping of assumptions and that he or she tends to mold his or her Behaviour towards subordinates according to these assumptions.

Under the assumptions of theory X:

- Employees inherently do not like work and whenever possible, will attempt to avoid it.
- Because employees dislike work, they have to be forced, coerced or threatened with punishment to achieve goals.
- Employees avoid responsibilities and do not work fill formal directions are issued.
- Most workers place a greater importance on security over all other factors and display little ambition.

In contrast under the assumptions of theory Y:

- Physical and mental effort at work is as natural as rest or play.

- People do exercise self-control and self-direction and if they are committed to those goals.
- Average human beings are willing to take responsibility and exercise imagination, ingenuity and creativity in solving the problems of the organisation.
- That the way the things are organised, the average human being's brainpower is only partly used.

On analysis of the assumptions it can be detected that theory X assumes that lower-order needs dominate individuals and theory Y assumes that higher-order needs dominate individuals. An organisation that is run on Theory X lines tends to be authoritarian in nature, the word "authoritarian" suggests such ideas as the "power to enforce obedience" and the "right to command".

In contrast Theory Y organisations can be described as "participative", where the aims of the organisation and of the individuals in it are integrated; individuals can achieve their own goals best by directing their efforts towards the success of the organisation. However, this theory has been criticised widely for generalisation of work and human Behaviour.

Contribution of Rensis Likert

Likert developed a refined classification, breaking down organisations into four management systems:

- 1st System – Primitive authoritarian.
- 2nd System – Benevolent authoritarian.
- 3rd System – Consultative.
- 4th System – Participative.

As per the opinion of Likert, the 4th system is the best, not only for profit organisations, but also for non-profit firms.

Frederick Herzberg's Motivation-hygiene Theory

Frederick has tried to modify Maslow's need Hierarchy theory. His theory is also known as two-factor theory or Hygiene theory. He stated that there are certain satisfiers and dissatisfiers for employees at work. Intrinsic factors are related to job satisfaction, while extrinsic factors are associated with dissatisfaction.

He devised his theory on the question: "What do people want from their jobs ?" He asked people to describe in detail, such situations when they felt exceptionally good or exceptionally bad. From the responses that he received, he concluded that opposite of satisfaction is not dissatisfaction. Removing dissatisfying characteristics from a job does not necessarily make the job satisfying. He states that presence of certain factors in the organisation is natural and the presence of the same does not lead to motivation. However, their non-presence leads to demotivation. In similar manner there are certain factors, the absence of which causes no dissatisfaction, but their presence has motivational impact.

Examples of Hygiene factors are:

- Security, status, relationship with subordinates, personal life, salary, work conditions, relationship with supervisor and company policy and administration.

Examples of Motivational factors are:

- Growth prospectus job advancement, responsibility, challenges, recognition and achievements.

Contributions of Elton Mayo

The work of Elton Mayo is famously known as "Hawthorne Experiments". He conducted Behavioural experiments at the Hawthorne Works of the American Western Electric Company in Chicago. He made some illumination experiments, introduced breaks in between the work performance and also introduced refreshments during the pause's.

On the basis of this he drew the conclusions that motivation was a very complex subject. It was not only about pay, work condition and morale but also included psychological and social factors. Although this research has been criticised from many angles, the central conclusions drawn were:

- People are motivated by more than pay and conditions.
- The need for recognition and a sense of belonging are very important.
- Attitudes towards work are strongly influenced by the group.

Vroom's Valence x Expectancy Theory

The most widely accepted explanations of motivation has been propounded by Victor Vroom. His theory is commonly known as expectancy theory. The theory argues that the strength of a tendency to act in a specific way depends on the strength of an expectation that the act will be followed by a given outcome and on the attractiveness of that outcome to the individual to make this simple, expectancy theory says that an employee can be motivated to perform better when their is a belief that the better performance will lead to good performance appraisal and that this shall result into realisation of personal goal in form of some reward. Therefore an employee is:

- Motivation = Valence x Expectancy.

The theory focuses on three things:

- Efforts and performance relationship.
- Performance and reward relationship.
- Rewards and personal goal relationship.

This leads us to a conclusion that:

The Porter and Lawler Model

Lyman W. Porter and Edward E. Lawler developed a more complete version of motivation depending upon expectancy theory. Actual performance in a job is primarily determined by the effort spent. But it is also affected by the person's ability to do the job and also by individual's perception of what the required task is.

So performance is the responsible factor that leads to intrinsic as well as extrinsic rewards. These rewards, along with the equity of individual leads to satisfaction. Hence, satisfaction of the individual depends upon the fairness of the reward.

Clayton Alderfer's ERG Theory

Alderfer has tried to rebuild the hierarchy of needs of Maslow into another model named ERG, *i.e.*, Existence–Relatedness–Growth. The existence group is concerned mainly with providing basic material existence. The second group is the individuals need to maintain interpersonal relationship with other members in the group. The final group is the intrinsic desire to grow and develop personally.

The major conclusions of this theory are:

- In an individual, more than one need may be operative at the same time.
- If a higher need goes unsatisfied than the desire to satisfy a lower need intensifies.
- It also contains the frustration-regression dimension.

McClelland's Theory of Needs

David McClelland has developed a theory on three types of motivating needs:

- Need for Power.
- Need for Affiliation.
- Need for Achievement.

Basically people for high need for power are inclined towards influence and control. They like to be at the center and are good orators. They are demanding in nature, forceful in manners and ambitious in life. They can be motivated to perform if they are given key positions or power positions. In the second category are the people who are social in nature. They try to affiliate themselves with individuals and groups. They are driven by love and faith.

They like to build a friendly environment around themselves. Social recognition and affiliation with others provides them motivation. People in the third area are driven by the challenge of success and the fear of failure. Their need for achievement is moderate and they set for themselves moderately difficult tasks. They are analytical in nature and take calculated risks. Such people are motivated to perform when they see atleast some chances of success. McClelland observed that with the advancement in hierarchy the need for power and achievement increased rather than Affiliation. He also observed that people who were at the top, later ceased to be motivated by this drives.

Equity Theory

As per the equity theory of J. Stacey Adams, people are motivated by their beliefs about the reward structure as being fair or unfair, relative to the inputs. People have a tendency to use subjective Judgement to balance the outcomes and inputs in the relationship for comparisons between different individuals. Accordingly: If people feel that they are not equally rewarded they either reduce the quantity or quality of work or migrate to some other organisation. However, if people perceive that they are rewarded higher, they may be motivated to work harder.

Reinforcement Theory

B.F. Skinner, who propounded the reinforcement theory, holds that by designing the environment properly, individuals can be motivated. Instead of considering internal factors like impressions, feelings, attitudes and other cognitive Behaviour, individuals are directed by what happens in the environment external to them.

Skinner states that work environment should be made suitable to the individuals and that punishments actually leads to frustration and de-motivation. Hence, the only way to motivate is to keep on making positive changes in the external environment of the organisation.

Goal Setting Theory of Edwin Locke

Instead of giving vague tasks to people, specific and pronounced objectives, help in achieving them faster. As the clarity is high, a goal orientation also avoids any misunder-standings in the work of the employees. The goal setting theory states that when the goals to be achieved are set at a higher standard than in that case employees are motivated to perform better and put in maximum effort. It revolves around the concept of "Self-efficacy", *i.e.*, individual's belief that he or she is capable of performing a hard task.

Cognitive Evaluation Theory

As per this theory a shift from external rewards to internal rewards results into motivation. It believes that even after the stoppage of external stimulus, internal stimulus survives. It relates to the pay structure in the organisation. Instead of treating external factors like pay, incentives, promotion etc and internal factors like interests, drives, responsibility etc, separately, they should be treated as contemporary to each other. The cognition is to be such that even when external motivators are not there the internal motivation continues. However, practically extrinsic rewards are given much more weightage.

OBJECTIVES AND ACHIEVEMENTS OF MOTIVATION

MAIN OBJECTIVES OF MOTIVATION

Self-preservation, whether this is pointed directly to survivial or towards our image of ourselves painted by our beliefs and ideals. What I mean by this is that we have in our mind a view point of who we are and we trive to accomplish this in either advancement or a continuation of our currant state. This personal view point might look down upon theft, and so seeing a theft we might feel "motivated" to call police, in order to up keep our currant view of what kind of person we see ourselves as.

ACHIEVEMENT

Over the years, behavioural scientists have noticed that some people have an intense desire to achieve something, while others may not seem that concerned about their achievements. This phenomenon has attracted a lot of discussions and debates. Scientists have observed that people with a high level of achievement motivation exhibit certain characteristics. Achievement motivation is the tendency to endeavor for success and to choose goal oriented success or failure activities. Achievement motivation forms to be the basic for a good life. People who are oriented towards achievement, in general, enjoy life and feel in control. Being motivated keeps people dynamic and gives them self-respect. They set moderately difficult but easily achievable targets, which help them, achieve their objectives. They do not set up extremely difficult or extremely easy targets. By doing this they ensure that they only undertake tasks that can be achieved by them. Achievement motivated people prefer to work on a problem rather than leaving the outcome to chance. It is also seen that achievement motivated people seem to be more concerned with their personal achievement rather than the rewards of success. It is generally seen that achievement motivated people evidenced a significantly higher rate of advancement in their company compared to others. Programmes and courses designed, involves seven "training inputs."

The first step refers to the process through which achievement motivation thinking is taught to the person. The second step helps participants understand their own individuality and goals. The third assist participants in practicing achievement-related actions in cases, role-plays, and real life. A fourth refers to practicing of achievement-related actions in business and other games. A fifth input encourages participants to relate the achievement Behaviour model to their own Behaviour, self-image, and goals.

The sixth Programme facilitates participants to develop a personal plan of action. Finally, the course provides participants with feedback on their progress towards achieving objectives and targets. Achievement motivation as a branch of study has greatly established its prominence. A number of companies are now training their employees in the same.

ENTREPRENEURIAL COMPETENCIES

Every career draws on the competencies of an individual. Some of these competencies may be general and some peculiar to the chosen career. You may understand competencies to mean abilities and skills.

However, we would desist from calling these as personality traits as such a conceptualisation only reinforces the mistaken belief that entrepreneurs are born rather than made. We believe that recognition of these competencies as abilities and skills makes entrepreneurship as a teachable and learnable behaviour.

We orient you towards a set of entrepreneurial competencies developed by the Entrepreneurship Development Institute of India Ahemdabad. These competencies were identified by a thorough research procedure based on critical analysis of the case studies of the successful entrepreneurs.

ENTREPRENEURIAL COMPETENCIES IDENTIFIED BY THE EDI

- Acting out of choice rather than compulsion, taking the lead rather than waiting for others to start.
- A mindset where one is trained to look for business opportunities from everyday experiences. Recall 'oranges' example.
- A 'never say die' attitude, not giving up easily, striving Information seeking continuously until success is achieved.
- Knowing who knows, consulting experts, reading of relevant material and an overall openness to ideas and information.
- Attention to details and observance of established standards and norms.
- Taking personal pains to complete a task as scheduled.
- Concern for conservation of time, money and effort.
- Breaking up the complex whole into parts, close examination of the parts and inferring about the whole *e.g.*, simultaneously attending to production, marketing and financial aspects (parts) of the overall business strategy (the whole).
- Observing the symptoms, diagnosing and curing.
- Not being afraid of the risks associated with business and relying on one's capabilities to successfully manage these.
- Conveying emphatically one's vision and convincing others of its value.
- Eliciting support of others in the venture.
- Providing leadership.
- Ensuring the progress of the venture as planned.
- Believing in employee well being as the key to competitiveness and success and initiating programmes of employee welfare.

The self-administered questionnaire in the annexure to this chapter would help you measure where you stand on these competencies. Given that these competencies matter in entrepreneurial success. EDI estimates that development of these competencies can substantially bring down incidence of business failures/industrial sickness.

DEVELOPING COMPETENCIES

'Awareness,' they say, is the first step towards 'improvement' and 'success.' Now that you are aware of the critical competencies for entrepreneurial success and also have a measure of your scores on these, it is appropriate that you also think in terms of how to improve your scores. Suppose, you find yourself lacking in the competency - 'opportunity spotting,' you may start practicing to think like an entrepreneur. With just a little change in perspective, the world changes for you. Similarly you may work on the other competencies as well.

MOTIVATION AND PRODUCTIVITY IN THE LIBRARY

Employee motivation is important in libraries, as in any other organisation. This chapter attempts to identify the place of motivation in developing human resources in the library. This attempt begins with the need to define human resources, human resources development, and motivation, and to discuss theories of motivation and the literature of motivation as they pertain to libraries.

THE CONCEPT OF HUMAN RESOURCES

UNECA conceptualises human resources as the body of knowledge, skills, attitudes, physical, and managerial efforts required to manipulate land, capital, and technology, to produce goods and services for human consumption and welfare.

Human resources includes:

- Technical skill and abilities acquired from education, training, and experience. It indicates the ability to use knowledge, methods, and techniques in the performance of library tasks.
- Human skills, which is the ability to work with and through people. It includes the understanding of motivation and the application of effective leadership.
- Conceptual skill, which incorporates the ability to understand the complexity of the overall organisation.

Human resources includes two major activities. The first is recruitment, selection, compensation, discipline, appraisal, and welfare of employees. The second is working with employees to improve their efficiency and productivity.

The activities that enable individuals and groups to acquire new knowledge and skills and assume new roles and responsibilities are usually referred to as human resources development.

HUMAN RESOURCES DEVELOPMENT

Nadler defines human resources development as a "series of organised activities conducted within a specified time and designed to produce Behaviour change" in individuals and organisations. The key point is learning. Ojo remarks that, the "organised activities contained in the definition provided above embraced a carefully developed learning activity with identifiable components of objectives, actions, and evaluation. These conditions must exist in all forms of human resources development." Ideally, human resources development should provide solutions to problems such as a shortage of employees, employees who are inadequately skilled and efficient, high turnover, organisational expansion, career planning, and training needs.

MOTIVATION IN THE DEVELOPMENT OF HUMAN RESOURCES IN THE LIBRARY

A library is an organisation whose mission is to provide information to its users. The library staff are the human resources, who provide information services using library resources. How well the services are provided depends on how well the human resources are motivated and developed. Motivation is crucial to the development of human resources in the library in the following ways:

- Maslow's hierarchy of needs is apparent in library employment. Acquiring a job and looking for job security help satisfy physiological and safety needs. When those needs are satisfied, employees look to their need for belonging and self-esteem. The need for self-esteem and self-actualisation are represented in library human resources development efforts that focus on training, creativity, problem-solving, and so on.
- The maintenance and motivational factors of Herzberg's two-factor theory play important roles in the development of human resources in the library. Herzberg's believed that motivators must be build into the job. These include responsibility, autonomy, respect and recognition from superiors, a sense of wellbeing, and the opportunity to have one's ideas adopted.
- Equity theory indicates likewise has a place in the library. Workers compare their pay, work schedules, benefits, or any reward with what is being received by other employees. Unless the reward system is carefully administered, it could result in problems of perceived or actual inequity.
- Expectancy theory can be used in the development of human resources in libraries. The logic of expectancy theory is that individuals exert effort for a performance that results in preferred rewards. Expectancy can be influenced by selecting individuals with particular skills and abilities, providing training, and providing support to achieve a particular level of performance.

STRATEGIES FOR INCREASING MOTIVATION

Job Enrichment

The idea of quality work life has received attention for several decades. Workers become increasingly dissatisfied and frustrated by routine tasks. The result may be lower output, poor attitude, lower quality, absenteeism, high turnover, and pressure for better conditions and greater participation in decision-making.

Herzberg contributed the theory of job enrichment as a motivational technique. Job enrichment provides employees with an opportunity to grow psychologically and mature in a job. Job enrichment attempts to make the job itself motivational. Research indicates that jobs higher in enrichment factors result in higher satisfaction; however, research also indicates that enriched jobs require more training time and result in slightly higher anxiety and stress. Job enrichment increases a job's range and depth, which refers to the number of activities and the autonomy, responsibility, discretion, and control.

Merit Pay

The money that employees receive is actually a package made up of salary, and other fringe benefits such as transport, housing, furniture, medical allowance. Others include meal subsidy and utility allowances. The motivation theories discussed, suggest that and fringe benefits can have some influence on effort and persistence. The money that employees receive is actually a package of salary and benefits.

Theories of motivation suggest that salary and benefits have influence on effort and persistence. Pay has the potential to satisfy each of the five needs in Maslow's hierarchy. In Herzberg's two-factor model pay is a maintenance factor that should not contribute significantly to motivation. In expectancy theory, pay can satisfy a variety of needs and influence choice and Behaviour, while in equity theory, pay is a major outcome that one compares with other employees.

A number of studies reveal that, in order to motivate, a salary plan must demonstrate that good performance leads to higher levels of pay, minimise any negative consequences of good performance, and relate other rewards to good performance.

Flexible Working Hours

Libraries are faced with an increasingly diverse workforce that includes nursing mothers, single parents with young children, employees with very different responsibilities, and those taking classes or pursuing degrees to improve skills and abilities or for self-improvement. The concept of flexible working hours has motivational appeal to many library staff.

Flexible time is intended to ensure that the work of the organisation is accomplished and, at the same time, to permit library staff and their supervisors to establish work schedules that recognise individual and family needs. Research indicates that flexible scheduling can be motivational in that job satisfaction is improved and absenteeism reduced. The ability to accommodate employee needs is a healthy and positive approach to motivation.

MOTIVATING EMPLOYEES IN ACADEMIC LIBRARIES IN TOUGH TIMES

Organisational effectiveness is largely determined by the quality of the employees and how the organisation develops them. Therefore, it is natural that high performing organisations try to recruit and retain the right people and provide them with training and professional development opportunities. However, abilities, skills, personality, and organisational support alone might not lead to individual job performance that contributes to overall organisational effectiveness if people are not motivated. It is possible that some employees choose not to perform even if they have the right qualifications.Managers face tough motivational challenges especially in economic downturns and it seems helpful to know key organisational Behaviour studies' findings related to human motivation. However, the goal is not manipulating and making people do what managers want them to do, but making people reach their highest job performance potential and getting them excited to do so.

The author's literature review revealed that motivation analyses in libraries as workplaces are limited and have been focused on content theories or what motivates people.This chapter attempts to build on the former analyses and explain applications of motivation theories that describe the motivation factors, motivation processes, effective job design, and conditions for sustaining motivation in the academic library workplace.

CONTENT THEORIES: WHAT MOTIVATES PEOPLE

The motivation theories that deal with the content of what motivates people are referred to as content theories or static-content theories as they look at only one point in time and do not predict Behaviour. The most well-known theories in this area include Maslow's hierarchy of needs, Alderfer's ERG theory, McClelland's theory of socially acquired needs, and Herzberg's motivator- hygiene theory.

Maslow organised the needs underlying human motivation in a hierarchy on five levels: physiological needs, security needs, social needs, ego or self-esteem needs, and self-actualisation needs.He further proposed that lower-level needs such as physiological needs and security needs must be satisfied before the individual can address higher-level needs. Although there is little evidence to support the concept of hierarchical progression and all individuals cannot be motivated in the same way, managers can attempt to influence their performance by satisfying employees' needs. Alderfer's ERG Theory, on the other hand, provides an alternative to Maslow's theory and is based on a 3-fold conceptualisation of human needs: existence, relatedness, and growth.

It does not assume lowerlevel satisfaction as a prerequisite for the emergence of higher-level needs. To test his theory, Alderfer surveyed 110 bank employees at several job levels.Although the results indicated stronger support for the ERG theory than Maslow's theory, both theories are similar in that people shape their actions to satisfy unfulfilled needs. McClelland identified three basic needs that people develop in the society: the need for achievement, power, and affiliation. He argued that each individual is likely to have developed a dominant orientation Towards one of these needs based on our life experiences. An obvious implication for managers might be to draw out those employees with a high need for achievement.However, McClelland suggested that motivation is changeable and that people can be taught to have certain needs through training Programmes. Herzberg's motivator-hygiene theory is different from other content theories as it suggested that motivation is composed of two dimensions:

- Hygiene Factors or the conditions surrounding the job and can prevent dissatisfaction; and
- Motivators, or the factors associated with the work itself and influence employees to grow and develop.

The hygiene factors include such things as salary, supervision, policies, working conditions, relationship, and job securities. The motivators include promotion, growth opportunities, responsibility, recognition, and achievement. The main implication of this theory is that for employees to be truly satisfied and perform above minimum standards, motivators had to be built into the job.

PROCESS THEORIES: HOW DOES MOTIVATION OPERATE

Although the static-content theories can provide a basic understanding of what energises people, they are not sufficient to explain the complex nature of human motivation as people respond differently to their needs. Factors other than unfulfilled needs also influence motivation, and various process theories were developed to explain how motivation operates.Expectancy theory, which is also known as VIE theory, assumes that motivation is a function of three components; for an individual to be motivated:

- The reward must be valued by the person;
- The person must believe that higher performance will result in greater rewards (instrumentality); and
- That additional effort will lead to higher performance (expectancy).

For example, if an employee perceives that high performance might not be achieved even after hours of effort due to lack of skills or self-efficacy, even if he or she desires promotion, the person might not feel motivated enough to achieve the goal.

Therefore, providing appropriate training, clarifying expectations, and providing guidance are important to strengthen this effort-performance link. Another example might be that if an individual believes that rewards might be given to people with higher seniority regardless of their performance, getting the reward might be perceived as unlikely for junior staff, thus undermining the person's motivation to perform.

Finally, if an employee can perform well but does not value the reward provided, *e.g.*, a gift certificate to a restaurant that the person does not care for, the person is likely to be less motivated. Goal-setting theory is another process theory and suggests the idea that setting goals can be a cause of high performance. Locke argued that a person's conscious intentions (goals) are the primary determinants of task-related motivation.

Managers should:

- Set specific goals;
- Make goals sufficiently difficult (but not too difficult);
- Involve employees in goal setting to ensure commitment;
- Provide feedback; and
- Link goal accomplishment with rewards that are valued by the employee.

This theory can be applied in various library tasks. For example, instead of asking employees to do their best in enhancing information fluency, the goal might be "implementing information fluency Programmes in at least 10 courses next semester." To gain goal commitment, it will be important for managers to provide clear direction and guidance to employees in addition to building their self-efficacy.

Organisational justice theories suggest that people's perception of fairness within the organisation regarding how and what decisions are made about the distribution of outcomes affects motivation. Justice theories are important given the current economy where many organisations have been forced to lay off people. Questions such as "Are we restructuring our organisation in a fair manner?" and "Were the layoffs perceived as fair by employees?" are important for managers.

The outcomes of justice perceptions can have an economic impact on the organisation such as absenteeism, withdrawal, theft, sabotage, or even lawsuits against employers. Justice theories consider both procedural justice and distributive justice. Distributive justice theory is also referred to as equity theory and suggests that people compare the ratio of their inputs (effort) and outcomes (rewards) to the input-outcome ratios of other comparable individuals. The research on equity theory is also more definitive on the reactions of people who perceive that they are under-rewarded. If an individual views a relationship as unequal, an attempt will be made to restore equality either by trying to gain greater rewards or by putting forth less effort. For example, if an employee feels that everyone gets promoted at the same rate regardless of their amount of inputs, he or she who feels under-rewarded might reduce the amount of the effort.

At the same time, the employee will not think it is unfair if another employee who contributes more to the organisation receives more reward. Colquitt *et al.* conducted a meta-analysis of justice theories and concluded that there was a strong negative correlation ($r = -.51$) between distributive justice and withdrawal, suggesting that if an employee views a relationship as unequal, he or she is likely to lose interest in the work or leave the organisation.

They also concluded that there was a strong positive correlation ($r = .56$) between procedural justice and performance, suggesting that employees are likely to perform better if procedures are perceived as fair. Other business literature also suggests that procedural justice increases performance significantly as managers gain trust, commitment, and voluntary cooperation from their employees.

It is possible that some managers might be fair in terms of distributing rewards such as recognition, promotion, pay raise, authority, responsibility, and resources, but not so in terms of process. Fair process involves engaging employees, providing opportunities for them to speak up, explaining why final decisions are made as they are, and clarifying expectations. Fair process is lost when information is filtered and managers retain power by withholding what they know to themselves. It is important for employees to be treated with sincerity and respect, and adequate explanation needs to be provided.

When the process is perceived to be fair, most people will realise that compromises are occasionally necessary and accept outcomes that might not be in their favour.

JOB CHARACTERISTICS THEORY: HOW CAN WE MAKE JOBS INTERESTING

Job design and job enrichment also affect human motivation and it will be helpful to know the characteristics that make jobs interesting. The job characteristics model developed by Hackman and Oldham identified five core job dimensions that should be enriched when jobs are re-designed:

- *Skill variety*—the degree to which a job requires a variety of activities that draw on different skills and talents of the employee.
- *Task identity*—the degree to which the job requires completion of a task, from beginning to end.
- *Task significance*—the degree to which the job has a significant impact on the lives of other people.
- *Autonomy*—the degree to which the job provides substantial

freedom, independence, and discretion to the individual in scheduling work and determining the procedures to be used.

- *Feedback*—the degree to which workers are provided with direct and clear information about their performance.

As the core dimensions are enhanced, the job characteristics model posits that they influence three critical psychological states:

- Experienced meaningfulness of work, which is increased by skill variety, task identity, and task significance;
- Experienced responsibility for work outcomes, which is enhanced by autonomy; and
- Knowledge of results, which is provided by effective feedback mechanisms.

For example, providing credits to individuals rather than to the department when preparing path-finders, instruction handouts, or other documents will provide opportunities for those employees involved to receive direct feedback from library users and establish client relationships with them. In addition, open lines of communication between employees and managers need to be incorporated into the workplace culture. The more people know how well they are doing, the better equipped they are to take appropriate corrective action. In terms of increasing autonomy, the first step will be to hire people who can do their jobs properly without close supervision. Second, the individuals will need to be trained to do their jobs effectively.

Finally, it should be clear that high-quality performance is expected. Loading jobs vertically by giving employees greater responsibility for their jobs and allowing them to make their own decisions, instead of micro-managing, increase the level of autonomy and sense of accountability that results in higher motivation. At the same time, employees should not be given a great deal of autonomy in any organisations where marginal work tends to be accepted without question. Autonomy will work only when everyone involved buys into the importance of performing at a high level. One approach in increasing autonomy might be to ask employees what goals they want to accomplish and what resources or support is needed as self-setting goals are naturally self-committed. It is important to note that the job characteristics model recognises the limitation that not everyone wants and benefits from enriched jobs and that people with a high need for personal growth benefit the most. In that sense, it will be essential for managers to hire people who are interested in growing professionally in the work instead of people who are attracted to the work because of work conditions or benefits.

ENVIRONMENTALLY-BASED THEORIES: HOW CAN WE REINFORCE AND MAINTAIN MOTIVATION

Let's now think about some of the ways in which motivation can be sustained. If we are rewarded for behaving in a certain way, we begin to make the connection between the Behaviour and the reward and continue to engage in the Behaviour. As B.F. Skinner's operant conditioning theory explains, Behaviours with positive consequences are strengthened and acquired, and Behaviours with negative consequences are eliminated. The positive consequences, such as recognition and reward, need to be tied directly to desired Behaviours and be given immediately and continuously so that the connection between the Behaviour and reinforcer is established. For example, staff recognition needs to be provided with an explanation of desirable Behaviour.

It should also be repeated if the staff continues to improve the work instead of choosing different employees to be rewarded when in fact the same employee performed the best. Additionally, rewards need to be distributed consistently so that recognition of good work will become part of the organisational culture. It is also important to know what you are rewarding. For example, if you reward someone because she or he answered the largest number of reference questions, the employee and possibly others might try to enhance the number of reference questions instead of focusing on the quality of the service and other ways that reference service can be improved. As social learning theory suggests, people acquire new Behaviours by observing the rewards and punishments given to others.

If you want to increase teamwork but continue distributing rewards according to individual performance only, your desired outcome, *i.e.*, teamwork will not be reinforced. In addition, if an individual performs fine in one area but not so in another, the explanation for the reward needs to be very clear so that the desirable Behaviour is strengthened while the undesirable Behaviour is not. When providing rewards, it will be helpful to know the difference between extrinsic and intrinsic rewards. Extrinsic rewards are contrived and some of them incur direct cost. They include such things as promotion, monetary reward, gifts, and bonuses. Intrinsic rewards involve no direct cost, and the examples include compliments, public recognition, opportunities, and a smile.

Thus, intrinsic rewards are closely related to the work itself and are motivators in the context of Herzberg's motivator. Therefore, intrinsic motivation is synonymous with a desire to work hard solely for the pleasure of task accomplishment. On the other hand, extrinsic motivation encourages us to complete the task to receive the reward. In other words, rewards motivate people to get rewards. Scholars research implies that the feedback and social reinforcers, such as recognition and attention, may have as strong an impact on performance as pay. Their research also indicates that extrinsic rewards can undermine an individual's intrinsic motivation. However, this is not to suggest that extrinsic incentives are unimportant. Good pay, benefits, and good working condition are often significant factors to attract and retain best people and cannot be ignored.

CONCLUSIONS

This chapter described applications of various motivation theories in the academic library workplace. Although those theories might not accurately explain Behaviour in all situations, they can still be helpful for managers who try to increase motivation among staff in academic libraries. Need theories can be used to satisfy employees' physical and psychological needs and hopefully to motivate them by enhancing their sense of self-esteem and self-actualisation.

Hygiene-Motivator theory makes us realise that job conditions such as pay and benefits alone might not motivate people. Therefore, it will be important for managers to provide motivators such as growth opportunities, sense of responsibility and accomplishment, and recognition as well as providing good working conditions. Expectancy theory suggests that managers need to provide rewards that are valued by their employees and that the employees need to feel they can achieve their goals and high-performance will result in the reward. Goals need to be specific, sufficiently difficult, accepted by the employee, and self-set if possible so that the employee becomes naturally committed.

In addition, process and reward distribution needs to be fair to enhance trust, job performance, and motivation. We also learned that characteristics of jobs affect human motivation. Jobs with a variety of activities, task identity, task significance, autonomy, and feedback mechanisms tend to increase motivation. Autonomy does not mean that employees can do whatever they want; instead, it involves hiring the right people, providing training, explaining that high-performance is expected, enriching jobs, providing respect and independence, and rewarding appropriately. Direct feedback channels should be established between service users and the employees who contributed to the work as well as between the employees and their supervisors.

Providing appropriate credits to work is important so that "thank you" notes and other feedback arrive to the people who were involved. Rewarding excellent work is essential to reinforce and maintain employee motivation. Intrinsic rewards such as compliments, public recognition, professional and opportunities are motivators according to the content theory and can be as effective as extrinsic rewards such as monetary reward and gifts, which might motivate employees to win the reward rather than to focus on the work itself. Nevertheless, extrinsic rewards encourage risk taking and for people to do extraordinary things and cannot be ignored.

At the same time, it will be important for managers to be mindful of those employees who get disappointed when their effort does not lead to rewards. Distributing rewards consistently instead of providing them only when accomplishment is visible will help strengthen trust within the organisation. Although most theories were tested in corporate settings, it appears they are also applicable in academic or non-profit workplaces. Peter Drucker wrote that "Non-profits need management precisely because they don't have a bottom line" and argued that non-profit organisations often end up becoming pioneers in the most crucial area—the motivation and productivity of knowledge workers—as non-profits start with the mission, which business will have to learn from them.

It seems that the key for the successful management is to clarify the mission of the organisation, hire people who have the right skills and agree with the mission, set goals, provide development opportunities, explain accountability, build trust through fair process, give autonomy and feedback, and provide appropriate rewards. Service excellence can be achieved even in times of budget constraints.

10

Need of Coordination in Library Staff

The term 'coordination' refers to syntactic constructions in which two or more units of the same type are combined into a larger unit and still have the same semantic relations with other surrounding elements. The units may be words, phrases, subordinate clauses, or full sentences:

- My husband supports and adores Juventus Turin.
- My uncle or your in-laws or the neighbours will come to visit us.
- I realise that you were right and that I was mistaken.
- The pope dissolved the Jesuit order, and all the Indian missions were abandoned.

All languages appear to possess coordination constructions of some kind, but there is a lot of cross-linguistic variation. Individual languages may possess a wealth of different coordinate constructions that relate to each other in complex ways. It is the purpose of this chapter to introduce and discuss a wide range of conceptual distinctions that are useful for describing the cross-linguistic and language-internal variation. This entails the use of a large number of technical terms, each of which is explained and illustrated as it is introduced. The particle or affix that serves to link the units of a coordinate construction is called coordinator. The coordinator is printed in boldface. By far the most frequently occurring coordinator is 'and' but coordinate constructions can also involve various other semantic types of linkers, such as 'or', 'but' and 'for'. 'And' - coordination is also called conjunctive coordination, 'or' - coordination is also called disjunctive coordination, 'but' - coordination is called adversative coordination, and 'for' - coordination is called causal coordination. Examples of each of these four types are given in:

1. (conjunction) Snow-white ate and drank.
2. (disjunction) She was a countess or a princess.
3. (adversative coordination) The dwarfs were ugly but kind.
4. (causal coordination) She died, for the apple was poisoned.

The units combined in a conjunctive coordination are called conjuncts, and more generally, the units of any coordination will be called coordinands here. Adversative coordination is always binary, *i.e.*, it must consist of two coordinands. Ternary or other multiple coordinations are impossible here.

This is illustrated in:

- The queen tried to kill Snow-white but Snow-white escaped but she went through much hardship.
- The mountain climbers were tired but happy but bankrupt.

By contrast, conjunctions and disjunctions can consist of an indefinite number of coordinands. The examples in show six coordinands each:

- You can vote for Baranov or Wagner or Lefèvre or McGarrigle or Ramírez or Abdurrasul.
- Cameroon, Nigeria, Niger, Libya, Sudan, and the Central African Republic have a common border with Chad.

Languages differ with respect to the number and the position of the coordinators used in coordinate constructions. For instance, while English generally shows the pattern A co-B, Kannada shows the pattern A-co B-co:

- So:mas&e:kharan-u: pe:t5e-ge ho:-d-aru. Narahari-and Somashekhara-and market-DAT go-PAST-3PL 'Narahari and Somashekhara went to the market.'

The patterns of coordinator placement and the types of linkers are discussed here. Many languages have several alternative patterns for a given semantic type of coordination, as illustrated in the English examples. Coordination with the two-part coordinator both ... and describes the coordinands as contrasting in some way: is appropriate, for instance, if the hearer expects only one of them to make the trip. These constructions will be called contrastive coordination in this chapter:

- Both Franz and Sisi will travel to Trieste.
- Franz and Sisi will travel to Trieste.

Moreover, many languages have special coordinators for negative contexts, as in the English example. This sentence is roughly equivalent semantically with, but again it has a more emphatic, contrastive Flavour. The construction in will be called contrastive negative coordination:

- Neither Brahms nor Bruckner reached Beethoven's fame.
- Brahms and Bruckner did not reach Beethoven's fame.

Contrastive and negative coordinate constructions are discussed below: We saw in above that a coordinate construction can consist of different types of coordinands: words, phrases, clauses or sentences. But as the definition of coordination says, each coordinand must be of the same type within a coordinate construction. Because the coordinands are syntactically different or at least semantically different:

- Guglielmo wrote to his bishop and to the pope.
- Guglielmo wrote a letter of protest and to the pope.
- Guglielmo spoke with the abbot and with the cardinal.
- Guglielmo spoke with eloquence and with the cardinal.

Different languages may require different coordinators depending on the syntactic type of the coordinands. Types of coordinands and their relevance for the structure of coordination are discussed below: In addition to the major semantic distinctions that we saw in, numerous more fine-grained distinctions can be made. For example, many languages distinguish between two types of disjunction: interrogative disjunction and standard disjunction. Mandarin Chinese uses two different coordinators for these two cases, haishi and huozhe:

1. You want I help you or want self do 'Do you want me to help you, or do you want to do it yourself?'
2. We at here eat or eat restaurant all OK 'We can either eat here or eat out.'

Next we discuss some special types of conjunction. Since, conjunction is the most frequent kind of coordination, it exhibits the greatest formal diversity. The most prominent "special type" of conjunction involves the use of a comitative marker, as in Hausa, where da means both 'with':

- I went to the market with Audu.
- Go market 'Dauda and Audu went to the market.'

In addition to coordinations in which each coordinand is a regular syntactic constituent many languages allow non-constituent coordination. For the sake of clarity, the coordinands are enclosed in square brackets in these examples:

- [Robert cooked the first course] and [Maria the dessert].
- Ahmed [sent a letter to Zaynab] or [a postcard to Fatima].
- [Martin adores], but [Tom hates Hollywood movies].

The first coordinand is an ordinary constituent but the second coordinand is not. Only the second coordinand is an ordinary constituent. In order to assimilate non-constituent coordinations to patterns found elsewhere in the grammar, linguists have often described them in terms of ellipsis. That is, abstract underlying structures such as those in are posited which show ordinary constituent coordination. In a second step, a rule of ellipsis of identical elements deletes the words underlined in resulting in the surface patterns:

- Robert cooked the first course and Maria cooked the dessert.
- Ahmed sent a letter to Zaynab or sent a postcard to Fatima.
- Martin adores Hollywood movies, but Tom hates Hollywood movies.

Finally, we discuss ways of delimiting coordination against less grammaticalised constructions and, perhaps most importantly, against subordination and dependency. The latter two notions will be discussed briefly here.

The primary contrast is that between coordination and dependency. In a coordination structure of the type A(-link-)B, A and B are structurally symmetrical in some sense, whereas in a dependency structure of the type X(-link-)Y, X and Y are not symmetrical, but either X or Y is the head and the other element is a dependent. When the dependent element is a clause, it is called subordinate clause. Although the distinction between coordination and dependency is of course fundamental, it is sometimes not evident whether a construction exhibits a coordination relation or a dependency relation. The best-known distinctive property of coordinate structures is that they obey the coordinate structure constraint, which prohibits the application of certain rules such as extraction of interrogative words from coordinate structures. This is illustrated, where the:

- Sentences show the basic structure, and the;
- Sentences show fronting of who.

As the examples make clear, only the dependency structures allow extraction:

- Dependency (subordination):
  - (basic sentence) You talked to someone before Joan arrived.
  - (who extraction) Who did you talk to _ before Joan arrived.
- Coordination:
  - (basic sentence) You talked to someone and then Joan arrived.
  - (who extraction) *Who did you talk to _ and then Joan arrived.
- Dependency:
  - (basic sentence) You saw Marvin with someone.
  - (who extraction) Who did you see Marvin with –.
- Coordination:
  - (basic sentence) You saw Marvin and someone.
  - (who extraction) *Who did you see Marvin and _.

Obeying the coordinate structure constraint is a formal property of constructions that is sometimes taken as the decisive criterion for coordinate status. As suggested, work with a primarily semantic definition of coordination, as given at the beginning of this section. The reason for this is that only semantically-based notions can be applied cross-linguistically – formal criteria are generally too language-particular.

DEVELOPMENT AND COORDINATION OF LIBRARY SERVICES TO STATE GOVERNMENT

In recent years the sise, complexity, pervasiveness and burgeoning growth of the federal government have made it a prime focus of the nation's news media, and it consequently has captured the attention of the general public. A similar expansion has occurred at the level of state government, but without as much commentary or analysis by the press. One author refers to the "surprising discovery that the largest growth sector in the 1960s and 1970s is not national Defence, automobile manufacturing, or even the federal government" but is instead state and local government.

When the broadened scope of responsibilities, services and agency functions are considered, the changing nature and importance of state government is even more impressive. Like the federal government, state governments have responded to the needs of a population beset by accelerating technological, social, economic, cultural, and political change. Thus there are state agencies, com- missions, committees, bureaus, councils, and departments whose responsibilities and concerns range from atomic energy to drug addiction treatment, and from medical care to the aged to the development of the arts. This expanding scope of interests has meant that the business of state government, in all its facets, requires an expanding variety of information sources and services.

Like the rest of society in this postindustrial era, state government has become heavily information-dependent. How have state libraries responded to the burgeoning information needs of state government? Almost every state library gives some kind of information service to other agencies of state government and, indeed, many have been doing so Since, the early days of the Republic. The standards for Library functions at the state level makes clear the state library's responsibility to provide quality services to other agencies of state government.

The ways in which state libraries fulfil this responsibility, the variety of services offered, the intensity of effort, and the degree of coordination with other agencies varies widely among the fifty states. As early as 1966, Phillip Monypenny noted a variety of provisions to supply service to legislative, executive and judicial branches of state government, with varying degrees of coordination between law libraries, historical societies, archives, departmental libraries, and general state library agencies.

Some indication of the variety of such services offered by state library agencies may be gained from the 1977 Simpson survey, where state library agencies listed the following: library services to state government, consultant services to state agency libraries, research library for state agencies, special collection for state agencies, cooperation with agency and departmental libraries, reference services to state agencies and officials, centralised purchasing for agency libraries, centralised processing for agency libraries, audiovisual production and direction for state agencies, legislative reference library, reference services to legislature, special administrative and legislative library, legislative research, computerised on- line bill status, state law library as part of state library, current awareness services, depository for state publications, depository for historical records, distribution of state publications, index of state publications, published checklist of state documents, records management service for state government, consultant services to state institutions, and library services to state institutions.

State library collections range in sise from the large and comprehensive libraries of New York, Illinois and California, to the more typical 100,000-200,000 volume collections held by many states. A few state libraries, such as Maryland's, do not maintain collections, but provide reference service by other means. In addition to the services and collections of the state library itself, agency or departmental libraries exist in many states. Although reliable and up to date data on these are difficult to obtain, a US Office of Education (USOE) survey conducted in late 1977 of special libraries serving state government will provide such data when compiled and published. It is known, however, that the number of such libraries varies from state to state (New York has nearly fifty, Texas twenty-three, New Jersey thirteen). Similarly, the collection sise, budget and number and level of staffing will vary widely from state to state, from major and sizable libraries (most typically court or law libraries) to office collections with part- time or no library staff.

The literature on the activities of state library agencies during the past fifteen years has clearly dealt more with statewide library development and extension services than with other functions. A similar bias was observed by Ralph Blasingame in a survey of library studies conducted between 1965 and 1969 based on an ERIC bibliography. He reported that only seven of the eighty-nine studies listed were concerned with services to state institutions (none specifically with services to state government), while two-thirds were studies of public libraries. A reading of the literature indicates that information services to state government have not been the leading edge of "state library" Programme development during this period. This emphasis on statewide library Programmes is not surprising in view of the passage of the Library Services Act of 1956, and the attendant in- flux of federal funds to support this type of development.

Forced to respond to pressure from the field and anxious to seise the opportunity to effectuate long-sought improvements in statewide planning and library system development, many state libraries clearly have not given the same attention to the development of information services to state government. Regulations of the federal Library Services and Construction Act specifically prohibited use of federal funds for service to state government. Several states, however, have commissioned studies during this period designed to improve information service to state government. Studies in South Dakota, Ohio, Indiana and New York do indicate a growing concern and offer recommendations for implementation of Programmes in this area. Michael Jackley, in a 1965 analysis of the functions of the South Dakota Library Commission, opted for greater centralisation.

His recommendations take the form of central purchasing of library materials, with those appropriate to departmental libraries being placed on permanent loan with the departmental library as a branch of the central agency. Better access to materials held by archives, history and law would be promoted by close coordination with these agencies and the central library. He suggested that those agencies of state government whose major function is research, such as the Legislative Research Council, should be housed with the state library on the Capitol grounds. Blasingame, in a 1968study for Ohio, advocated that the Information Resources and Services Division of the state library become a govern-mental service unit with three new staff positions.

Each of these new staff members would work with a specific group of logically chosen state agencies in order to become knowledgeable about the concerns and problems of these groups.

This would enable the state library to provide strong leadership in planning the development of information services in state agencies, and provide individual advice and assistance to those agencies with their own libraries. Duplication of effort and materials would be avoided, and maximum exploitation of existing resources inspired. Recommendations by Genevieve Casey were made in 1970 in a study for the Indiana State Library. Detailed recommendations for the coordination of services to the legislature and to state agencies include: consultant services to agencies desiring aid in cataloging and classifying materials; better circulation procedures; the provision of more sophisticated bibliographical services; centralised purchasing and processing; periodical print- outs and centralised records in the state library of the holdings of agencies; some form of current awareness service, with staff members working with administrators and librarians in the agencies assessing information needs and helping to establish acquisition policies; the use of existing TWX facilities by state employees; contracting for access to the collection and services of the Indiana University Medical Library for all state employees, especially those in the fields of health and environment; and the evaluation of the state library collection in terms of state government.

To provide guidance in establishing priorities for comprehensive information services, a council of persons responsible for department libraries and staff libraries in institutions would meet regularly with state library staff to discuss common problems and concerns. Work with large state agencies might be organised with small advisory councils within the agencies to work directly with the staff member from the state library responsible for that agency. Financial arrangements could take the form of either in- creased budget for the state library to support additional services to agencies, or an inter-accounting mechanism between the library agency and departments receiving special services.

The state library would require additional funds in any case, primarily for new staff to implement these activities, but also for materials and equipment. In 1974, the New York State Library undertook a major review of information services to state government in other states. To obtain up- to-date information on existing patterns of service from the other forty- nine state library agencies, a brief but pointed questionnaire was developed and distributed in autumn 1974.

Follow up visits were made to Texas, North Carolina and Ohio in this study, and additional data were gathered from Washington State. These visits provided information on both innovative Programmes and the varying approaches to state agency services taken in each of the states. The Texas State Library, employing a former public library consultant, has emphasised cooperative activities with other state agency libraries in Austin, resulting in the development of a lively organisation called State Agency Libraries of Texas (SALT). SALT publishes a news-letter, holds regular meetings and workshops, and has developed a number of cooperative projects, including a union list of serials and a Texas state documents project. Building on the recommendations of the Blasingame report summarised above, the Ohio State Library has expanded its services in recent years through an aggressive campaign to create awareness. Acting Head, Information and Reference Division:

- Active marketing of the information provision capabilities of the State Library of Ohio is emphasised -through "sales calls," by presentations before department groups, through orientation and familiarisation classes and tours, with follow-through in the form of individualised current awareness services which provide an ordering tool to the recipient. In the last year, more than a third of the circulation to state government personnel can be traced to the stimulus provided by the direct mail current awareness Programme. An important positive aspect is the system for delivery to the requestor whether he is remotely sited or contiguous to the library.

Like Texas and Ohio, the North Carolina State Library created a special unit to provide service to state agencies, entitled the "Library Services to State Agencies Branch." The Programme differs from Texas's and Ohio's reference-centered operations in that a considerable portion of the unit's thrust is in the area of technical services. In 1973-74, this unit provided cataloging, consultative and other support services to fourteen agency libraries, including the large Public Health Service library, the Department of Public Instruction, and newly organised libraries in the Labour and State Personnel departments. In the latter instance, the state library provided the necessary in-service training to assist the agency in starting the new library and the department provided staff, furnishings, shelving and a card catalogue.

Central to an understanding of the Washington State arrangement is the fact that the state librarian is a cabinet officer reporting directly to the governor, and the state library is responsible for all library services for state government (except law), no matter where the facility served is located. The former Washington State Librarian, described the Programme in refreshingly non-bureaucratic language:

- Some departments want us to operate fully and where they can generate federal funds for the service we enter into a "contract".... We pay no attention to the actual dollars so generated but render the service as needed. In some instances the department prefers to have the library staff on its payroll. . . . All materials are purchased and processed by us so that our catalog reflects the total information resource. The staffs are given orientation here so they realise we are back-up to their limited collection. The collections are weeded frequently and materials returned here for final decision as to retention. Some offices around the state have small collections but we encourage the employees to use their local public library and to call us directly. In addition to subscribing to key professional publications, we Xerox tables of contents and route them around. People write their names by the article desired and we send a Xerox copy which they can keep or throw away. It is a very wide ranging, flexible and effective programme.

Special consultative services are also available to state agencies by contract and have resulted in a comprehensive bibliography on disasters in Washington State for the Department of Emergency Services, and a combined subject index for environmental impact statements for the Department of Ecology. The New York State Library, building on an 86-year history of special services to the legislature, established a Legislative and Governmental Services unit in 1977, directed by a member of the top-level administration. This unit will promote library services to state agencies aggressively, pro- vide special research and bibliographic support, and conduct orientation and other Programmes for legislative and agency staff.

Publications currently issued by the unit include Legislative trends (an annotated list of state library acquisitions on topics of interest to the legislature), Spotlight (guides to basic resources in selected subject fields), Topics on top (short bibliographies on topics of current interest), and comprehensive literature searches on requested subjects. Resources offered include free search services on twenty-six computerised data banks. Despite the considerable variety of state library Programmes, certain general norms or patterns emerge which suggest the following elements as essential in developing an effective Programme of state library services to state agencies:

- *Attitude:* An aggressive, outreach approach is needed, based on a commitment to service and a wide-ranging, well-defined Programme to meet the needs of state agencies, officials and employees.
- *Organisation:* The state library should serve as the hub or center of library activity for state government, and should create a special office or unit which will provide leadership, coordination and the necessary monitoring of the programme. At the least, it should assign one or more staff members to carry out this outreach Programme on a continuing and preferably full-time basis. Staff should be carefully chosen for many of the same qualities which characterise successful field consultants, as well as for their perception of reference and bibliographic needs, and of the operation and structure of state government.
- *Agency Involvement:* As many agencies as possible should be involved, not only in the planning of service patterns, but in their

refinement and evaluation as well. Even if the cooperating agency has no library *per se,* it should assign someone to work with the state library coordinator.

- *Shared Activities/Shared Financing:* Services which are beyond the capability of the individual cooperating agency should be explored care- fully and implemented as practicable, including centralised ordering and processing of library materials, union lists and other methods of bibliographic control, central computerised data banks with terminal access as required, cooperative storage and materials retirement plans, etc. Shared financing on some unit cost basis, by means of contractual or other arrangements, is desirable and tends to stimulate mutual involvement, respect and commitment, and provides a basis for evaluating cost-effectiveness.
- *Visibility, Direct Contact with Administration:* In order to gain the support of the administration and the legislature, the state library and its Programme of service to state government needs visibility, a voice and some degree of clout. This may be achieved organisationally, with cabinet rank for the state librarian or with strong advisory groups who can make their voices heard by the power structure. It may like- wise be achieved personally, through the visibility and personal dynamics of the chief state library officer and the programme specialists; and functionally, through the provision of services of demonstrable value and reliable quality. All these avenues may be necessary and should be bulwarked with an effective public relations Programme including publicity, orientation workshops and appropriate accountability through regular reports.

The data assembled in this chapter indicate that state library agencies generally accept information service to state government as a primary responsibility. Although this function does not appear to have been the "leading edge" of state library Programme development in recent years, there is evidence of increased interest and innovative activity in a number of states. As state government expands its interests, as legislative, judicial and executive agencies become increasingly information dependent, and as the relationship of information availability to cost-effectiveness and productivity becomes clearer, it may be expected that information service to state government will become an increasingly critical area of state library agency activity.

11

Librarianship

To some people, librarianship may sound like an old-fashion term - something that smells of mothballs and is wrapped in parchment. The term librarian already evokes image of a certain type of staid personality and putting the suffix "ship" to it only adds lead to its weight. More than twenty years ago, when I started out in this field, I confess that I was not very keen to call myself a librarian too, preferring something with the word information or some other technically sounding clang in the job title. Somehow the transition from being an engineer to a librarian seemed a bit too drastic in those days. However the words "librarian" and "librarianship" became more endearing to me as I grew older.

At this point, I thought it aptly described what we do as a profession. Like many of you, I have a graduate degree in Library and Information Science, but what we do is not a science, not in the strictest sense of it. The word librarianship is better for it encompasses humanistic elements that define our ethos and more importantly, puts the place of libraries as an institution squarely in the centre.

I know that some people will disagree with this and want to rip the library out of their information persona just as digital information now exists without being associated with any one media. Actually I am sympathetic to this view. Labels and their connotations can be devastating and create obstacles to the good things that we can do. However, I think there is much strength to be gained from libraries as an institution and it would be wise for librarians not to disassociate ourselves from it.

WHAT IS LIBRARIANSHIP ABOUT NOW

So what is librarianship? Particularly, what is it about now? We can take a very broad view, such as "the preservation and transfer of knowledge in all recorded forms across time and space for the benefit of humankind", which is part of the LAS Ethical Statement or we can draw on our practical day to day work and define librarianship as "being concerned with the principle and practice of selecting, acquiring, organising, disseminating and providing access to information in accordance with the specific needs of groups of people or an individual". Both definitions are my own formulation, expressed in response to various demands in the course of my work. What we need is an empirical, up-to-date and aggregated view of what librarians today really think. So I turned to my colleagues at NTU Library for an answer. I asked each of the professional staff to give me a short spontaneous response on what they think librarianship is all about now. After going through all the responses, which ranged from one liner to 3 pages of passionate text, I manage to distill it into the chart. Basically I just tick the number of times a facet or its equivalent is mentioned – not very scientific but what I needed was just some indication. Note that no questionnaire was used and the categories listed in the chart are created by me. Though the responses may be coloured by the nature of the work we do in NTU, I think it might be a fair representation of what most librarians in Singapore think. We have a very diverse group of staff representing many age groups, prior occupational backgrounds, fields of study and duration of library work experience.

A DEFINITION OF LIBRARIANSHIP

Many of the key elements of librarianship identified in the informal e-mail poll are what we would expect. What is interesting but not so surprising is that there is a strong emphasis on users and less on library collections and resources. This is probably one of the major but subtle changes in librarianship in the last 20 years. When I started out in librarianship there was much more focus on building and organising library collections. Even reference work was very dependent on good cataloging and organisation of library resources. Though everything we did then was also aimed at helping the users, it was more implied than obvious. Today we seem to be more obsessed and anxious about our relationship with users, and for good reason as we shall discuss. Nonetheless, going by the e-mail poll, there seem to be some agreement on the shape and structure to the profession. There is a unique "aboutness" of the profession that can be articulated just as in the discipline of science, engineering, law, medicine, etc., Based on various sentiments expressed in the poll, I attempted to provide a collective view in the following definition of librarianship for the purpose of this presentation. "Librarianship is the discipline and profession that is concerned with helping individuals obtain reliable information to increase their knowledge in all spheres of their lives from the cumulated information store of mankind". This definition focuses on the intermediary or bridging role of libraries. One of the respondents put it more colourfully as follows:

- "Librarianship is a bridge between two entities; people and information. Librarians consider who may need this bridge, when and where a bridge is needed, how it is to be built, how it can be best utilised. We are the planner, architect, builder, and marketer of bridges".

To play this role adequately, it is implied that libraries need to have a clear understanding of the needs of the user on one hand and the knowledge and availability of relevant information resources on the other. The definition also assigns an end purpose for our roles, *i.e.*, to help users obtain information that will increase their knowledge in all spheres of their lives. It makes a distinction between information and knowledge, as the latter is part of an individual's makeup and cannot be disassociated from it. We help people obtain useful and reliable information but it is up to the each individual to assimilate it and make knowledge their own.

It is clear that most librarians in the survey look at librarianship as a predominantly intermediary function. The question is whether this is relevant today. Do users need or want us to help them obtain information? Are the information resources that libraries provide - the evidence base of knowledge cumulated in the past, highly desired by users anymore? Are people concerned enough about using reliable sources of information to make an effort to obtain it? There are many questions and exciting developments in library land today and it might not be possible to touch on all of them in this short presentation.

USERS

Librarianship has always been about serving the individual, whom we call by different names such as user, patron, customer, etc. Books or information resources are purchased for the individual because he or she needs them or we anticipate his or her needs. They are catalogued with great consideration of appropriate access points so that the individual may find them precisely.

We lend out materials to individuals or provide databases for them to get the information to increase their knowledge and perform their work effectively or help in their personal development. We have specialist reference librarians to answer questions from individuals and guide them in finding information. Librarians in public libraries run reading promotion Programmes to encourage the reading habits of individuals, from children to adults. What is more, individuals get these services mostly for free. Therefore all the work that librarians do leads to the satisfaction of the needs of individuals. However although we focus exclusively on the user, the user-library relationship has not always been equal.

Generally users depends a lot more on librarians for access to information in the past than at present. The librarian had a strong intermediary function then as there were various kinds of obstacles to access. These could be physical, administrative, system or skills related. For example, a researcher in the 1980s wishing to have a comprehensive literature search done would have to go through an expert online searcher in the Library to interrogate online systems such as DIALOG and BRS both for skills and cost reasons. Libraries then could therefore afford to treat their users with less alacrity. They either came to the Library or did not get the information they need. However that is not to say that libraries were not user-oriented.

It is just that user-centred issues were not accorded high priority over other concerns. The relationship changed drastically with the beginning of the end-user revolution. It started with bibliographic databases on cd-roms which enable users to use to their hearts' content without incurring expensive online charges or the librarian watching over their shoulders. Soon after that, purchased content became more convenient to use as they migrate to the web which gave users 24/7 access.

The power of convenience cannot be underestimated. It is probably the single most important factor that determines the use of an information resource or system. In the last few years, the advent of Google, the proliferation of free content, the massive worldwide digitisation projects and the wide spread use of social networking tools have completed the end-user revolution. Not only is it easier and more convenient to gain access to information but there is also an abundance of free information to be had. Today the perception among many people is that they can find decent amount of information on the Internet for their work or leisure without venturing into the Library or gaining access into its vault of online resources or print collection.

Thus the alarming results from the 2005 OCLC study on college students that shows that 84 per cent of respondents use search engines to begin an information search and only one per cent start from a library web site. Thus it would appear that the relationship between libraries and their users have turned 180 degrees. Today, there is much more thinking and activities among librarians on getting the attention of users and bringing them back to the fold of the library.

This then is the first big change in librarianship today. Librarianship today demands much more thought and effort on connecting with users and maintaining their engagement. This emphasis did not appear overnight but has been gaining centre-stage gradually Since, the balance between libraries and end-users tipped towards the latter due to technological and societal changes. Users now have an attractive alternative to the Library. The goals of librarianship, particularly its role in transmission of knowledge cannot be achieved without users occupying a huge chunk in the equation.

Therefore there is an almost frantic rush to pamper to the whims and tech savvy habits of users, particularly those from the new generations who are more at ease with the QWERTY keyboard than with chalk and blackboard. This preoccupation has implications for how librarianship is and will be practiced. As suggested, see more librarians going to bed with users or being embedded in the working and social environment of users. This is a logical development as the Internet and its attraction will remain and grow and users will not divert from it to the Library unless librarians go out and lead them through our pathways, virtual or otherwise. Furthermore, as users have less contact with libraries, there will be fewer opportunities for libraries to observe and study their real information needs to develop effective plans and services to achieve our mission.

In a rapidly evolving environment it is critical to have this information and only by working closely with users can we achieve this. These imperatives require librarians to have the disposition and the interpersonal skills not traditionally associated with library work. Librarianship is no longer centered in the backroom but in the frontline where the users are. Besides possessing knowledge and expertise in information content and users' information seeking Behaviour, librarians now need to be able to strive in the hustle and bustle of human-tohuman relationships and have strong advocacy and marketing skills.

The key to making an impact on users is to raise their expectation of libraries and librarians. This can be done by librarians demonstrating our value directly in the work and interests of users. Librarians could offer to participate as information architect and manager of specific research or study groups in a learning environment or workplace. For example, a librarian could set up highly specific information portals for individual research teams, linking them with resources from the library or elsewhere.

He or she could be more involved in the informat on flow of the group by being their dedicated reference librarian. Librarians could also host blogs for a course of study and contribute to discussion or provide pointers when matters relating to information sources and access surface. They can help individual users set up their own personal virtual libraries to aid them in their learning activities and studies.

This type of approach goes one step beyond merely providing resources, tools and services for users to make use of on their own initiative or through the encouragement of the Library's outreach activities. It creates and constructs a mini infrastructure that engages specific users with library expertise. It is highly targeted. Such close activities between librarians and users have advantages for both parties. The users will benefit from better information management and flow in their research or learning activities and the personal attention of expert librarians.

They will also have a more heightened awareness of what libraries and librarians can offer. Librarians will have a more intimate knowledge of the real needs of users and the problems they face in information access and use by actually being involved in the users' workflow and processes. This will lead to new initiatives in services and products that will solve real information problems and thus create greater value for libraries. Objections to such intense engagement with users would probably center on lack of resources and problems of sustainability. It could be argued that there is just not enough manpower resources in a typical library to sustain such schemes. However, not to find ways to do so would mean further disengagement with users and possible decline in the role of libraries.

INFORMATION RESOURCES

A key visible role of libraries in the past as well as the present is to provide access to information. If we go back to a few decades ago, information provided by libraries came exclusively from its print collection. A Library then was in total control of the information materials that it provided. It owned everything that it had.

A typical user saw his library forming a huge part of his information diet. Today, a large percentage of what a library provides, particularly electronic resources is leased and can be taken away when subscriptions are not renewed. With the continued rise and supply of information in electronic format, libraries will own less and less of what is provided over time. If we look at the total universe of information available to a typical user today, the library owned resources, including leased resources form only a small proportion. Despite their pedigree and high potential value, library resources are hardly noticed in the sea of information. Much of the information diet of the ordinary person comes from the vast Internet.

Though most librarians complain about the quality of information available on the Internet, this is slowly changing. The massive book digitisation projects by Google, Microsoft, Open Content Alliance and others have put many hitherto inaccessible titles online. Many universities are putting up institutional repositories of their academic staff publications. There is an increasing number of open access journals. For example, more than 3,000 are listed in the Directory of Open Access Journals which is about 12 percent of total peer-reviewed journals.

Scholars now have greater incentive to submit their publications to open access repositories due to increasing numbers of open access mandates by research funding bodies. Recently the US Congress passed a law that requires beneficiaries of National Institute of Health to submit publications arising from their funded research work to PUB-MED Central within one year of their publication. Similar mandates have been initiated by other major agencies in UK and Europe.

There is also an increasing number of educational resources from the *Open Educational Resources* (OER) Movement, which started in 2001 when MIT started to offer free access to a wide range of their courseware. Unlike the earlier days of the Internet, there is much more serious and quality information available for free on the Internet, though these are mixed with all the chips and chaff of web chatter. How will the explosion of free online content and their easy accessibility affect the way that librarianship is practiced? One of the key contributions of librarianship is the development of sophisticated methods of organising information or bibliographic control that allow information to be accessed efficiently. Put simply, given a large collection of information objects, the librarian can organise them to allow people to find an item or related groups of items with great precision and efficiency. Consider a library. Every item in the library has a corresponding record in the Library Catalog. Everything is ordered, structured, controlled, accountable, retrievable and traceable even when there are millions of items.

The Library Catalog is the heart of the Library – it symbolises the power of libraries. Its classification system, authority and vocabulary control, tracings, finding rules, even the dots and commas on catalog cards are marvels of organisation. Within seconds and without the aid of computers, one can collate comprehensively all books on the economy of Singapore or the treatment for depression. You can drill down on a record and identify the date the information first appeared, identify the person who produce the information and find his other works.

In other words, catalogs or other index systems create a network of relationships between information items that allow users to draw conclusions, make inferences and act on them. Strangely with all the computing power of the Internet, Google cannot do this. You can never be sure if the list you get is comprehensive. Most times, you cannot even establish the date the information was produced and who produced it. Behind the power of the catalog lies the Labour and skills of librarians who painstakingly look through each book to create handles for users to find and collate it with other books.

This is an example of the invisible intermediation role of librarians. There is of course no such intermediation on the Internet. Is the first 10 items listed in a Google search result good enough or is deeper investigative and research work still valuable? Is the core competency of librarians in making sense of information through systematic organisation still relevant in the new information environment? The answer must surely be the yes. However the problem is the scale and perhaps the common sociological phenomena of diffusion of responsibility.

The amount of information pages in the Internet is astronomical compared to a typical library collection. Even if we just take the good bits to catalog, it would still be daunting to even think about it. Also many of the digital files are updated and changed frequently and have many characteristics that are not amenable to traditional form of cataloging. As most web resources are not under the custody of libraries, there is also a question of who should do the cataloging which is where the diffusion of responsibility phenomena applies. The opening paragraph of the Report of the Library of Congress Working Group on the Future of Bibliographic Control summarises the state of thinking on the above in noting that,

- "The future of bibliographic control will be collaborative, decentralised, international in scope, and Web-based. Its realisation will occur in cooperation with the private sector, and with the active collaboration of library users. Data will be gathered from multiple sources; change will happen quickly; and bibliographic control will be dynamic, not static. The underlying technology that makes this future possible and necessary—the World Wide Web—is now almost two decades old. Libraries must continue the transition to this future without delay in order to retain their significance as information providers."

Without going into the current controversy over RDA (Resource Description and Access) development by the Joint Steering Committee for the revision of AACR2, it is clear that the library community is divided over the approach that future bibliographic control should take. I joined the library profession about 5 years after the publication of AACR2 and I remember having been tutored on the difference between AACR1 and AACR2 as a rookie librarian.

The transition from AACR2 to RDA or its variants will be much more radical as it has to seriously take into account the new information environment which is much more global, user controlled, dynamic and complex. Changes in our approach in dealing with the organisation and access to information largely mediated by the web will have great impact on the theory and practice of librarianship. We have to watch this space.

INTERMEDIATION

In my interaction and work with librarians, including interviews with potential employees, I noted that one of the most common roles of librarian they cite is that of an intermediary between users and information. This implies that there is some kind of barrier or obstacle between users and the information out there which requires the mediation of a library or a librarian to connect the link. This is largely true in the pre-Internet era. However it would appear that this is no longer true in an era when everyone can have access to global information sources from the desktop of their homes or offices.

The emergence of the global information network and its accompanying social upheavals has led many people to predict the death of the middle man and intermediaries not only in library work but in many other areas of commerce and society. However the deluge of information and the convenience and ease of access to it also creates new problems and issues that are fertile grounds for librarians to explore and to establish their presence. Disintermediation in one area often cause shifts in others.

In other words, life usually gets more complex, not simpler. Complex lives often require a greater variety of support systems and intervention. Though we often think of intermediation in terms of a librarian assisting a user in getting the information he or she wants, the intermediary role of librarianship can be expressed in many other forms. For example, the detailed bibliographic information that cataloguers provide to lead users to the appropriate text is a form of mediation. The classified arrangement of books on the shelves allowing users to browse related work is another.

The librarian's negotiation for a right price with vendors in getting a database for users' access is yet another. Intermediation is therefore multi-dimensional. It happens and will be sustained when there is value in the intermediation act. We use an intermediary when he or she saves us time, does the work for us better, or does things that we have no expertise to do ourselves. Therefore as long as librarians can add value and demonstrate it visibly in a middleman role between users and the information environment, intermediation will always occur.

So, what are the possible intermediation roles for librarianship in a highly networked and content rich world? For an indication of this, it is instructive to read some of the recent literature on users' Behaviour on the Internet. One of the latest, from UK, was commissioned by the British Library and the U.K., Joint Information System Committee to investigate the searching and researching Behaviour of young people. The study found that despite early exposure to technology and regular use of digital resources, the information literacy skills of young people have not improved.

It pointed out that "digital literacies and information literacies do not go hand in hand." Conclusions from logged files of user searches indicated that everyone exhibits a "bouncing/flicking behaviour, which sees them searching horizontally, rather than vertically". They spend a lot more time navigating online than viewing and reading and are not able to develop effective search strategies. They have a poor understanding of their information needs and do not have a good grasp that the Internet is a collection of networked resources from different providers.

Young people also have difficulties making relevant judgments about the pages they retrieve. It suggests that plagiarism is a serious issue for this "cut-and-paste" generation. Are similar Behaviours prevalent among Singapore's Google generation and other Internet users? Only parallel studies can tell. However anecdotal information does suggest very similar characteristics. It is not surprising that people have problems using the Internet to seek information effectively.

Behind the Google search box lie billions of documents that are not structured or organised systematically for retrieval by all manner of people and organisations with various agendas, motivation and interest in offering their content. Finding relevant and reliable information in an environment with abundant information is as problematic as in an environment with scarce information. When there are tremendous choices, the ability to pinpoint and select reliable, credible and useful information requires knowledge, expertise and experience. Interpreting the authenticity and reliability of what is found on the Internet with confidence would be difficult for most people due to the lack of context, explicit cues and metadata common in library and traditional information systems. Even before one starts typing on the keyboard, the ability to formulate the search question is a great hurdle. In short, information literacy or fluency skills is not a given.

It requires investment of time and effort to acquire. Given the common skimming and horizontal searching habits identified in the UCL study, it is unlikely that the majority of online users will acquire the necessary skills to get the most out of the information global house. They are going to need help. Although the librarian has the skills to help users mediate and maximise their use of global information environment, it does not necessary follow that the skills will be demanded by users. The convenience and ease of use and access to the Internet has lulled many Internet users into a sense of mastery over their information environment. In a survey of findings on end-user searching Behaviour, Markey concluded that "end users rarely use advanced system features and when they do, they are quite likely to use them incorrectly.

Although research findings demonstrate that end users are not conducting sophisticated online searches, the vast majority are satisfied with their searches. In fact, percentages of users who express satisfaction with the results of their searches reach into the high seventies and beyond". Libraries and librarians face two major obstacles in trying to play the intermediary role. Firstly, libraries are not on the radar screen of users as much as we would like. Secondly, even if libraries are, users will need to be convinced to make the effort to use libraries, whether online or offline.

This brings us back to our first point of discussion on the importance of advocacy work. Like many things else, development of good habits of people during their formative years are crucial in influencing their Behaviour later. Good library Programmes in schools therefore play critical roles in influencing students to learn and develop good information literacy skills. It is unfortunate that there is no concerted effort in this direction here in Singapore. As noted in the UCL report, "Emerging research findings from the US points to the fact that these skills need to be inculcated during the formative years of childhood: by university or college it is too late to reverse engineer deeply ingrained habits, notably an uncritical trust in branded search engines to deliver quick fixes".

Libraries in tertiary institutions here can still play an important role. They will have the last opportunity to influence students in acquiring information literacy skills before they disperse into the working world with less opportunity, and lesser motivation and time to learn to get the most out of a complex information environment. Sometimes simple acts can go a long way. For example, one feedback we had from a teaching staff after our instructional classes for his students is that he noticed a remarkable change in their citation patterns. Instead of citing mainly Internet resources and Wikipedia articles, the students had changed to using scholarly materials in academic journals which they learned during the library classes. This small change will have profound effect on their information seeking habits in the future.

Active intermediary functions performed by libraries need also to take into account the Behavioural traits of users, particularly the young generation. Though there are many studies on user Behaviour in U.S., U.K., and other places, there is a paucity of such national data in Singapore. Availability of such studies will be important for libraries here to address users' needs effectively.

At this moment we could only assume that the effect of globalisation has produced an internationally homogenised student profile that is applicable in our case as well. We know from various studies by Frand, Oblinger and others that users today learn by doing, using trial and error methods rather than systematic approaches, spent most of their time online, prefer to work in groups, are producers as well as consumer of information, etc., Libraries need to fit their intermediation approaches around these Behavioural characteristics. Traditional hard-core approaches in imparting knowledge will probably be less effective today.

I would suggest that we take a "tourist guide" approach in our intermediation effort. A tourist can visit any place he wants in a country, but he will get a much better understanding and insight into the culture, history and social norms of the place and all the interesting nooks and corners if he is led by an expert tourist guide. Similarly, anyone can wander around the global information environment, but experts such as librarians can provide tremendous added value by showing and leading users to unexpected resources, explaining their intricacies, pointing out trusted sources as well as "dangerous" areas.

Such intermediation work is not only confined to librarians but libraries as institutions. Just as a country's tourism agencies build infrastructure, coordinate resources and provide support to the tourism trade, libraries can do similar things in the networked online environment to provide the facilities, tools and Programmes that will make learning in the virtual as well as the physical world a much more enriching place.

PUBLIC RELATIONS IN LIBRARIANSHIP

It is the relationship of your library with its borrowers, with the non-borrowers of your community, with your trustees or library committee, with dealers, collectors, salesmen of equipment; with scholars and contest solvers, with your staff and the administration for which you work. Public relations is with the public, and as true as in its Biblical context is the admonition, "Whatsoever you do unto the least of these . . ." "Curse or blessing," C. D.

MacDougall calls public relations. Either is possible. For your public relations is what you make it. It cannot be shuddered at and wished away, but it can be welcomed and made to serve you well. It is with you every minute of every day.

It is waiting at your library doors. It is observing the cleanliness of your hallways and public rooms. It is reacting to the service of all your staff, listening in on telephone conversations, reading your mail. It follows you home, into your personal life. It accompanies you on all your ventures into the life of your community. Public relations has been endowed with a kind of twentieth century magic by the corporations and their P.R. officers. Neither the corporations nor the P.R. men invented public relations. It has been with us Since, the beginning of trade. But the American business man has learned the foolishness caveat emptor of as a motto, has learned the dead end of selling wooden nutmegs.

He has made the good will of his public part and parcel of the assets of his business. Public relations is as much a part of the daily life of a library as it is of any business. Perhaps more so, for a library is not self-supporting and depends, even more than the usual business, primarily on the good opinion of its patrons. It is the day-to-day building of the atmosphere of good will in which a library can operate most widely and most effectively to give the best possible service to its public. As R. L. Heilbronner wrote in Harper's Magazine for June 1957: "In a word, public relations covers a lot of acreage-blurring out into advertising, slopping over into selling, dipping down into publicity, and touching-or at least aspiring to-the 'making' of public opinion itself."

Edward W. Barrett, dean of Columbia University's School of Journalism, praises J. W. Hill, himself the ungowned dean of American P.R. men, for seeing "public relations as a broad management function - more precisely . . . as the management function of giving the same organised and careful attention to the asset of good will as is given to any other major asset of the business." Public relations may well be the most important asset - "the priceless ingredient," to quote the phrase that one firm's advertising Programme has made famous - for bad public relations can cancel the good of every other asset.

With a knowledge of the experiences of other libraries and other types of organisations, public relations becomes perforce a do-it-yourself Programme. Public relations is the asset, is the Programme, most expressive of the individuality, the personality, of each separate library. It may be patterned emulatively, but never imitatively. It must be done according to the needs of your library. It must express as attractively as possible your library to the public. First, public relations must be properly fitted into the administrative pattern of your library. Few libraries can afford the services of a special public relations officer. For those that can, fine. University and college libraries often can work through a campus public relations office. In some cases, a city P.R.

man is available to public libraries. Where a trained professional is available, it is an error both factual and tactical to direct public relations except through that individual.

In other cases, public relations must be conducted as an auxiliary responsibility of the librarian or delegated to some other member of his staff. In both of these alternatives, however, it remains a function of management and the responsibility of the librarian. A library's policies in many fields must be worked out thoroughly and wisely by the librarian and his governing board. nce worked out, policy must be implemented by actions which elucidate it in every function of the library and by every member of a library's staff.

The right hand must know what to expect of the left hand. It is of basic importance for good public relations that all staff be kept as fully informed as possible, both of long-term library policy and immediate newsworthy developments which relate to that policy. If not with a single voice, the library must at least speak in a consistent accent. •The extent of a library's services and resources must be well enough known for any and every employee to respond with accurate answers or definite and proper referrals to patrons' questions.

There is hardly a greater disservice that a library can do its public relations Programme than to permit an employee to answer an enquiry with a "that's-not-my- business" type of reply. It matters not how extensive a library's services are if the attainment of those services becomes a dismaying pursuit of referrals from one functionary to another. Good service is the handmaiden of good public relations. This does not mean that every library must provide every service.

It does mean that whatever service a library provides must be done well. A well considered "no" can be much more effective public relations than an ill considered "yes". Public relations is as important within your organisation as it is without. Staff relations are a part of public relations. Ability to work with a governing board is a part of public relations. And, once these relationships are satisfactorily established, each member of your staff, each member of your board becomes a part-time P.R. man for your library. But the more apparent aspects of public relations are those outside your management family. Public relations is with the public, but each library has several publics.

There is its public which borrows books. There is a public made up of others in the same profession. There is a public, in some libraries at least, of scholars or professional users of materials. Relations with the general borrowing public are broadest, most demanding, and, yet, easiest. Here the field is reasonably well defined. Here publicity can be effective. Here patrons' response is quickest and most vocal; if you are taking the wrong tack, someone will tell you so. Librarians generally have done good work with publicity, but it is too easy to forget that not all publicity is good publicity. Publicity begins at home, at least, in the library profession itself. Staff news sheets, exhibits, guides to exhibits are all part of a library publicity Programme. The incidence of library publicity material of this type pitched at a kindergarten level is more appalling than appealing.

Is it necessary that adult human beings approach the problem of announcing a staff party as if they were writing for the amusement of low grade morons? The same approach pervades much of the material issued in the name of recruiting for librarianship. If these things are done well, they make for good public relations. But there is no middle ground. It is better that they not be done at all than that they be done badly. Newspaper publicity must be controlled within the management function of public relations, but it is practicably possible to delegate responsibility in this area. It is helpful both to the library and to a paper that one person be responsible for newspaper publicity.

A minimum of experience can establish a satisfactory working relationship between a library and a reporter. He will know what he wants. It is your business to give him the facts. Handout journalism has been a corollary development of public relations as a profession. It is certainly not its healthiest aspect. Make information available to newspapers, but don't try to style it for them. Reporters are better reporters than are librarians. Notices and articles in the library press are another aspect of continuing public relations.

The unfortunate proliferation of library periodicals makes complete coverage impossible, cuts down the readership for any single journal, and lowers the average quality of writing on librarianship; but this is, nevertheless, a legitimate area for use in furthering public relations. Wide knowledge of one's own profession and of his colleagues in it is a prerequisite for general recognition of librarianship as a profession. Librarians are inclined to write too much solely for other librarians, talk too much to other librarians. Participation in national, regional, and local organisations of professional librarians is good public relations, particularly if such organisations reach other professions and the public in general.

Individual participation by staff members is also good for a library. Individuals should be encouraged in membership in civic groups, professional organisations in specific subject fields, and in activity in communuity projects. As useful as professional exchange is, articles in the non-library press, speeches before Rotary, Kiwanis, and other civic or special interest groups are especially rewarding. Publicity and participation are merely vehicles of public relations. The public as a mass can be effectively reached through newspapers, radio, and television. The public as a special force in promoting the welfare of a library can be better and more directly reached through individual participation in the widest possible variety of activities. Public relations as a continuing function is a more important and a slower process. It is axiomatic that repeated incidental mention of a celebrity is more important to his reputation than one large splurge of publicity about him. Every time the library is mentioned favourably, every time an individual connected with the library appears in the community in a favourable light, good public relations are being built. Every time a library is listed among the acknowledgments in a published book, every time an individual sees a creditable publication from the library, every time an organisation or an individual is helped by the library's services, the library increases in stature.

The cumulative effects are unlimited: better budgets, adequate staffing, more books, finer buildings, easier recruiting-in a word: better libraries. "Good will" is often listed in corporate assets as valued at $1.00 not because it is worth little but because it is an intangible beyond practical evaluation. Good will is priceless. It is public relations that build good will. Libraries are a public or institutional service, tangible examples of good public relations on the part of a municipality, a corporation, or an educational institution providing informational and recreational resources to its constituency. Librarianship is a service profession. If librarians are to emphasise their work as a profession, interpreting as well as making available knowledge, this emphasis must be based on good service. It must be quality service at all levels of operations. Good service, conceived to support community and institutional goals, will automatically result in good public relations. Good public relations will create lasting good will.

ETHICS IN LIBRARIANSHIP: A MANAGEMENT MODEL

The study of ethics in the information professions is a subset of the study of ethics in general. Thus, a definition of ethics may be helpful in clarifying this concept. There is no agreement on the exact definition of the term ethics. Some use it to refer to the art of determining what is right or good.

It is also used in three different but related ways signifying:

- A general pattern or "way of life,"
- A set of rules of conduct or "moral code," and
- Enquiry about ways of life and rules of conduct.

As a concept, the purpose of ethics is to establish principles of Behaviour that help people make choices among alternative modes of action. Making such choices of ten involves ethical and lemmas, because these are marked by multiple and non-comparable dimensions. The dimensions are the results - both benefits and harms-that are going to affect the organisation, the society, and the individual as a result of a decision or action. In essence, ethical behaviour is what is accepted as "good" and "right" as opposed to "bad" or "wrong" in the context of the governing moral code. The determination of what is right rather than what is wrong has been generally codified in the form of law, although not all situations have been, and can be, covered by any such codification. Laws are rationalised for the welfare of society; thus, any Behaviour considered ethical should also be legal in a just and fair society. This does mean, however, that simply because an action is not illegal it is necessarily ethical. In other words, just living up to the "letter of the law" is not sufficient to guarantee that one's actions can be or should be considered ethical. The following examples of ethical questions can be considered in this context:

- Is it ethical to take longer than necessary to do a task.
- Is it ethical to do personal business on the employer's time.
- Is it ethical to call in sick to take a day off to catch up on chores at home.
- Is it ethical to fail to report rule violations by a co-worker.

None of these examples is illegal. But many individuals would consider one or more of them to be unethical. The values held by an individual, group, or society are the basic components of an ethical system. Yet uncertainty is a fact of complex dynamic organisational life. The interests and values of another individual, group, or society and laws regarding both are unclear. Ethical standards, therefore, are not universally accepted, but rather they are the end product of discretionary decision-making Behaviour affecting the lives and well-being of others. Ethics in the information professions is concerned with the application of moral standards to the conduct of librarians and other individuals involved in information dissemination. It is a type of applied ethics concerned with clarifying the obligations and dilemmas of librarians and other information professionals who make decisions regarding the acquisition, processing, and dissemination of information to individuals, groups, and society at large.

EVOLUTION IN/ OF ETHICALCONCERNS INFORMATION PROFESSIONS

Tracing the development of ethics as an area of concern for information professionals will help in identifying the factors that are responsible for and that influenced the evolution of ethical Behaviour. Although ethical issues in librarianship were of some concern prior to the 1960s, it was the rise of the social responsibility debate in the decade of the 1960s that caused ethical concerns to become of major importance to librarians and other information professionals.

The concept of social responsibility is fundamentally an ethical concept. It involves changing notions of how human needs should be met and emphasises a concern with the social dimensions of information service that has to do with improving the quality of life. Social responsibility provides a way for the information profession to concern itself with the social dimensions of service and be aware of the social impact of that service. Historically, librarians saw that their major responsibility was to the collection; caring for the materials within the library building was their primary concern. Many modern information professionals now acknowledge that they are responsible to any individual or group with an information need.

These stakeholders can be any constituency in the library's environment-users, non-users, employees, suppliers, government agencies, public interest groups, and host communities. Stage one encompasses responsibility for the library collection. Stage two adds responsibility for employees. Stage three includes responsibility to library users-those individuals who have made a conscious decision to use the library's information resources. Stage four expands responsibility furthest by proposing that information professionals are responsible to society in general and includes users and non-users alike. What information professionals do in terms of pursuing social goals depends on to what or to whom they believe they are responsible.

A stage one information professional promotes collection development and maintenance. At stage two, information professionals accept responsibility for the employees in their organisation and focus on human resource concerns. Because they will want to get, keep, and motivate good employees, they are concerned with appropriate education and training, improved working conditions, expanded employee rights, increased job security, and the like. A stage three professional expands goals to include high quality service, an excellent collection, good relations with the public, and the like. A stage four professional aligns with an active interpretation of social responsibility. At this stage, professionals see their responsibility to society as a whole. Their service is defined in terms of advancing the public good.

The acceptance of such responsibility means that such information professionals actively promote social justice, support social and cultural goals, and take political positions even if such actions are perceived negatively by some. Each stage carries with it an increasing level of discretion. As professionals move to the right along the continuum, they have to make more decisions based upon situational variables not of their own making. By the time professionals reach stage four, they are required to think about ethical dilemmas not necessarily solely within the context of their organisations but to decide what is right and what is wrong from a societal perspective. They may follow self-chosen ethical principles, upholding values and rights regardless of majority opinion.

Obviously, not all professionals perceive reaching stage four as an appropriate goal. Some stay in stage one, which emphasises responsibility for collection maintenance and development, or stage two, which emphasises appropriate Behaviour for a librarian as a professional, or stage three, which emphasises fulfilling the duties and obligations of a professional librarian through high quality service to users. There never has been established any simple right-wrong dichotomy to help information professionals make decisions regarding their appropriate domain for ethically responsible action.

The social responsibility movement of the 1960s did provide fuel for debate. The concept of intellectual freedom, called the profession's "central ethic", was used to frame issues as diverse as civil rights, the war in Vietnam, women's rights, and the war on poverty.

On one side, there were those who were in stage four on the social responsibility continuum, defining intellectual freedom as a series of value judgments supporting a radically pluralistic egalitarian society. On the other side were those who viewed social responsibility from stages one and two of the continuum, defending intellectual freedom from a position of collective and individual neutrality. As the debate waned in the 1970s, it was obvious to many proponents and opponents of the social responsibility movement that there were several key issues in the debate that had not been, and perhaps cannot yet be, settled. One key issue concerns the operational definition of social responsibility.

How shall a library's resources be allocated to help solve social problems? With what specific problems shall a given library concern itself? What priorities shall be established? What goals or standards of performance shall be established? What measures shall be employed to determine if a library is socially responsible or socially irresponsible? In the, past, the traditional library environment provided little or no information to the decision maker that was useful in answering the above questions. The concept of social responsibility itself provided no clear guidelines for ethical Behaviour. Given this lack of clarity, librarians who wanted to be socially responsible were left to follow their own devices or relied on some rather vague generalisations about social values and public expectations.

Another problem with the concept of social responsibility is that it has not always taken into account the environment in which the library functions. In the past, many advocates of social responsibility treated the library as an isolated entity that had the ability to engage in unilateral social action. Eventually, it came to be recognised that libraries are severely limited in their ability to respond adequately to social problems. There are physical, organisational, and attitudinal barriers that have to be overcome. The last issue that remains unresolved in the debate about social responsibility concerns the moral basis of the notion.

The term responsibility is fundamentally a moral one that implies an obligation to someone or something. It is clear to most people that librarians have professional responsibilities to acquire, process, and disseminate information products and services efficiently to users of libraries. These responsibilities constitute the reason for the existence of libraries. But why do librarians have social responsibilities and to whom? What are the moral foundations for a concern with the social impact of information services? The proponents of social responsibility, though well intentioned, have produced no clear and generally accepted moral principle that would impose on the information professions an obligation to work for social change. Various arguments have been made to try to link moral Behaviour of the profession to the performance of libraries. Little has been accomplished, however, by way of developing a solid and acceptable moral argument for the notion of social responsibility.

Thus, although those promoting social responsibility are wry moralistic in many of their statements, in debate with others, they do not articulate a philosophical basis for the social responsibilities discussed. The emotionally laden nature of the discussion on social responsibility presents the possibility that debate on the subject will continue indefinitely with little prospect of agreement being reached on the scope of the issues involved or their solution. Beginning in the late 1970s and continuing through the 1980s, a theoretical and conceptual reorientation has begun to take place regarding the information profession's obligations to its various constituencies. The new approach can be labeled "social responsiveness" and it has become clear that the shift from responsibility to responsiveness reflects a significant change of focus.

This new focus has shifted the discussion from moral imperatives related to social responsibility to a more technical and neutral approach that includes social responsiveness. The Public Library Association's guidelines for identifying roles for public libraries reflects this shift. The process described in the guidelines includes identification of both internal and external mechanisms, procedures, arrangements, and Behavioural patterns of the library's constituent groups taken collectively. It establishes mechanisms to judge the capability of libraries to fulfil certain roles. Attempts are made to identify key variables within the library that relate to its responsiveness and discover structural changes that will enable the library to respond adequately to social demands.

The important questions are not moral, related to whether a library should respond to a social problem out of a sense of social responsibility, but more pragmatic and action oriented, dealing with the library's ability to respond and the changes necessary to enable it to respond more effectively. One of the advantages of this approach is its managerial orientation. The concept ignores the philosophical debate about responsibility and obligation and focuses on the problems and prospects of making libraries more socially responsive.The process lends itself to analytical techniques in utilising specific methods, such as data collection and analysis and numerical interpretation of results.

The utilisation of data through this process can help decision makers determine how best to institutionalise social policy throughout the library. Organisational structures can be evaluated; the roles of information professionals can be delineated; personnel policies can be structured to reward appropriate "socially responsive" Behaviour; and goal statements can be formulated that reflect the roles identified. Even though this approach seems to answer many of the questions faced by those concerned with the social responsibility debate, social responsiveness does not offer answers to all questions. The concept of social responsiveness does not provide guidance on how resources should be allocated to fulfill the various library roles. Libraries respond to the same problems in different ways and to varying degrees.

And there is no clear data as to what pattern of responsiveness will be the most successful. The philosophy of responsiveness does not help a library to decide what roles it should have or what priorities should be established. In the final analysis, social responsiveness provides no better guidance to management than does social responsibility on the best strategies or policies to be adopted for library service. It appears that library personnel, by determining the degree of social responsiveness and the pressures to which they will respond, decide the meaning of the concept and what services will be developed as a result. There is still a lack of moral principles or theory on which to base decisions.

Societal pressures are assumed to exist, and libraries must respond to these in some manner. Social responsiveness assumes a passive attitude to such pressures. The concept of responsiveness provides no moral basis for information professionals to respond to social problems. There is no explicit moral or ethical theory and no specific values for personnel to follow in making responses to societal demands. This position becomes quite evident when examining the statement of professional ethics developed by the American Library Association (ALA) in 1981. The 1981 statement makes neither mention of the Library Bill of Rights nor any other philosophical statement as a source of the foundational ethics of library service. Although a 1980 draft spoke of the need for "participation in professional associations [and] community activity in support of library Programmes and legislation", this point was left out of the adopted version.

Criticism of the draft document includes the assertion that, "it does not deal adequately with the ends and means of the library profession. Rather it is primarily a guide to attitudes Towards work, without examining the mission of that work". While the presence of an ethical code can stimulate debate and strengthen professional autonomy, these results can only take place if the effect of the code is one of clarification of the practice of librarianship rather than a clarification of the appropriate demeanor of the professional.

In responding to such criticism, the question of managerial guidelines and principles becomes relevant. What criteria, other than self-interest, are relevant to guide information professionals in the development of socially responsible strategies? Shall these strategies be judged solely on their short term effectiveness, *i.e.*, in helping a library respond to a patron who wishes to remove a certain book from the shelves? Can libraries retain their neutral posture and still support those government leaders who support the interests of libraries and share traditional values of intellectual freedom and access? The nagging question of defining the social good or, in a public policy context, of defining the public interest, appears. And finally, the absence of a clear moral underpinning for whatever strategies are determined continues to present a problem.

If information professionals become proactive, does such Behaviour mean that they are attempting to minimise the impact of social change? Do not information professionals have a moral obligation that goes beyond their identified mandate to acquire and disseminate information? If information professionals do have social and political responsibilities as well as professional responsibilities, what is the moral basis for these responsibilities today?

ETHICAL DIMENSION OF DECISION-MAKING

In answering the preceding questions, the major premise is that management is basically an ethical task, and that many management decisions have an ethical dimension. An ethical decision can be further defined as a decision where questions of justice and rights are serious and relevant moral considerations.

These concepts are central ethical considerations in human affairs, and an ethical decision is one where a consideration of them is an important dimension of the decision. Can the decision be defended on grounds of justice? Is it fair and equitable in some sense to all the parties affected? Does the decision violate some basic human rights, such that it could be labeled an immoral decision? These are the kinds of questions that must be asked. Bucholz has identified three levels of ethical issues which vary in scope and breadth-the individual level, the organisation level, and the system level. At the individual level, one makes day-to-day decisions that mostly involve the application of institutional policy to specific situations.

When dilemmas arise, judgments must be made, some of which have ethical dimensions. At the organisational level, decisions are made for the organisation that will guide the Behaviour of employees. These decisions may be broad in scope and involve consideration of social responsibility. At the system level, broad questions can be raised about the ethical foundations of information service; such questions are not tied to a particular organisation. The specific nature of the decisions involved at each of these levels can be seen if a concrete example is used. Information access issues are fraught with ethical dimensions and provide a useful vehicle to illustrate ethical dilemmas at each of these levels.

Let us assume that the basic organisational policy in regard to access is one of "free access to all library materials for all individuals." Ethics enters into access decisions at the individual level in borderline or exceptional cases that policy does not seem to cover. For example, does free access really mean that a ten year old can take out an "R" rated video? At the organisational level, the ethical dimensions of decision making come into play when selection decisions are made.

Decision makers must make certain that the criteria and procedures that are established to make selection choices do not discriminate against certain writers nor points of view nor on the basis of irrelevant factors such as race, sex, or religious preference of either the author or selector. Self-censorship of controversial materials is a constant problem that must be addressed. At the system level, ethical questions relate to information dissemination. Who has access to information and at what cost? How does information format affect access? Who is responsible for providing information for those who have limited skills to acquire it? These kinds of questions are settled through the public policy process and the eventual outcome is reflected in laws and regulations related to information access at local, state, and federal levels. These various levels of decision making and the ethical issues relevant to each level.

Potential clashes exist at all levels. Institutional policy may require that a decision maker go agains this or her own ethical standards, producing significant internal conflict for one so involved. Institutional policy may not always reflect the ethical standards of the society at large, which may force society to develop laws and regulations to bring about change in institutional Behaviour. Another example can be taken from the hiring process for librarians. Many libraries make an ALA-accredited degree an entry-level qualification for a professional librarian.

Applicants for professional positions lacking this qualification are rejected. The ALA-accredited degree thus becomes a standard by which libraries hope to assure the recruitment of a high quality staff. Ethics enters into a decision to hire at the individual level in borderline or exceptional cases where applying the policy in a mechanical fashion does not seem just or equitable. For example, if an applicant does not have an ALA-accredited degree, should he or she be automatically rejected without looking at other information such as previous work experience or other academic credentials? Such a decision may not seem fair given the subjective nature of the hiring process in general.

Suppose a candidate with previous work experience, but without an ALA degree, is narrowly rejected for an academic library position and another candidate with an ALA-accredited degree, but no work experience, is accepted for a position. Is that fair considering that the work experience and academic credentials are not really comparable. And what about exceptional cases in which applicants may have other credentials, including doctorates? Should they be mechanically rejected without some special consideration? At the organisational level, ethical considerations come into play when one considers justice and rights in relation to the hiring policy itself.

Does a hiring policy discriminate unjustly on the basis of race or sex, or can it be defended as fair and equitable? Are written employment tests biased in favour of white middle class applicants due to the concepts and language used in examinations: Is an applicant's right to equal treatment violated by the use of such examinations? And, given the fact that grades mean different things depending on the school one attended, is it fair that grades are used as a factor in making employment decisions? At the system level, questions can be asked about the justice of public service institutions such as libraries hiring only those who are citisens or legal residents of a given community. Do not all individuals have a right to apply for employment for which they feel qualified, regardless of their legal status or place of residence? These are serious ethical questions worthy of debate. These examples serve to illustrate where ethical questions arise at different levels of decision making in libraries.

The decisions made at all these levels benefit and burden individuals and groups differentially. Some individuals gain and others are affected adversely. Questions of justice and individual rights become relevant. The question for the manager to answer is, Whose rights should be respected and what concept of justice is appropriate?.

ETHICAL CONSIDERATIONS FOR MANAGERS IN LIBRARIANSHIP

Librarians as managers are constantly making ethical decisions whether they know it or not. They are constantly directing people. Towards or away from information resources that may directly impact their ability to enhance their lives or the life of their community. They are creating the future for their organisations, for their employees, for their users, for those who fund the service, and for society as a whole.

Decisions about information access can affect human well being and social welfare, having ethical impacts that are significant for all those touched by the decisions. A recent article in the chronicle of higher education discussed "a revolution in the nature of resources that provide power". The suggestion is made that access to information resources must now be counted as a source of world power. As the ability to access information across the globe becomes possible through the use of technology, librarians will have more and more opportunity to influence decision making on a worldwide scale through appropriate information provision.

This is an awesome responsibility and one that calls for ethical reflection of the highest order. Librarians must be encouraged to think more broadly and highly of their task. They must recognise that libraries are multiple purpose institutions that have many impacts besides cultural enrichment or recreation. Moral leadership of such institutions means recognising information agencies as part of an ethical system havingvarious values that are important to human welfare. The challenge to librarians is to incorporate these values into routine decision making and develop methods of analysis that are applicable to identifying appropriate goals for themselves and their organisations.

AN ACTION PLAN

The implementation of an ethical vision in librarianship requires action in several areas. An ethical perspective must be incorporated into the workplace as well as into the curriculum through which future librarians are being educated. The following areas constitute what could be called an ethical agenda for librarians in both of these settings:

- In the educational setting, such a plan calls for a thorough integration of moral and ethical concerns into the library/ information science curriculum. Although separate courses in ethics may also be offered, integration of ethical concerns into basic courses such as Management or Reference is essential to make ethics more directly related to the roles and responsibilities of information professionals.
- Continuing education Programmes need to develop parallel efforts to maintain the work begun in the academic setting. Questions about ethics and moral aspects of librarianship must continue to be addressed as professionals move through their careers.
- Library boards of trustees and/or advisory boards must demonstrate a concern about ethics by raising ethical questions when appropriate. The moral implications of decisions and actions must
- Boards can acknowledge the significance of ethical issues by raising them in relation to goal setting and long-range planning.
- Information professionals at all levels must recognise the important role they play in institutionalising ethical responsibility throughout their organisations. Professional librarians have many channels open to them to shape the library/information center, including the setting of objectives for units and individuals, developing and implementing the reward structure of staff, modifying organisational structure to accomplish goals, and developing and utilising appropriate measures of performance. Professional staff not only have responsibility for efficient and effective use of material and human resources but also must be willing to create a responsible institution that cares about and responds to the ethical and moral imperatives of its policies and actions.
- Information policy-making by various government bodies must be considered from an ethical point of view. Librarians have a role to play in the debate; they can make contributions to the discussion

and provide insight into the formation of regulations regarding the dissemination of information. Librarians must be given the freedom to respond to information policy issues out of a sense of ethical responsibility; rules and regulations for the control of information flow must be evaluated as well as the inherent limitations of information dissemination systems.

- More research must be considered by both library school faculty and professional librarians into the ethical aspects of decision making by librarians. One of the themes of this article is that many in the profession of librarianship are ignorant of ethical issues, not having a good understanding of how such matters should be analysed and discussed. Research into ethical and moral issues can help overcome this ignorance. Scholars in the field need to apply their expertise to ethical questions and combine this with the work of those from other professional disciplines who have similar concerns.

This action plan suggests that a consideration of ethical issues must become a familiar comfortable part of librarians' thought processes. Ethical ambiguities are always present because no one can formulate policies that are going to be morally justified in all circumstances and in all places and times. It is important that those responsible for formulating, implementing, and evaluating policies should be made aware of these ambiguities and be ethically aware so as to act in a responsible and moral manner. Ambiguity, it should be noted, does not diminish the significance of ethical issues, which this discussion implies are pervasive in librarianship.

In point of fact, the ethical dimension of librarianship represents a generalised concern for the improvement of quality of library service and professional conduct of librarians. A final caveat is in order. Ethical Behaviour in librarianship does not mean that one should take no action, that is, avoid certain actions or books or ideas in an effort to keep out of trouble. On the contrary, the notion of ethics suggests that librarians take actions that are socially just. Only by actively pursuing social aims can librarians be ethically responsive. There is evidence to suggest that librarians choose not to choose, to "play it safe" with services and collections. Instead, librarians ought to exercise ethical judgement in their duties. Only by demonstrating the highest standards of ethical decision making will librarians inspire confidence and respect in the information arena.

THE EFFECTS OF LIBRARIANS' BEHAVIOURAL PERFORMANCE ON USER SATISFACTION IN CHAT REFERENCE SERVICES

As library users become more comfortable with using the Web for services and to search for information, librarians often have led the way in making reference services available to patrons online. Online real-time chat reference services have become increasingly prevalent in many types and sises of libraries, and, as with any other library service, it is important to evaluate the effectiveness of, and user satisfaction with, those services.

This research reports the results and conclusions from a case study of a chat reference service intended to assess the usefulness of the 2004 revised "RUSA Guidelines for Behavioural Performance of Reference and Information Services Providers". These were originally developed by the Reference and User Services Association (RUSA) in 1996 as Behavioural guidelines to support reference staff working at a physical reference desk. The purpose of this study is to:

- Investigate, in a series of chat interviews, the extent to which librarians' Behaviours reflected those recommended in the revised guidelines;
- Assess the influence of those Behaviours on user satisfaction; and
- Examine the revised guidelines as a useful assessment tool in evaluating the efficacy of a chat reference service.

The results of this study will provide library professionals with a better understanding of the nature of chat reference interviews as well as test the usefulness of the revised guidelines in the context of chat reference services. The results of this study will better elucidate effective teaching methods and techniques for library educators within the area of virtual reference with respect to the reference question negotiation process.

BACKGROUND OF THE STUDY

The Original Guidelines and the Revised Guidelines

Perhaps one of the most important roles of professional associations is to establish benchmarking standards and develop useful guidelines to assist their members' practice. RUSA has been at the forefront in offering its members such support. Beginning in the 1980s, RUSA began developing reference interview guidelines intended to delineate those librarian Behaviours most likely to lead to an effective face-to-face reference interview. This effort resulted in the publication of the "RUSA Guidelines for Behavioural Performance of Reference and Information Services Providers" in 1996.

A handful of research studies conducted Since, that time have consistently indicated that use of the Behaviours prescribed in the original guidelines is positively associated with reference success. The original guidelines thus became widely recognised as the only Behavioural guidelines of its kind for reference staff. Besides the fact that the original guidelines were prepared by RUSA, a leading professional association among reference librarians, the continued use of the original guidelines in practice seems to suggest their usefulness as standards for reference staff training as well as performance evaluation. A revised and extended version of the original guidelines was published in June 2004. This revision reflects the increasing need for Behavioural standards that can assist personnel who provide virtual reference services. Maintaining the five-component structure of the original guidelines, the revised guidelines subcategorised each of those five components into three settings: general, in-person, and remote. The five-component structure is summarised as follows:

- First, approachability refers to Behaviours that ensure easy access to the reference staff by lowering barriers to personal assistance. Example Behaviours include making instructional and directional signs clear, making the presence of reference assistance visible, and establishing "word" contact with the patrons.
- Second, interest refers to Behaviours that exhibit librarians' interest in patron enquiries so that patrons can ask questions without hesitation. Example Behaviours include focusing attention on the patron, maintaining and re-establishing "word" contact, and clarifying the scope of the questions.
- Third, listening/enquiring refers to Behaviours that exhibit good listening and questioning skills so that librarians can identify patrons' real information needs, which sometimes are buried or poorly expressed. Example Behaviours are communicating in receptive and cordial ways, using proper written language, ensuring adequate probing, and rephrasing questions to ensure adequate understanding.
- Fourth, searching includes the application of effective search skills and related Behaviours that can enhance searching effectiveness and result in finding accurate answers. Example Behaviours include explaining search strategies, escorting patrons in the search process, and providing pointers and information sources.
- Finally, follow-up refers to the Behaviours involved in bringing proper closure to the reference transaction. Example Behaviours include asking patrons if their questions were completely answered, asking if they need additional information, referring them to alternative sources or agencies if their questions were not answered, and urging patrons to return if they need further assistance.

The revised guidelines have incorporated many Behaviours that pertain specifically to virtual reference. Yet, the core components and ideas remain the same as those set out in the original guidelines prepared for face-to-face reference service practice.

Librarians' Behavioural Performance during Chat Reference Service

The body of the reference service literature has consistently emphasised that the quality of the reference interview is an important factor in reference service effectiveness. In their seminal research, scholars demonstrated that reference librarians' verbal and non-verbal communication skills during the reference interview are crucial in delivering reference services successfully. This research has had a great affect on the research and the practice of reference services, and has brought attention to the need for pertinent staff training that can provide instruction in, and emphasise the importance of, verbal and non-verbal communication skills in the reference interview. Saxton reported that reference effectiveness was most consistently predicted by the presence of verbal and non-verbal Behaviours prescribed in the original guidelines.

Subsequent studies also reported similar findings, substantiating RUSA's initial intent to provide the original guidelines as a service assessment tool. Yet, many issues remain veiled regarding the interactions between librarians and patrons in virtual space in general, and reference interviews during chat sessions specifically. Some of the important but unanswered questions are:

- How do reference librarians interact with their patrons in chat reference settings.
- Are the interactions in chat reference similar to, or considerably different from, those in traditional reference service.
- What staff Behaviours would be most conducive to user satisfaction with chat reference services.

Regarding these questions, some would argue that the interactions between patrons and librarians in chat settings should not be fundamentally different from those involved in the physical reference setting because both ultimately serve the same purpose—resolving information problems by answering questions. In essence, proponents of this position view chat reference as the same service delivered via a different medium, much like the telephone reference service that was new in the 1930s. In contrast, others would contend that the particular mode of virtual communications is the very factor that makes chat reference different from the face-to-face or the telephone reference interview. After all, virtual communication lacks facial, aural, or environmental cues, which are crucial components in the physical reference setting, as well as the voice cues that are so crucial to phone reference.

In the absence of clear understanding of the nature of chat reference interactions, identifying effective librarian Behaviours in the chat reference interview will be an important first step in helping librarians to achieve higher levels of service performance. In this regard, specific Behaviours prescribed in the revised guidelines can be utilised as effective Behavioural standards to examine librarians' actual Behaviours while answering questions during chat sessions. Thus, the purpose of the present study was to investigate the extent to which the Behaviours prescribed in the revised guidelines are observed in chat reference sessions, and whether the presence of those Behaviours increases user satisfaction with chat reference. For this purpose, three specific research questions were proposed for investigation:

- *Research question 1:* To what extent is each RUSA Behaviour observed in chat reference interviews.

- *Research question 2:* Is user satisfaction with chat reference higher when librarians perform the RUSA Behaviours during reference sessions than when they do not
- *Research question 3:* Which of the RUSA Behaviours performed during chat reference interviews could predict higher user satisfaction.

The findings of the present study will enable us to determine whether the RUSA Behaviours can lead to more effective reference services performance. Ultimately, the results of the study will help us to resolve the question of whether the revised guidelines can be effectively used as a pertinent training and service assessment tool for chat reference services.

METHODS

Setting and Participants

The present study examined chat reference services delivered through the Broward County public library system, the largest such system in Florida, with thirty-three regional and branch libraries. Since, August 2002, the system has used a chat reference service dubbed "24/7 Reference" delivered by the Metropolitan Cooperative Library System (MCLS), an association of libraries located in the greater Los Angeles area funded by a federal Library Services and Technology Act grant.

MCLS's 24/7 Reference was merged with Online Computer Library Center's (OCLC) QuestionPoint in August 2004. The data examined for the present study were online chat reference transactions initiated by patrons of the Broward Countries library system, along with survey responses submitted by the patrons. While the patrons were mostly users of the Broward County system, the reference staff members who provided the service were from forty-nine library systems across the United States participating in the MCLS 24/7 Reference Programme.

During the six-month duration of the research study, between January and June 2004, a total of 1,387completed or transferred transactions took place. As the intention of this study was to analyse the influence of librarians' Behaviours on user satisfaction, only the transactions that had a corresponding completed self-report user satisfaction survey were selected for data analysis. Thus, the total number of transactions analysed for the present study was 422, comprising 30.4 percent of the total analysable transactions.

Coding RUSA Behaviours

RUSA Behaviours refer to the Behaviours prescribed in the revised guidelines. These Behaviours were coded through the analysis of 422 chat transcripts that show all patron-staff interactions as well as search activities, including co-browsing. Initially, librarians' Behaviours were coded against all fortynine items in the revised guidelines, which include all three modes of transactions. This decision was made because certain items listed under the in-person category also were applicable to the chat reference setting. Later, the initial forty-nine items were collapsed into ten types of Behaviours after merging similar items together and removing items that were either unobservable or irrelevant for chat reference.

For example, some items describe thought processes rather than actual observable Behaviours. Some Behaviours, such as providing information sources, were observed across multiple items. Finally, some items are applicable for physical setting transactions only. pecific items in the five RUSA Behavioural areas were coded into ten Behavioural types in the present study. Approachability was observed by two Behavioural types: welcoming and the use of patrons' name.

First, welcoming was coded to be present either when an initial word contact was made or when a general welcoming atmosphere was observed from the librarians' written communications. Other than these examples, the revised guidelines do not include many clear Behavioural indicators of approachability Thus, the second Behavioural type, the use of patrons' name, was adopted from the Guidelines for Chat Sessions within "IFLA Digital Reference Guidelines"; the assumption here is that the Behaviour could lower the patron's emotional barriers and thus enhance the librarian's approachability.

Currently, there is no consensus about the effectiveness of using a patron's name during the chat session. Some think it is effective because it could make the reference interview more personable and approachable. Others think that it may intrude upon personal privacy. By observing its use, as suggested, be able to determine whether the use of patrons' names affects user satisfaction. Interest was observed by using two items in the revised guidelines: focusing attention on the patron and maintaining word contact. The remaining items were excluded from coding because they were mostly applicable to the physical reference setting, e-mail, or pre-interview stage. Listening/enquiring was observed by two Behavioural types: receptive and cordial listening; and enquiring by rephrasing, clarifying, or asking questions.

The rest of the items were excluded from coding because they were not easily observable or overlapped with other items. Searching was observed by two Behavioural types: searching for or with patrons, and offering pointers or information sources. Some Behaviours, such as co-browsing, were coded as both when they involved searching and offering information sources. Four items were excluded from coding because they either pertain to listening/ enquiring or follow-up, or indicate a cognitive process rather than an observable Behaviour.

Finally, follow-up was observed by three Behavioural types: proper closing, offering alternatives or making referral, and asking to come back for further assistance. RUSA Behaviours were coded by two independent coders for intercoder reliability in order to ensure the consistency. First, the primary researcher coded the entire 422 transactions. Then, the second coder, a reference librarian who received training for coding the RUSA Behaviours, coded every fifth transaction.

This sample for intercoder reliability comprises 20 percent of the total transactions, which is the recommended percentage for social science research. Finally, the percentage agreement between the two coders was calculated for each Behaviour, which informs the level of agreement between two coders. The agreements were Welcoming, Use of patrons' name, Interest, Listening, Enquiring, Searching with or for patrons, Offering pointers and information sources, Asking if answered completely, Offering referrals, and Asking to come back for further assistance.

All these intercoder percentage agreements were either above or close to the generally acceptable threshold value of 80 percent. It should be noted that the use of the RUSA guidelines in the current study is differentiated from the approaches of the previous studies. While the earlier studies did not observe librarian Behaviours with respect to actual items in the guidelines or measured with a few items only, the present study used the entirety of the items in the revised guidelines as the coding scheme to analyse librarians' chat reference Behaviours.

RESULTS

User Satisfaction

User satisfaction has been one of the most frequently used outcome variables that measure reference service effectiveness. In the present study, user satisfaction was assessed through user responses to the following four questionnaire items: satisfaction with the answer, perceived staff quality, willingness to return to the service, and positivity of service experience. First, satisfaction with the answer was assessed by asking the question, "Were you satisfied with the answer you received to your reference question?" Among the 417 respondents who answered this question, 65.2 percent reported that they were satisfied with the answer received, and 21.1 percent of the respondents were not sure whether they were satisfied or not.

Finally, 12.6 percent of the respondents reported that they were not satisfied at all. Perceived staff qualitythe second indicator of user satisfaction, was assessed by the user response to the question, "The quality of the library staff service in answering this request was _________." Among the 416 people who responded, 68.2 percent of the respondents answered that the librarians handling the reference questions were excellent.

About 19.5 percent evaluated the librarians' performance as good, and 11.3 percent as poor. Willingness to use the service again, the third indicator of user satisfaction, was measured using the questionnaire item, "Will you use this service again?" Among the 417 people who responded to this question,

77.2 percent answered that they were very likely to use the service again, 19.0 percent of the respondents answered maybe, and only 3.8 percent said they would never use the service again. Regarding positivity of service experience, among the total of 422 survey responses, 183 offered open-ended comments on the service.

Sixty-three percent of the respondents evaluated the experience positively, and 28.4 percent evaluated it negatively. About 10 percent of the respondents described it as either a mixed or neutral experience. Frequently mentioned expressions among the positive open-ended responses included "wonderful service," "quick," "helpful," "innovative," "cool," "good use of public money," and other comments indicating immediacy, convenience, and ease of use, including "human contact," "anytime 24/7," "likable," "interesting," and "time saver."

Frequently mentioned expressions among those reporting a negative experience include "hard to use interface design," "didn't answer the question," "slow response time," "virtual librarians should access account," "virtual reference service coverage should be clearly indicated," technical problems, "waiting," "service delay," misunderstanding, hasty ending, listening skill lacking, and "poor service." In addition to the patrons' negative and positive experiences expressed via the responses, mixed comments also were observed. An example of a mixed comment is "the idea of the virtual service is great but I didn't get much help." Comments that were categorised as neutral included suggestions for additional features, unawareness of the service's nationwide nature, additional information about the patrons' information needs or their background, or reports about problems experienced after the session ended.

Finally, overall user satisfaction was computed by summing up the first three questionnaire items that measured different aspects of user satisfaction. This computation was necessary because the user satisfaction items in the survey questionnaire were measured on a simple three- or four-point ordinal scale. These ordinal level measurements are not suitable for undertaking the inferential statistical tests that are crucial to answer the research questions of the present study. To resolve this problem, the three ordinal level variables were summed to create a composite variable, which increases the variability of the measure.

This data management procedure allowed the researchers to conduct necessary inferential statistical tests. Survey research literature indicates that a composite variable is generally more valid and reliable than a single question item because it increases variability of the measurement. The transformation of the existing three questionnaire items into a composite variable involved a series of conversions from a natural language answer choice to a numeric value. By carefully analysing the wording of the answer choices, a set of logical numeric values were assigned for answer choices of each of the three questionnaire items on the same five-point Likert scale. First, for the satisfaction with the answer item, the numeric value assigned for "unsatisfied" was 1, 2 for "not sure," and 5 for "satisfied."

For the perceived staff quality item, the value assigned for "poor" was 1, 3 for "average," 4 for "good," and 5 for "excellent." For the willingness to return item, the numeric value assigned for "never" was 1, 3 for "maybe," and 5 for "very likely." In order to determine the composite variable's reliability and validity, a classical theory alpha reliability and factor analysis were performed, respectively.

First, the reliability test generated a score for the sample that had a Cronbach's alpha reliability coefficient of.845 for user satisfaction. This score is greater than the customary threshold value of .70, indicating that the composite variable is reliable. Second, the factor analysis result showed that the three questionnaire items were loaded on one-factor solution, with factor loading scores of .868, .916, and .876. All three items explained 78.64 percent of variance in the factor.

This result indicates that the composite variable is measuring a single construct with a high score validity, suggesting that the composite variable is a valid measure of user satisfaction. The mean of the composite variable, user satisfaction, was 12.69, with a standard deviation of 3.44 in the range between a maximum value of 3 for "highly dissatisfied" and the minimum value of 15 for "highly satisfied."

The Presence of RUSA Behaviours in Chat Reference Interviews

Research question 1 of the present study asks to what extent reference staff members employ each of the ten RUSA Behaviours during their chat reference transactions. The presence of the ten selected RUSA Behaviours ranged between 28.7 percent and 63.7 percent. The three most frequently observed Behaviours were comeback, interest, and welcoming. A complete comparison of this finding with those reported in the previous studies is not feasible because none has used the complete revised guidelines as a coding scheme.

A couple of studies allow a partial comparison in the area of follow-up. Follow-up Behaviours were observed in approximately one-third of the total in-person reference transactions. Also in the physical library setting, Gatten and Radcliff reported that 29 percent of the proxy patrons were asked by the librarians if their questions were answered.

In the present study, however, the three follow-up Behaviours appeared with greater frequency, ranging between 46.9 percent and 63.7 percent. Their frequent appearance may reflect the use of the scripted words stored in the chat reference software Programme. It should be noted that not all RUSA Behaviours are expected to appear in a single reference session. For example, probing is not generally expected to occur in response to directional or circulation policy questions. Similarly, offering alternatives or making referrals are expected to occur mostly when reference staff is not able to provide a complete answer. Rather, the information about the RUSA Behaviours should be more useful in its relationship with user satisfaction.

RUSA Behaviours and User Satisfaction

Research question 2 relates to whether chat reference users would be more satisfied with the service when librarians demonstrate a RUSA Behaviour than when they do not. Where the means of the user satisfaction are compared between when librarians showed the Behaviour and when librarians did not. Across all but two Behaviours, user satisfaction was found to be higher when librarians performed the RUSA Behaviours than when they did not. A series of statistical analyses was conducted to determine the statistical significance of the difference in user satisfaction between when each RUSA Behaviour was present and absent.

Both parametric statistics and non-parametric statistics were considered in our study to determine the most appropriate statistical technique for the tests. In general, parametric statistics are recommended when a test variable:

- Is measured on an interval or ratio level;
- Is measured on a sample size of sixty cases or more; or
- Is normally distributed.

When the data were examined with respect to these three criteria, the answer was not clear-cut. The test variable, user satisfaction, is an interval-level variable measured on the sample sise of 422, but is not normally distributed.

Hence, the data were examined using both parametric and non-parametric statistical techniques, and the test results were compared. If the two statistical techniques generate identical results, parametric statistics are recommended to present the data, which is the case in the present study. When tested using SPSS 14.0, it was revealed that test results from both techniques were identical across all ten RUSA Behaviours.

This result indicates that the Mann-Whitney U test results corroborated the results from the t-tests. User satisfaction was statistically significantly different in six out of the ten RUSA Behaviours at the significance level of α <.05.

Satisfaction was statistically significantly higher when reference staff showed the following six Behaviours than otherwise; that is to say, chat reference services were perceived to be more satisfying to the patrons when librarians:

- Used the patron's name during the reference interview;
- Communicated more receptively and listened more carefully;
- Searched with or for the patron;
- Provided pointers;

- Asked the patron whether the question was completely answered; and
- Asked the patron to come back if they needed further assistance.

This result is consistent with the findings of the previous studies conducted in face-to-face reference setting, which reported the positive influence of the original guidelines on reference success. Thus, the findings of the present study indicate that performance of RUSA Behaviours also are effective in the real-time chat reference setting.

Index